# PICNIC IN BABYLON

# PICNIC IN BABYLON

## A JESUIT PRIEST'S

## JOURNAL 1963-1967

by JOHN L'HEUREUX

THE MACMILLAN COMPANY, NEW YORK

COLLIER-MACMILLAN LTD., LONDON

Library of Congress Catalog Card Number: (67–24288)

FIRST PRINTING

*The Macmillan Company, New York*
*Collier-Macmillan Canada Ltd., Toronto, Ontario*

Printed in the United States of America

# ACKNOWLEDGMENTS

The author wishes to thank the following for permission to reproduce copyrighted material: Harper & Row for *Ariel* by Sylvia Plath; Farrar, Straus & Giroux, Inc. for *For the Union Dead* by Robert Lowell, copyright © 1964 by Robert Lowell, by permission of Farrar, Straus & Giroux, Inc. and Faber & Faber Ltd., London; Doubleday & Company, Inc. for "Intermission," "The Imperfect Eye," "Psalm," "Radiators," copyright © 1964 by John L'Heureux, from *Quick As Dandelions*, by John L'Heureux, reprinted by permission of Doubleday & Company, Inc.; Alfred A. Knopf Inc. for *Of the Farm* by John Updike and *The Mandelbaum Gate* by Muriel Spark; *Columbia Daily Spectator* for an excerpt from a review of a poetry reading by Allen Ginsberg and Peter Orlovsky, by Alan Feldman, in the December 3, 1964 issue; The Macmillan Company for permission to reprint the following poems, in whole or in part, in this volume, from *Rubrics For a Revolution*, copyright © by Rev. John L'Heureux, S.J., 1961, 1964, 1965, 1966, 1967: "Compliance," "The Concert," "The Exile," "Marginal Note in a Theology Text," "The Measure," "The Unlikely Prophet," and "The Window."

FOR *DAVID*

# CONTENTS

# PREFACE

I DON'T KNOW why I became a Jesuit. I cannot recall as a child or later in college ever wanting to say Mass, administer the sacraments, save souls. Indeed I cannot recall any particular urgency to save my own soul. Further, I did not like vestments, incense made me sneeze, and I had a positive dread of delivering a sermon. I became a Jesuit, paradoxically, on the grounds of coldest reason: I felt God wanted me to, I could, and therefore I should. So I did. In the past fourteen years I have regretted it often; still, I am aware it is one of the few sensible decisions I've ever made. I rejoice in it.

I was born of two very agreeable people who paint pictures, give presents to their numerous grandchildren, and—think of it—love one another. It is not their fault I grew up to be only me; they deserved better; they are, however, fond of the clergy and fonder of me and seem eminently satisfied with things as they are. I have one brother, four years older, who is a civil engineer. My father is a civil engineer. My mother is a housewife. None of us had any reason to expect a Jesuit.

Growing up in South Hadley, Massachusetts, can be a lonely business. Almost nobody there was ever my age. I had one close friend who moved to St. Louis when we were both in third grade. We wrote back and forth for a few years. His letters stopped abruptly and I discovered later that at this time his father, a rather proficient embezzler, had been found out and had hanged himself from the bedroom chandelier. A bad end to my first friendship. Most of the other neighborhood children were my brother's age, and since I was four years younger, they hated me. So I read and wrote and dramatized my infinitely dull existence. By the time I was nine I had written a novel about a lizard and a rat, a hundred poems or more on Things Adventurous, a play in two acts about poor children on Christmas morning. I guess things looked pretty bleak at age nine. Then again, of course, nine is a tragic age.

In high school I fell hopefully in love with a dazzling girl who is today a dazzling woman. Our romance followed the normal adolescent pattern: my finding her more beautiful and more fragile and more desirable in direct proportion to her finding me less interesting in every way. Eventually she lost interest altogether and, painfully, I recovered. I love her still; she and her husband and I have very pleasant times together.

Upon leaving high school I spent a summer at the National Academy of Theatre Arts and in fall entered Holy Cross College, where I spent most of my time in the cafeteria and, undisturbed by the sobering processes of thought, was supremely happy. Two years later I gave up altogether and entered the Society of Jesus. My college friends took bets on how long I would last as a Jesuit; the most benevolent prognosis was two months—"Jack will stay that long out of spite"—and the least benevolent was two hours. Friends of our family were not surprised. They "always knew he would be a priest." Against such certitude there is no effective argument. And because I could offer no satisfying reason for my becoming a Jesuit, I had to bear with people saying I "had the call." "Having the call" always reminded me of Edith Wharton's lady who "had complications": you might get very ill from a normal sickness, but there was not a chance of recovery from complications. So I had the call.

Fifteen years ago the ordinary course of Jesuit training involved two years, novitiate, working and praying and familiarizing oneself with the principles of the spiritual life. Vows of poverty, chastity, and obedience marked the culmination of the novitiate and the beginning of the properly Jesuit life: there followed two years of classical studies, three years of philosophy, three years of practical experience called Regency (usually spent teaching in a Jesuit high school), and three years of theology, after which the Jesuit was ordained priest. Ordination was followed by still another year of theology and a third and final year of novitiate. The course of studies, therefore, was usually a fifteen-year affair. Today this has been modified and varies somewhat with each Jesuit.

On the feast of St. Ignatius in 1954 I began this course of studies, entering the Jesuit Novitiate at Shadowbrook in Lenox, Massachusetts. Shadowbrook was the beautiful old Carnegie estate, called the Ruby of the Berkshires for the crimson tile roof that rambled over the sprawling mansion. It had been an ideal home for ten very rich people; it was somewhat less than ideal for one hundred and twenty poor ones. Still I was very happy there for a year, gradually growing less so, however, under prolonged self-scrutiny, an inflexible rule, poor spiritual guidance, and worse spiritual conduct on my own part. It was all a bad mistake, I thought, and was giving serious considera- tion to leaving the Society of Jesus when in my second year novitiate, in the middle of an icy winter night, Shadowbrook burned to the ground. Four Jesuits died in the fire and several were injured. I very nearly slept through into eternity. Though I grieved for the dead Jesuits, I rejoiced that I was sent to Wernersville, Pennsylvania, to finish my novitiate. There, under a wise and liberal Master of Novices, I learned to think less about my self, learned to stop trying to strong-arm the Holy Spirit into making me a saint. The religious life became once more possible for me. I took vows in July, 1956.

Because of my two years at Holy Cross, I skipped one year of classical studies, went on to three years of philosophy at Weston College in Massachusetts, spent two of my three years of teaching at Fairfield Preparatory School in Connecticut and the third at Boston College High School. During this last year of teaching, I also studied at Boston College, so that when I arrived at Woodstock in 1963, it was with the B.A. degree I had begun in 1952, and with two incidental M.A.'s, one in philosophy, one in English. By the time this journal is pub- lished I shall be studying for a Ph.D in English at Harvard University. With luck I shall finish school before I am thrust upon Medicare.

The journal selections that follow were written during the three years of theology prior to my ordination as priest. Dur- ing this time I published a book of poems, *Quick as Dandelions,* which had been many years in preparation, and completed a second book of poems, *Rubrics for a Revolution*. While writing these books, I was deeply involved in trying to come to an understanding of my own vocation within the Society of Jesus. The first three years of theology are perhaps the most crucial years for the individual Jesuit; he is called upon to examine more closely than ever before what it means to be a priest, what it means to be himself, what it means to square away the disparity between the two. It is often a time of personal crisis, always a time of personal intensity. It was this and more for me. With this excuse then—that my experience of coming to the priesthood is essentially the experience of all priests and at the same time is unknown and a mystery to all nonpriests—I offer to both the interested and the merely curious this rather personal record of my three years of preparation.

A word about the journal itself. Like my life, *Picnic in Babylon* is an amalgam of lies and half truths and a larger more important care for that truth which can be approached only tangentially. It is precisely through half truths and indeliberate lies, through distortion of the real and a determined rendering of the illusory, that we compose our souls, fabricate our minds.

So it happens that not all passages in this journal were written on the date assigned them, though indeed most of them were. Similarly there were many occasions when my concern for living interfered with recording experiences both important and formative. And often the ennui of life in a seminary forbade my writing anything at all. Finally the first half year was not written as a journal; it was assembled from letters returned to me by friends, from carbon copies of business letters, from random notes I kept by accident rather than design.

For whatever its small worth—here. I have tried to write honestly; the untruths are Adam's, the price of being a very limited man.

By the waters of Babylon,
  there we sat down and wept
  when we remembered Zion.
On the willows there
  we hung our lyres.
For there our captors
  required of us songs,
and our tormentors, mirth, saying,
  "Sing us one of the songs of Zion!"

How shall we sing the Lord's song
  in a foreign land?
If I forget you, O Jerusalem,
  let my right hand wither!
Let my tongue cleave to the roof of my mouth
  if I do not remember you,
if I do not set Jerusalem
  above my highest joy!

Remember, O Lord, against the Edomites
  the day of Jerusalem,
how they said, "Rase it, rase it!
  Down to its foundations!"
O daughter of Babylon, you devastator!
  Happy shall he be who requites you
  with what you have done to us!
Happy shall he be who takes your little ones
  and dashes them against the rock!

PSALM 137

# I
# SETTING OUT

AUGUST 1963–AUGUST 1964

## Wednesday, 28 August

WOODSTOCK. Here I sit surrounded by a disarray of abandoned furniture, an unpacked trunk, two great book boxes, clothes, papers and—broken and neatly bundled up in the corner—an old venetian blind. I feel like a wealthy refugee, someone who even in his flight didn't have enough sense to abandon the useless but familiar claptrap that assures him he exists. At noon they will come and hang me.

Outside there's an impenetrable mist, which I'm told surrounds us every morning and clears off as the day gathers momentum. We're like a hump in the middle of a saucer. Woodstock sits on a hill completely surrounded by valley; beyond the valley there are mountains. It's an admirable spot to do battle from, a miserable one if we should ever suffer prolonged siege; the trouble with cutting off the world is that you are also cut off from it. I'll never understand why our Jesuit predecessors felt the forests the best place for houses of formation.

My room is something out of *Jane Eyre*, the attic closet sort of thing. The floors and walls are ancient beyond belief and the air tastes of dust. Spiders here have died of old age. The house itself is a fortress, all stone and mortar and cold forbidding windows. It may well be the most depressing building I've ever seen. You approach it from the valley by crossing a little wooden one-lane bridge that spans a muddy stream called the Patapsco River. Where on earth have you seen a bridge of wooden planks which, when a car drives over it, lets go with a sound like a Gatling gun. Enough of this. I faint, I die, I . . . the hell with it.

## Friday, 30 August

I JUST SAW our swimming pool, an enormous number in tur-
quoise. Apparently some enterprising theologians built it with
refuse cement and fieldstone some years ago after a fellow
theologian drowned while swimming in the Patapsco. I find
it hard to imagine anyone getting wet in the Patapsco, let
alone drowning in it, but I guess everything has run down a
little with the years and that poor trickle was once a torrent—
of sorts.

What astounds me here is the size of everybody. Woodstock
doesn't admit you unless you're over six feet. Or maybe they
have all developed some unspeakable thyroid condition since
coming here and I may yet live to see myself six feet seven.
Age twenty-eight is no time to embark on a basketball career.
And they're not a very friendly bunch. You'd think that with
three hundred men you could find somebody to talk to. It's
such a crazy situation: I'm so eager to meet people and to be
friendly and yet I'm terrified at the same time—of making a
fool of myself, I suppose, or of alienating them, or of creating
a "poet image" with which they'll label me for the next four
years. Oh well, he said, shrugging. Oh well.

Later. Naomi Burton just phoned me from New York to
tell me Doubleday is going to publish my book of poems. After
all these years of waiting. This will be my fourth book of
poems written and my first to be published: one burned, one
abandoned as hopeless, one abandoned with pale hope, one
published. Not a particularly high percentage of success, is it?
But I exult anyhow in this one. Now, dammitall, if only I had
somebody to share the excitement with.

## Saturday, 31 August

RETREAT BEGINS tonight. I understand the chap who will give
it is the twenty-fourth person asked, all the previous requestees
having engagements or an overriding terror of Woodstock
which forbade their giving it. Doesn't sound too good for num-

ber twenty-four. Or for us either. But you can't tell; the Holy
Spirit is capable of using the twenty-fourth to as much advantage as the first. Of course, you don't like to put a strain
on the Spirit unless you have to, and if the retreat master is
that far down the line, it's folly to hope for a John Courtney
Murray.

My first impressions of Woodstock remind me of a trip
I made to see the Old Man of the Mountain in New Hampshire when I was eleven. After a long and tiring drive, we
finally reached the place and paid our fee and wound down
a long rocky path where I kept expecting to stumble on a
snake and came to a place by a brook where we were told we
could lean forward and scrootch our necks up and over our
right shoulders and we could catch a perfect profile of the
Man of the Mountain. I leaned and scrootched and looked
and, sick to my stomach, realized I had left my glasses back at
the car. Dad was angry—we had come so that I could see it—
and everybody else was depressed except the people standing
around; they were amused. Everybody waited while I ran wildly
to the car to fetch my glasses. I returned exhausted and drip-
ping with sweat and muddy where I had tripped going up the
path. Again I leaned and scrootched and looked and yes, it was
there, the rocky profile of an old man with an Indian nose and
a New England jaw. It looked like any of its photographs. And
I was only tired and sweaty and dirty from having fallen down.
There was nothing special or surprising or even very satisfying
about it. It was big and made of stone; everybody had heard
of it and anybody—who didn't forget his glasses—could see it;
and its one recommendation seemed to be that you could now
go away and say "I have seen the Man of the Mountain in
Laconia, New Hampshire." That's how I feel about Woodstock
as retreat begins. I'd be perfectly content to go away forever
with only the memory of having been here, tired and dirty and
sweaty.

Well, retreat will be good. I'm still prostrate from a summer
school session in which I took a course, wrote a master's thesis,
and passed oral comprehensives, but I'm eager to begin praying full time, rising at 5:30 God help me, and going through
the routine that makes up the externals of religious life. I do

want to pray. And I do want to see if I can live the religious life with its built-in loneliness without the support of my many friends in New England. I want to discover if I can survive on merely what I am, if I can manage to be alone with God and find that enough. This was the reason I asked to come here, and so I must give Woodstock a fair try. Otherwise I'll never know. So here goes, survival without props. No looking back. Think glad. I'd never go over on Madison Avenue.

And I am excited about my book *Eye of the Spider*.\* The contract sounds awfully good: 10 percent royalties on the selling price of each volume. Granted there won't *be* any sales; still it's nice to think that every relative and every abandoned student who purchases a copy contributes 10 percent of the price to the slender coffers of the Society of Jesus. I've written home about it and to my friends at Weston. I asked Fr. Minister if I might call home, collect, to tell the folks and he gave me an emphatic no. That seals that, I guess. Fr. Minister is not terribly social. He chops trees.

Last night as I lay awake listening to the trains thunder through the valley, and then the local cars lambaste that poor wooden bridge, it occured to me that this place really is a fortress. Replete with moat. My room is on the top floor, way up among the eaves. The roof slopes at a ninety-degree angle and today, to my understandable surprise, as I stood musing, looking down the alley at the end of which my window does its futile best to admit light and air and mosquitoes, a gentleman walked by the window, on the sloping ledge of the ninety-degree roof, upright and kicking madly at a two-by-four a couple of feet from where the roof drops off four or five stories. They do things like that here. Fun and games. I presume he was testing the stability of that two-by-four in the eventuality of our having to cling to it during the fire that many fervently await. I've had my fire. No thank you.

My room is furnished, in a menacing sort of way. There is a funny deformed chest for clothes with a little skinny section where you hang coats and things, a desk made for a doll's house, a bed I'm going to keep quiet about as a penance dur-

---

\* Later entitled *Quick as Dandelions.*

ing retreat, and a white wicker rocker that has been badly damaged and repaired in such a way that whenever you sit down it clutches your behind and gives you a horrendous pinch. The place is rigged with booby traps. I expect whenever I open a desk drawer that a land mine will go off, and the whole theological endeavor will end in a powdery explosion.

## Wednesday, 4 September

FOURTH DAY of retreat. I wrote Dave Morrissy today, assuring him perhaps too profusely that I pray for him daily at Mass and in meditation. David is one of my closest friends, an outrageous wit and a very good Jesuit.

Funny how you make friends in the Society of Jesus. Paul and I entered the same day and became close immediately: we were from similar backgrounds, hated organized joy, exchanged vulgar jokes. I remember during that first week when everybody else was playing compulsory baseball, Paul and I slipped off to the lake and went swimming. Nongroup activity, singularity—those two will never last, people thought. We have. Leo, on the other hand, I knew for years before we became friends. Only about three years ago we began talking at summer school and discovered that, whereas we have almost nothing in common, we feel the same about the things that really matter: loving God and people and being a religious. David has always been a delight, treating me when we were novices with benign indulgence during my corrupt period and with reserved scorn during my pious one. We have everything in common, except that he's a Baghdad missionary who studies economics and I . . . well, I'm not.

Anyway, I wrote David effusively because I feel I've failed to communicate the great fondness I bear him and I feel bad about that. He is a swamp and a wart hog and a sack of guts, to quote the greater authors, but he is dear to me. Why do we never communicate the things that really matter? Life is like that. Though, God knows, I *try* to let people know I like them and am grateful to them. I guess I succeed better at letting them know when I don't like them. Negatives are easier.

### Thursday, 5 September

I'VE JUST FINISHED a new poem called "Psalm for an Exile." Which gives you an idea of how things are going. Retreat is awful. This is the fifth day and it seems like the fiftieth. Praying is the hardest thing, though getting up at five-thirty takes a bit more oomph than I can customarily raise at that unseemly hour. I drag myself out of that ditch they've disguised as a bed, lurch around sickish with diseased and disintegrating sinuses most of the day, and then flop back in the ditch and konk out. Will I survive this, even for a year? And why? To be a priest. I guess it's worth it, though from this point it requires a bit more faith than I've got handy. This is my tenth year, and all the externals I found so frightening before I entered look even more frightening now. Getting up in the middle of the night, answering bells promptly, never doing or saying outrageous things, surrendering your will to Superiors. Surrendering your will to Christ, really, but he operates through Superiors, and it takes a humble eye to see him in their commands.

### Friday, 6 September

SIXTH DAY. I have read *Jacob's Room* and *The Waves*, Virginia Woolf again. I've also reworked "Psalm for an Exile," which wasn't finished after all. I'm still not sure it's much good. Here it is.

#### Psalm for an Exile

> Let him read
> *Mansfield Park* or listen
> Bach and counterpoint;
> These help distill
> The poison. He *can*
> Sing Christ, of course,
>
> In foreign lands. Even
> With a hoarse throat.

He misses leeks
And garlic or hates them,
Depending on the place
He left, the place

He waters with just
Salt tears. For him
We recommend prayer;
Psalm 137—salvific
For the exile, seeing
In the course of praise

He sings blessed is he
Who takes the little ones
Of Babylon and dashes
Out their brains
Against the walls:
Strangers, take notice.

And then he laughs,
A Lazarus out of season.
He must, or miss—
Mourning exile in a land
Of exiles—our part
In the cosmic joke.

It's all right, I guess. Better perhaps without the last stanza?

Later. Here's something for *you*, L'Heureux: "A fool takes no pleasure in understanding, but only in expressing his opinion." Proverbs 18:2. Ouch.

Still later. At Rahner's cue, I have been praying to the Unseen God in whom I hope. I trust that through his mercy and grace even I may see forever. "You shall not finally break the bruised reed." And he won't. He won't.

## Saturday, 7 September

SEVENTH DAY of retreat. Note. The Woodstock toilet tissue is unusual: one side is made of wax paper and other of sand paper (fine grain).

Here's one resolution shot. Some imaginative person joined a spring to a frame with a piece of string (not rope, string) and threw a straw sack on it. And that's my bed. It has gullies. By planting one elbow firmly in my stomach and curling up so that the heavier portion of my body rests in the bigger of the two gullies, I can get quite cozy. Except I can't breathe that way. My pillow is stuffed with acorns, rocks, and pine cones. And I won't say another word about it.

## Tuesday, 10 September

RETREAT ENDED yesterday after eighty-seven days in the Sahara. What do I have to show for it? Not much. I'm tired to death; I've had a headache practically without interruption for the entire retreat; yet it's all been profitable. Though the worst-preached retreat of my last ten years—the eight days seemed somewhat longer than those ten years—the director was unable effectively to hinder the work of the Holy Spirit, and I discover it is possible to pray even in a wind tunnel. God help me to get through this year; it looks so difficult.

Discovery: people here are not really so big. They just look that way because I feel so small. It's the damned gray coat they make you wear around the house; you feel like a prison inmate on his first day in cell block. Men here aren't so big as they are old; everybody seems to have gray hair and wrinkles. And they're tired. What are they tired *from*, I wonder? There are some weirdies, as in every community. And also as in every community, there are some really fine men. I met a wonderful chap from Detroit this morning at breakfast. Bob Fitzgerald; a fine sort. He said he had read my last poem in the *Atlantic*, which made me choke on the orange I was eating, probably because the poem is about an orange, and I immediately went to pieces and apologized for writing and for being in the *Atlantic* and for being. Why do I do that?

## Wednesday, 11 September

I SPOKE to Fr. Fitzmyer today about making up the work I missed this summer. The Gospel background material I must do on my own, the Weigel Introduction to Theology I lose forever, the Greek must be done by mid-November. Greek. I scarcely remember an alpha from an omega. Fitz is grand: getting a little pudgy, jowls just beginning, intensely alive, a delightful conversationalist. He pounces on ideas, chews them, chatters. He is like a squirrel with a speed thyroid. Delightful. Delightful.

## Saturday, 14 September

FRENCH LITERARY criticism is funny. The French let their tongues run on until they stumble against an idea; they roll *that* around for a while and then start off again, running, in any direction.

## Wednesday, 18 September

I FINISHED a poem today, "Psalm," generated some days ago in Gus Weigel's class when he said: "Nothing is reliable these days except dying. It's rather easy to die in 1963; you just lie there and they give you an injection so you don't feel the pain and, pffft, pretty soon it's all over." The last part of the poem is particularly Weigelian, and good, too, I think.

> Dying today is rather easy.
> The clergy, on vacation, spares
> Us medieval scenes of sin,
> Regeneration, Christ. Antiseptic
> Nurses give injections; pain
> Becomes a memory, a bright flash
> On the eyelid, quiets to eternal
> Dark. And shall there be no night?
> Even now the shadows lengthen.

Gus is a great soul, hearty and a little vulgar and altogether without pretense. He's a huge gruff man who woofs and gargles when he talks. He looks and even walks like a disappointed bear. I find his classes stimulating, offbeat; many don't like him, feeling that he's just bazzooing when he should be teaching. To an extent they're right. I suspect, however, that he himself feels—as I did when I taught school—that the only really important stuff he says is the persiflage, the obiter dicta struck from the flinty texts of Denzinger. Gus loves the Church incredibly and so he chastises it, as indeed I suspect he chastises himself. He is brutally honest. He says wonderful, amusing things too: "I've always felt that the man who invented the distinction between mortal and venial sin must have gone to hell." And others, which would never survive the perilous passage through censors. He is a great man. It's a privilege to study under him.

### Friday, 20 September

WOODSTOCK DOES NOT exactly overpower you with its friendliness. I'm lonely, dammit. At age twenty-eight that's an awful admission to have to make, but I miss my friends at Weston terribly. I've made friends here—and I suppose enemies too, already—but I lust after the leeks and garlic of New England. Ironic, I suppose. Oh well. And he sighed.

Look at the positive aspects. This place is alive with ideas. An astonishing number of people *do* things: make movies, write books, teach correspondence courses in theology, edit *Woodstock Letters* and *Theological Studies*, write and produce musicals of extraordinary competence. We have a band of at least fifteen pieces, a fire department (honest to God, with two fire engines, and some of Ours ride off crazily to rescue mothers and babes from burning cow barns, etc.), and a student body which is at least unusual: 20 percent have Ph.D.'s, 85 to 90 percent have at least one M.A., many have a couple of M.A.'s. I guess it's a wonderful place to be. I wish I *felt* that way.

I sent my long long poem "A Solemne Musick" to *Thought* today with an apologia perhaps better omitted. I find it distressing to have published in places like *Atlantic, Kenyon, Yale*, etc., and never in any Jesuit periodical. Jesuit editors don't want me and I belong to them. Thinking back, I suppose it was imprudent to inflict my master's thesis on *Thought* without so much as a revision (the topic was Albee's plays); pitching "Solemne Musick" on top of the Albee heap may be the last straw for *Thought*.

One of the few fellows I've gotten to know is a great soul named Justin Kelly. He looks sort of like me but with all the bones drawn to their logical conclusion. He's witty and intimidatingly well read. We walk now and again and he patiently explains that he is not from Cincinnati but Cleveland, a purely logical distinction to me but an important one to anybody from Cleveland. He told me an amusing anecdote today about some character called David Jones. He's an English or Irish poet and is said to be whacking good; shamefully, I've never heard of him. Justin told me of attending a lecture by Fr. Noon, S.J., on the subject of David Jones, a talk largely incomprehensible to most of the audience and further irritating by reason of its having been advertised as a lecture on the contemporary English novel. Two love-doves were sitting in front of Justin, and shortly after the lecture began She passed a note to Boyfriend saying "Davie Jones. A joke?" Halfway through the lecture Boyfriend passed Her a note saying "Davie Jones. No joke." And this sustained them for the rest of the time with its built-in giggles. It's great to be in love; it can even get you through an impossible lecture. Maybe that's what's wrong with studies in the Society.

The weather staggers me. I wake in a pool of sweat, crawl out of the ditch, swim for the shower; all day the great problem is to keep from melting into an uncomely puddle.

### Saturday, 21 September

CHURCH HISTORY is good. Fr. McNally is droll and perceptive, if at times a little chaotic. How does he organize a book—and he does—with his mind leaping centuries, without so much as the grace of a transition sentence?

### Monday, 23 September

THOUGHT WROTE today accepting my Albee thesis as an article, with provisions, naturally, for rewriting. No word about my poem, which wouldn't have reached them at the time they wrote me. I'm pleased out of my wits. This will be my first prose published.

## Tuesday, 1 October

WHINE, WHINE, WHINE. That's all you ever do. Why don't you try to develop a little moral fiber; it would be a new experience for you. Isn't it D. H. Lawrence who said that he preferred dogs to human beings because dogs at least were not always whining about their lot?

## Thursday, 3 October

WELL, HERE GOES: charity to the winds. Religious are people too, you know. They have emotions and dispositions, good days and bad ones, virtues and—alas, he said, beating his head against the chair leg—vices. And *I* especially have my good days and bad ones. Let me record a bad one. Good therapy.

Evening recreation is impossible. From ten to twenty men skulk about the room snatching at whatever shred of paper there might be (in addition to three or four dread local papers, we get one *New York Times,* a day late, for over two hundred fifty people), and even while you're talking to someone, his eyes rove the room for a chunk of paper that might be dropped while you are in mid-sentence. Few men talk. In another room, a jam-packed smoke-filled dungeon, great numbers commit themselves irrevocably to bridge. And in a third room Where Men Alone Tread another group plays pool and ping-pong and table shuffleboard. Pandemonium. It's awful. I've taken to walking during evening recreation or disappearing to the periodical room. How I would like to unsheathe my tongue and lacerate people sometimes; flail them with some of the frighteningly uncharitable things I often think. Tell people that so-and-so is a mushroom with a face and a disposition to match. Or that the only difference between Blank and civilized man is civilization. Or that Fr. X. is a withered shank of sacrificial lamb who appears to be ineffably miser-

able and undoubtedly has good reasons. Tell another etc.,
etc. Cruelty is easy. And I suppose they—some of them anyway—think the same unkindnesses about me. My loneliness,
I suppose, when compounded with all those defense mech-
anisms I am aware of and the others I'm not aware of, must
come across as belligerence or snobbery or an affable disdain.
And yet I shouldn't moan. People come and talk to me in
my room; nice people, Justin and Bob Fitz and Jim Linehan. Jim is from New England also and his survival (he'll
be ordained in June) ought to give me encouragement. No
more of this; it's unhealthy and, to put it in a slightly more
significant realm, it's unchristian.

You can't tell people in the world things like this. Why,
I wonder? Religion as a state of perfection means that we
*strive* for perfection, not that we necessarily have it. *They*,
world-people, know that. They suffer few delusions about us,
especially if they've studied under us. We get cross. Why
deny it? Maybe we don't deny it; we just don't advertise it.
You win. Bravo. Now, go take an aspirin and lie down. Peace
to all.

Later. I finished a poem yesterday which I think rather good.
I had just read a touching article by Leonard Woolf on his
wife in that absurd *Show* magazine. In the course of the article
he mentioned that passage in her diary—the one I read and
was so struck by a year ago in Aileen Pippet's biography of
V. W.—describing the several phenomena of her occasional
insanity. I returned to my room and in only a few hours put
together "Intermission."

> *Intermission*
>
> Sometimes
> when the fire
> burns wild
>
> and mind pursues
> blistering voices
> I see how
>
> it could end:
> a plunge
> down sides of cliffs

rising straight
from green
white water.

Among the slimy
stems of lilies
the fire

is quenched
voices silent
mind drowned—

while I,
crouched above the cliffs,
clack

a wooden tonque
trying to say lost
and lost.

I feel a great affinity for Virginia Woolf; I don't know why.
Probably because our temperaments and the way our minds
work have some similarity. With the obvious distinction—her
talent was immense and I have no reason to suspect mine is
anything more than slightly unordinary (and maybe just quite
ordinary). But I react to criticism and to insensitivity in the
same disproportionate way she did. Could it be that I'm a
potential psychotic? I don't think so. Losing my mind, however, would be the most complete and most horrifying gift
of self to God I can imagine. I pray he doesn't want that of
me. The poem: it's only a little thing, but it has something
very immediate and real. Maybe.

### Friday, 4 October

I AM A BIT incoherent at the moment. I served the Dean's Mass
this morning and got the Latin all tangled up in the cotton
ball that mops about where my tongue should be at the wee
hours. So bad. And now it's getting on toward eight-thirty and
I must strap myself into my Greek chair. Every morning I
have my Greek session all by myself. It's great for discipline,

## Sunday, 20 October

THOUGH I SUPPOSE I've been doing my best to get far away, I remain in God's clutches; you know how painful that can be. It's different from being merely close to him. It's being squeezed: if you don't struggle, you're o.k.

## Monday, 21 October

SORTING PAPERS TODAY—teaching notes mostly—I came across a little sheaf of memoranda I recorded one Saturday morning following a prefecting assignment at a Friday-night record hop. What follows is almost literal transmission, committed to memory as I sat, having a coffee and doughnut, between two mothers of students I then had in class.

"He loves school. I did too. I always did. I always loved school. We had the good teachers too. Parochial."

"I didn't. I hated it."

"I loved my school." Shakes her head "no," apparently in regret at such early folly.

"I hated it. I couldn't wait to quit, I was so anxious. It was during the war, you know, and all the teachers joined the war and you had those practice teachers, I mean student teachers, who were just about nineteen and they had to just follow the book. . . ."

"I know what you mean. I was lucky. I always had good teachers. Parochial schools. You can't beat parochial schools."

"And all the boys were joining the war and everybody wanted to go into war work, there was a lot of money in machine shops and everything, and the boys were getting furloughs and everything was confused. That was the big problem, really, everything was confused. And you know, nobody cared. I mean they really didn't. It was all the war. The war. So I appreciate the need of a good education for my children. Believe me, I know."

"So do I. We had real good teachers and they taught us our books. None of this high stuff. I think there's too much of that today. [Here I get a dirty look; I am guilty of the high stuff.] But the real arithmetic and spelling and writing and like that. They knew. Our teachers knew."

"It all balances out. Sure. It all balances out."

That can stand, I think, without comment.

## Tuesday, 22 October

TRAINS SKREEK and grundle in the valley. I like that. The wooden bridge guns down a few more cars. I was about to say I am in love with God when a wave of sobriety swept over me, leaving me beached and too self-conscious to protest.

## Saturday, 26 October

I AM TWENTY-NINE today. Feel ninety. My tenth year in religion. It is good after the years of uncertainty, of wavering decision, to want unequivocally to be a priest. I do. And I must act accordingly. I must pray more. Take theology seriously. Be more careful in future about my relations with women. Let's face it. I love deeply and I'm as inclined to sex as any man. And my love for God, parents, Jesuit friends, and female friends are widely differing kinds of love. I do not love David (who ever loved a giraffe?) the same way I love Adria . . . for which, I suppose, they're both grateful. With women, sex rears its lovely head and what began as a solid love friendship can, with a little imprudence, become a profoundly disturbing love affair. I narrowly escaped disaster twice during regency, not so much because of overfamiliarity with women but because of a certain *kind* of familiarity. To find women attractive, sexually desirable, is all very well (thin cool blondes, for instance), but as a priest I must be clear that deep personal friendships with women must remain friendships. And only that. A certain kind of familiarity—a way of talking and looking, the facile social excuse for a kiss of greeting and parting—turns friendship into something else . . . and I can't really see myself as a fugitive priest. So I must be more careful. All this is much too depressing for a birthday.

My orlon sweater "that laughs at washing" stopped laughing when it met our laundry service this week. It looks like that proverbial rat who tried to desert the sinking ship and, having swum its best, came at last to grief in a watery death. Rest in peace, sweater.

And here's a birthday goodie from Proverbs (27:14) that ought to be branded on the arm of every morning exercitator: "He who blesses his neighbor with a loud voice in the morning will be counted as cursing." I think we can conclude from this that God is definitely not in favor of our rising at five-thirty. Which I'll never accustom myself to anyhow.

## Monday, 28 October

I HAVE BUNDLES of birthday greetings from kids I taught at Fairfield Prep and Boston College High. Amazing. And lots of nice birthday things have happened to me: letters, *Thought* is going to publish "A Solemne Musick," the Albee rewrite problem seems soluble.

Fr. O'Neill, the editor of *Thought*, writes that he wants a moral and critical evaluation of Albee's plays and, unnecessarily, he adds that I ought to avoid the *PMLA* type of language and documentation. The biggest problem I foresee is introducing critical appraisal naturally; that is to say, letting judgment flow logically from my treatment of Albee's peculiar structures. You must know what a work is trying to do and how it's trying to do it before you can say how well it succeeds or how badly it fails. I have until June 1 to work on this paper; by then I should have things well in hand.

Later. I've written a poem on one of my theology professors. I wonder do I dare publish it? It's a complimentary poem, mirroring and explaining my admiration for him; still most teachers don't care to see their photo peeking from the local bookstands. It is an accurate poem.

### Marginal Note in a Theology Text

All bones and ashes. And not
that either, for he is coat
hangers and rake handles and

all things awkward. Bolts
and pincers. Some careless god
tired by the elegance of lesser

men chose metal pipes to make
him, put him together haphazard
and with joy, confident that

everything would be all right.
He lopes. He gestures silent
movies. Flesh clings for life

upon his rack. And somewhere
in the wire tower Christ has
pitched a tent and keeps night

fire; his smile is conquest
of all bones and ashes. He is
epiphany. It is little wonder.

I shall now begin work on a larger project; turning the Code
of Canon Law into rhymed hexameters.

### Tuesday, 29 October

IT'S VERY LATE and all the mice are playing charades in my
little attic ceiling. My mind is soggy with moral theology and
Fr. Reed's time systems, which help you calculate how many
minutes you have to eat a ham sandwich in Boston, Philadelphia, Calcutta when the clock says twelve but it really isn't.
This is one of the ever-expanding body of things I do not wish
to know. Listening to him explain the system, I sighed and
made a rather desperate resolve to just simply follow the clock.
By the time it would take me to finish assessing hemispheric
and local time, dividing and adding and square rooting, the
sandwich would be stale and my stomach sick.

### Tuesday, 5 November

I SPENT A long long time this morning writing a letter to a
fellow who attended a school where I taught during Regency.

Though I never taught him, I used to see him occasionally at football games and around the school; he frequently dropped into my classroom to talk. Now he's involved in an awful emotional tie-up with some other kid at college. I record my letter to him here as a sort of exorcism, I guess; I'm very worried about him; I've offered Mass for him every day for a week now; I've consulted a priest on what I ought to say to him. Gosh, kids can break your heart. I'm praying he will get over this and not be scarred forever.

Letter: No, I am not shocked; just very very unhappy for you. Knowing you and being fond of you, I can empathize somewhat and realize the terrible divided loyalties you must feel. Your Catholic upbringing and beyond that the promptings of conscience which go back to Eve and the serpent must be at violent warfare with your manifestations of love for this boy. And that must cause you great pain. You say "sex is not the basis of our relationship, but it is there." You're anxious, I think, and naturally so, to establish that this isn't park-bench lust but a very genuine love you feel—a giving not of body only but of personality and of self. And that this *is* love is evidenced by your being so upset, I think. Of course you love him, ——, but—and of course there is always a but— you can't love him in this way. For one thing, it is mortal sin; a disagreeable way to put it, but that's how it is. And, negatively, that is the main consideration. Positively, the main consideration is that your relationship with God is being effectively done in. Cut off. Okay, so we'll forget that for the moment. The second thing wrong is that your "possessing one another" is destroying your relationship to each other. Real love can never flower in a setup like this. It will decay and become a bitter memory and possibly a psychic sore as well. And third, the relationship—carried on as it now is—is an incredible drain on your psychic life and on your social life as well. You must, all spiritual and moral and psychological considerations aside, live in society and you cannot live any life worth living so long as you're an alien. But all this is mere argumentation and we both know what that's worth. Not much. You have to see it yourself. And you ought to talk about this to a spiritual guide, and talk and talk and talk, and eventually you would find things clarifying themselves. I think you would find that your love for the boy is a lot more emotional and sexual than either of you suspect. But now I'm doing precisely what I had resolved not to do; I'm rattling on about things you can't say in a letter. They are hard things and disagreeable to hear and you may resent them. We ought to talk. Perhaps we can meet sometime during this coming summer. I'm afraid that things I say in writing will be misunderstood. I can't approve, you know that, and I can't really guide you when I know so little about the situation and about yourself and your present dispositions. All I can say is that I understand your unhappiness and that I pray for you every day and I am not going "to spurn you forever because you are a sinner." I am most eager for you to resolve your problems and return to a more stable emotional life and most of all of course return to Christ, who loves you more than either of us could understand. He does, you know. He does.

## Saturday, 9 November

WHILE I WAS walking with Justin today, we suddenly discovered ourselves in one of those serious conversations about truth and reality. I said to him with an exaggerated didactic tone: "I have long since ceased, Justin, to believe in the relevance of truth." Justin: "Relevance of truth to what?" I: "To anything." And then we laughed. Why is that funny? Maybe it isn't; maybe we're both a wee bit dingy dingy upstairs.

David Morrissy sent me another of his marvelous letters today. They're so witty, so damnably learned. I'm going to keep them and publish them as soon as he has the tact to die or leave the country.

Later. At recreation tonight I heard about one of our Fathers who gets off statements that are a variety of the malapropism and that are the more marvelous because they escape him altogether. He said—in class, mind you—"The fact that monkeys have hands should give us pause." And: "If Darwin were alive today, he'd turn over in his grave." And: "Many remains of primitive man have been found in old pots." And:

"I almost always agree with Betty Salmon. In fact, I feel certain I would embrace Betty Salmon in any position she wished to assume." And others, hilarious ones, which are better not committed to writing.

## Sunday, 10 November

EVERYBODY'S FAVORITE ATHEIST, Madelyn Murray, once told reporters that people think "that all they talk about in Baltimore is politics and sex, but it's not true; all they talk about is the goddam Orioles." Even Madelyn occasionally hits upon a truth. Sports are so important to the Jesuits here. Do you suppose it would be heresy to propose that possibly, just possibly, the world was created in some primal cosmic football match?

## Thursday, 14 November

NED LYNCH. Let us say a word of thanks for the Ned Lynches of this our time. He'll be ordained this year, which is nice because the world needs more priestly Ned Lynches; he is a hulk, a bit shy, a man who admires wit and mild malice but who is himself solidly good and kind. The first time I met him he was friendly and accepting; you know what I mean: he accepts you for what you are, not for what you look like or what people say you are like or what your poems indicate you must be like. Good. And simple. Actually he didn't know until today that I even write poems; that pleased me very much. *He* pleases me very much.

## Friday, 15 November

AS A BREAK from my Shakespeare regimen—since coming here I've read fourteen of his plays from *Titus Andronicus* right on through *A Midsummer Night's Dream*—I'm reading W. H. Lewis' *Sunset of the Splendid Century*. There's a marvelous passage speaking of Louis XIV's dislike for Mme. Scarron: "She had a reputation for wit. . . . She was the widow of that rackety poet whose circle had, in his [Louis'] mother's time, been one of the most brilliant in Paris; she was a well-known figure at the Hotels de Richelieu and d'Albret; she was the sort of woman who read poetry, and the king, darkly but unjustly, suspected her of writing it. On the whole, he thought the widow Scarron would not do."

### Saturday, 16 November

REJECTION FROM *Kenyon Review* today. My own fault. It was stupid of me to send *Kenyon* a poem in which the name of Christ appears twice—*Kenyon*, one of whose principles is that all gods are created equal.

Our theology discussion group today convinced me that the rationalism of the nineteenth century has influenced our ways of thinking much more extensively than most Jesuits believe. There was talk of "greater truth value in propositional logic" than in "a mere image." Certainly Christ did not feel images were such poor tools; he very rarely used an abstraction in his discourses. And the Gospel of St. John, the most purely theological of the Gospels, is full of concretions. "I am the vine; you are the branches" can scarcely be said to have less truth value than "I am your ultimate principle in the tendency toward which you must discover your relational significance." How we enjoy our little semantic waltz. How I wish we would join the twentieth century.

### Sunday, 17 November

TOMORROW I SHALL send Naomi the little autobiography Doubleday requested for their publicity department. Since publishers never ballyhoo a book of poetry and since there will be no danger therefore of my little true confession ever seeing print, I've opted for drollery over fact. There are enough facts in this world already. Here's an excerpt:

I was born inopportunely in a car on a bridge during a hurricane; it was the only exciting day in a univocally dull life. I was a normal happy child: destructive, malicious, and thoroughly self-centered. My parents read to me each night little anecdotes from Saintly Children of Our Own Times and I was inspired to become a great saint. When with the passage of a year of rather ostentatious prayer it became clear there would be no vision, I turned my energies to writing. By my ninth birthday I had written an ambitious novel of one hundred twenty-four pages called Lizard, a sequel to something I had been reading; and by my tenth, a play and some one hundred poems. Since the age of ten, I have gradually deteriorated as a writer.

I had the usual New England adolescence; I worked after school, fell in love with the village sorceress, grew desperately self-conscious. I was very lively and very stupid in high school; people tolerated me because my brother was a football player. After high school I attended the National Academy of Theatre Arts and acted, while attending Holy Cross College, on television and in summer stock. Since I had a weird voice and a frightening physical presence, it was a tribute to my gall and the critical incapacity of my employers that I was allowed to act at all. Actually it is the only thing I have ever done with any degree of competence. I entered the Society of Jesus at the age of nineteen, will be ordained in 1966 barring divine and/or ecclesiastical interference. I paint and write and try to grow in the Spirit who somehow has chosen me and, having made his choice, sticks by it to the wonder of not a few.

## Tuesday, 19 November

THEOLOGY IS FUNNY, isn't it? There are so many things I really want to read, but I never seem to have the time. When I make the time, they suddenly turn dull or excessively abstruse or just headachy. I guess I'm not a scholar, not even a student. I'm incapable of more than an occasional bright flash; sustained work makes me crumble. Even the Albee paper has become a burden. I look at it now and say, so what. I'd like to forget it and go on to something else, wondering if Albee is worth all that effort. I could more profitably spend the time on St. Paul. Resolution: I will do the Albee thing because (1) I have committed myself to *Thought* and (2) it will be good discipline to fulfill an unpleasant contract by a given date and (3) it will be my first appearance in prose . . . and the only way poets ever get readers is by writing prose. Seems we sidetracked theology somewhere early in the paragraph.

St. Paul is the answer or at least a good part of the answer to my spiritual problems: the jansenism and the self-hatred and the guilt. Read St. Paul.

## *Thursday, 21 November*

I'VE JUST NOW come in from a terrific handball session, still excited about my poem. For the first time in a very long time I've written something that strikes me as instantly good. I wrote it during lunch—stayed in my room and ate a sandwich I had made earlier and balanced a pad on my knee and wrote it, a rather long poem called "An Investigation into the Nature, Function, and Attendant Circumstances of Radiators." Snappy; a rather nice satire on scholasticism, on radiators, on poets, and on me. People will think I've taken to writing light verse . . . they may even begin to *read* me. I like the first part, describing radiators.

> Fat ones like men
> at doorways of tobacconists forty years
> waiting, skinnies like Miss Twiddle,
> little puffy ones (a favorite aunt
> scrunched up in the best seat by the window),
> slouch radiators that hug the wall so close
> they disappear (mice play their harpsichord
> at midnight), baseboard ones and grates
> in floors and little apertures behind
> the draperies, all pretending we are warm;
> and I cold now eighteen years.

And there are some other nice things in it. It goes off to *Harper's* as soon as I can get it back from the censors.

I feel really great these days; I wonder what's up. Will I be stricken with some fell disease? Will erosion of the mind, or at least of the gums, set in? The weather is clear and the nose has stopped its incessant harangue; perhaps that has something to do with it. The world rejoices, the trees clap hands—even though it is a kind of pallid fall.

## Friday, 22 November

PRESIDENT KENNEDY was assassinated this afternoon. May his soul rest in peace. I loved him.

## Wednesday, 27 November

I CANNOT BELIEVE he is dead. I can't talk about it nor can I stand to hear others talk about it, even when they speak of a genuine and simple grief. For the most part I stay in my room. And this afternoon I wrote him a poem, "Death of a Man." It's not bad. It's objective at least and strong and illumined by a conviction (faith, I guess), the strength of which I hadn't really expected in myself. Maybe I shall send it out to the *Atlantic*.

## Saturday, 30 November

JIM LINEHAN and I went to Arlington Cemetery today and waited in line with anywhere from two to ten thousand other people to view the President's grave and stay there long enough to say one Hail Mary. It is a marvelous spot, isolated from any other grave, and approachable in a great snaking twist right from the main entrance. It was a sad thing but good. Freezing, freezing cold. We witnessed the changing of the guard as we entered the grave inclosure; a display in itself.

The whole long wait was marred only by a priest and two ladies who crashed the line right near the head to the scarcely repressed annoyance of the guard (I winked and he shook his head and lifted his hands in mock despair) to whom this had obviously happened often in the preceding week and to the unrepressed embarrassment of Jim and myself. The three of them were so secure and self-satisfied and, I suspect, a little self-congratulatory for having gotten out of their car on a freezing cold day just to see a grave. Strange; at the time I was only ashamed for them and now, much later, I'm infuriated. There is a solemnity about the grave procession that makes one excuse boors like that, I guess, even clerical ones.

Returning home tonight, I decided it would have been wiser not to send that poem to the *Atlantic*. It falls hopelessly short of what I had intended. As soon as it returns I shall destroy it.

## Monday, 9 December

TELEGRAM TODAY from *Atlantic*: "Delighted to publish your 'Death of a Man' with opening eulogies. February *Atlantic*. Many thanks. Edward Weeks." I should be grateful and I am excited but mostly I am overwhelmed with embarrassment; the poem is not good enough. Period. And I find myself still unable to talk about Kennedy's death.

Later. I suppose I should remark here that twice each year we spend three days in prayer and meditation on the vows; on the morning after the third day we repeat our vows at Mass. We can't renew them, of course, because they're perpetual, so we just sort of refresh our commitment. All this is by way of saying that our most recent triduum—December 4, 5, 6—was a nightmare for me, a *crise*. But I *shall* work it out.

## Wednesday, 11 December

ATLANTIC WRITES SAYING they are going to use my poem along with the eulogies of Samuel Eliot Morison and Archibald MacLeish. Rather exclusive company.

Later. Fr. Weigel, just home from the Vatican Council, seems quite discouraged. He gave us a talk this evening on the goings-on in Rome. A fascinating hour. When he prepares a talk or a press interview, he is smashing. "The Christian unity movement is warming up but nobody should take off his coat yet." "Give man time and strength and wisdom and let him go ahead and work and everything will turn out . . . terrible." Gus is wonderful: Christian pessimism. But he says profound things: "The Continental mind holds that you do not have any kind of agreement unless it is written down or spelled out in law. The Anglo-Saxon mind, on the other hand, believes that the less law there is the better—leave as much as you possibly can to the moral sphere."

## Monday, 16 December

GUS'S CLASSES ARE terrific these days. Full of grace for me. St. Paul is rising to the surface. During the triduum early this month and during the prolonged depression that followed it, I reviewed and resumed all the puritan, jansenistic, legalistic, negativistic, self-centered errors of my pitiable spiritual career. They became so overwhelming that . . . well, they became overwhelming. And there were the guilt feelings that have stalked me since I was seven and have grown stronger with each successive failure. And I couldn't pray. I was at my wit's end, not doubting that I wanted to be a priest, but wondering whether I should or could be one. Then finally a series of graces began. In moral class I was bored to tears during a lecture on love and law; the words were aimless; they carried no conviction: it began to bother me, though, that love and law are at the very roots of our existence and I didn't even care. Then Gus mentioned St. Paul and his liberation from law—just in passing, you know. Then one evening I mentioned it to a young father I admire for his transparent holiness, and I added: "I think I'll be all right if only I can discover St. Paul." He all but leaped out of the chair, waving his arms (he's usually quite rational) and shouting "That's it." So now I've been reading St. Paul and trying to *think* with him. I become more and more convinced that this is the only escape for me from a self-orientation and a guilt syndrome that could easily become debilitating to me as a priest and as a person, even as a writer. I wonder, in fact, if I didn't first discover the difficulty in my writing and then work back to it in myself.

Later. After dinner I must chew away at that stack of unaddressed Christmas cards. Study some ecclesiology. See the treasurer. Send poems to censors. Wrap and mail two little book packages. Why is it I can never seem to *do* things?

Gus says this limerick was making its rounds of the Council Fathers:

> Gus Weigel, John Murray, Hans Kung
> Today are on everyone's tongue,
>   But Ottaviani
>   Will get off his fanni
> And see they're all properly hung.

## Tuesday, 17 December

"AND IF HE should delay, wait on him. For he will come. He will surely come."

## Thursday, 19 December

ADVENT. I love Advent. During these days I'm learning that we have liberty and that love extends even to me and so does forgiveness and mercy. I don't really believe these things yet —a sort of shadowy knowledge is the best I can muster now. But real knowledge will come in time.

Later. In the absence of real knowledge, I received a long delightful letter from Leo Fahey today. I've neglected writing him; disgraceful. So I wrote him a long letter this afternoon about St. Paul. Now that I think of it, it is Leo who first preached Paul to me.

## Friday, 20 December

POETRY AND LIVING. You cannot be a first-rate poet so long as you let your work be peddled about, so long as you let yourself be tricked into poetic self-defense or self-explication. I refuse to define or defend; I must beware of wanting to show people my verse, of wanting to "be appreciated."

### Saturday, 21 December

LATE AT NIGHT. At Woodstock I try. I try so hard. I suppose it's rather pitiful. I want to be liked. And then I go ahead and confuse people terribly by my frankness and directness and that other thing—whatever it is—my self-reliance. They don't know how to handle it. Maybe it's just my insecurity turned inside out, though I don't think so. I haven't yet capitulated to the theologate-ethos; that is to say, I haven't yet been whirled into the emotional vortex. I'm a little outside, seeing what goes on, the convolutedness and invertedness of so many, and I marvel at the grace of the Spirit heaped on me more and more each day, making me desire the priesthood more than anything, even while I fear it and doubt my capability of being a good priest. I love God, you know, I really do. With a distant, distrusting, jansenistic, semi-pelagian love—but the love only *I* can give him and, unfortunately, the *only* love I have to give. If I could only love God the way I love other people and do things for them and give things to them; perhaps in loving them I *am* loving him . . . I wish I were more theologically grounded in what it means to love God. In any case I want to grow in love, fear law less, realize what it means to be a good man: I am becoming convinced that unless I realize and accept my own minimal goodness, I shall never be able to do anything for Christ, others, myself.

### Christmas

MIDNIGHT MASS was beautiful. The day was trying, as Christmas in the Society always is.

Tom O'Gorman, who says Mass for the workmen here, told me this story. While the priest says the Gospel in Latin, one of the workmen reads it aloud in English to the little congregation. Tom says he distinctly heard the chap say in his Negro velvet voice: "And the wise men brought gifts of gold and mirth and frankenstein." And no one laughed. Terrific.

## *Friday, 3 January*

FR. GUS WEIGEL died today in New York. It was a shock to everybody. He was a great man, will be much missed.

## *Monday, 6 January*

WE BURY Fr. Weigel tomorrow. The house is swarming with people. Everybody has been given some crazy job—I was a busboy and have been promoted to waiter—and the chaos will reign until the guests go home. How amused Gus would be.

He talked frequently of death since his return from the Council. He had just had a complete physical, had been pronounced in good health, and nonetheless remarked to someone: "I'm going to die soon anyway." And when he last addressed the community, he concluded with the statement that the Council may or may not reconvene, may or may not handle certain problems. Then he said: "That however is your worry; for me, it is getting late, very late."

Later. There is no way to determine from mere phenomena the true nature of persons. A chap, a great ape of a chap, said to me this afternoon that he was afraid for two months to speak to me because I "looked like one of the few really sane persons in the house, as if I were passing through and collecting information for the FBI." So what do you make of *that*? I assured him that—though I am working for the FBI—I am not certifiably sane. That helped.

## *Wednesday, 8 January*

A BAT FLEW into our recreation room yesterday evening. Ned Lynch killed it with a broom. An incredible scene: men who are quiet as virtue sprang up and began flailing away at the thing with papers and magazines and one even grabbed the wastebasket and tried to trap the bat. Killing the bat was a community project bringing us close together "in the bond of charity." I wrote a poem about the little situation. It's kind of ironic and nice: "A Bat in the Monastery."

### Thursday, 9 January

TODAY HAS OVERFLOWED with God's goodies: a minor nervous breakdown in the face of thirty-three pages "on the theological virtues" in opaque and prolix Latin, a social crisis as unnecessary as it was painful to me, several other things I pass over in anguished silence, and now two letters, one a rejection slip from *Commonweal* and one from David reminding me in jocular fashion that I haven't written in seventy eleven years. And of course I forgot his birthday on top of everything else. So now I have a blinding headache and am miserable unto death, fed up with studying moral theology and with my brethren and with Woodstock and most of all with myself. Ugh. Gach. And foof.

### Saturday, 11 January

AMONG THE OTHER disasters of Thursday was my letter to Naomi Burton suggesting that I get out another book through another publisher since I have so many poems just piling up around my ankles. Today she phoned and we talked for about twenty minutes. She is good; kind and patient and knowledgeable as to what to say to neurotics. After she had settled my business hash (*no* other book), we talked. She had just written a long letter about me to "Tom Merton," whose agent she was long before he began Trappisting and mentioned to him that she hoped to get me to write occasional prose. She likes my letters, which she finds "terribly amusing" and, God help me, "sane." (Why do they all mention that I am sane? It must surprise them.)

The question of keeping a journal came up again—she suggested it months ago in a letter—but, though I've often kept notes and memos and so forth, I have never really seriously contemplated keeping a journal. Especially for publication. However, I've decided to give it a try. Certainly this is the ideal situation: the making of a priest, four years of theology in a seminary that is rather famous—what with Fathers Murray, Weigel until his death, Burghardt, Fitzmyer, Dulles on the faculty. The difficulty of course is that nothing ever happens here, at least to me, and so the journal would tend to be awfully intramental, personal, reflective—an account of conscience spiced with uncharity. Another thing; you tend to write about one side of yourself. You record the same mood over and over, partly because the same mood propels you to confide in a chunk of paper instead of in God or in a friend, partly because writing something that somebody is going to read induces a certain formality, a certain persona, and then you're just playing a part. There is the further difficulty of censors. How extensive do they consider their job? Root out heresy and scandal? Or root out anything the smallest most parochial mind might find offensive? Perhaps I should load the book with uncharities and verbal outrage as booby traps; let the censors fatigue themselves on weeding out the truly scandalous and then they might let the pleasantly malicious slip by.

Anyway I've decided to try it for a while. I've been reading Virginia Woolf's *A Writer's Diary*, a selection from journals she kept over the years, and I find it fascinating. She used her journal entries to store ideas, to provoke new ones, to unbend her style. Of course the reason *A Writer's Diary* makes such fine reading is her greatness as a writer, grounds which make *my* keeping a journal indefensible. Nonetheless . . .

Later. I skipped lunch to play handball today—two violent games that left me with my stomach shifting about in search of a comfortable position—and now my poor head feels like one of those puffballs we used to gather from oak trees. If some smart aleck whacks me, my head will just go "guuunch" and all the brown fluff will fall out.

And my mind won't stop whizzing. It whizzes: moral theol-

ogy—hope—Virginia Woolf worrying herself sick over the success or failure of her next book—Albee and *Who's Afraid of
Virginia Woolf?*—despair—my friend Ralph who, as he had
promised he would years earlier, shot himself through the head
while getting ready for Mass one morning—the little boy I
heard about yesterday, perverted by his own father at the
age of seven, and now at thirteen so vicious and corrupt he
has to be kept in isolation from other people—and God, who
is merciful. How do you understand these things? How do
you explain them? As his love, I suppose; a love we do not
ripely understand. In moral class we skipped the notes on hope.
Too banal for our selective attention? It's a shame; despair is
the most meaningful theological problem for me. Perhaps
because I've seen some. But here we chew up day after day,
establishing the three principle kinds of dirty thoughts, the
rules for determining whether or not you are obliged to denounce your brother-Christian (and *that* whether to him or
to the Church), and meanwhile half the world walks around
crazy because it does not know or love God and has no hope
of anything better than its present state of inconsequence.
Well, I suppose if we had treated hope in class, I'd be moaning
now about how dull it had been. Every cloud has its rainy
lining.

## Sunday, 12 January

HOPE. We cannot be saved despite all God's grace unless
we also will to be saved, unless we exercise some personal
choice—and so hope is really the virtue of the personalist.
It is understandable therefore that in our personalist age—
the canon law professor referred to it yesterday as "the age
of love" with not a little sarcasm—Edward Albee should write
in *Who's Afraid of Virginia Woolf?* a study of despair. He is
approaching the hopelessness of modern man from the back
door. Count the number of times he uses the name of Christ,
the prominence he gives it, the caustic ring he sounds upon it.
Hollow. Whatever Albee's intentions, his play is a strong commentary on the hopelessness of modern society.

How hot this house is. My room especially. Some unhealthy
Father must have charge of the heating system. The window
is wide open and a wonderful black bird just flew right up
to the window ledge and looked at me with some alarm—the
look you try not to give when there is a knock at the door and
you shout a joyful "come in" and then it isn't the person you
expected but some talkative lemon—and then he flew away.
It was nice.

Night. It's snowing, and though it has been for most of
the afternoon, the driveway is only dusted with powdered
sugar. When I was little I used to love those thick yellow
pound cakes that were sugar-sprinkled. I'd like one now—
instead of quick-frozen pies. Time for Vespers. I don't like
Vespers.

### Sunday, 19 January

FOR THE PAST WEEK I've been living underwater with fever. It
all began last Monday, was it? with chills and fever, then a
cold that cut off my respiratory system, and finally a crick
in the neck that rendered me as foolish looking as I felt. Gosh,
what a time.

The mind goes racing along logical pathways and suddenly
runs smack into a great brick wall, and while it lies there
stunned, an infinite number of new thoughts and images race
back and forth, tugging it in all directions and somewhere deep
in the background there is a song, one or two notes coming
back again and again as counterpoint to the mental chaos.
And then the mind struggles to its feet and for a minute
everything clears; the song straightens itself out into a real
melody with real lyrics; the ceiling steadies, now becomes
now and last year becomes last year; and you know that by
tomorrow you'll be all right. Tomorrow, of course, you aren't
all right.

Meals were nightmares. I couldn't quite hear what anyone
was saying . . . and of course you can see a person's lips purse
slightly and his jaw muscles flex as he swallows his annoyance
at having to repeat everything two or three times . . . and

the procession of wet vegetables and dry meat and uninteresting dessert . . . it was all unreal. It was like watching a
scene on a defective television set, everything wobbly and bent
at the edges. Then back to bed and again the crazy songs go
whistling in the mind and I am conscious only that I've got
to get over this by Wednesday because that is the day when
Ours will stage their musical. Which was terrific.

Called *Tender Is the Knight* and bristling with dragons and
knights and Merlin and a wonderful witch named Malvooda,
the play was a slamming satire on education, venerable socie-
ties some four hundred years old, tradition, pomposity, everything. One refrain keeps coming back to me: the headmaster,
telling young and inexperienced Gawain that he must slay
dragons at night (despite occupational hazards) "because we
have always slain dragons at night," concludes his admoni-
tion with a song that has these lines: "Don't analyze the enterprise, just memorize the magic word." Ouch. The show was
staged in only two weeks, brilliantly done, with an expenditure
of imagination that was Christianly lavish.

## Tuesday, 21 January

WHAT A DAY. I read Virginia Woolf's *A Writer's Diary* as an
appetizer before class, followed by a little moral theology in
English to work up real hunger. Then, as you'd expect, class
was a famine. And I was in such physical discomfort, still
restless and floppy from my disease, that I kept wanting to
shout: "Would you stop. Would you just stop this garbage
and let us all go to our rooms." I didn't shout, whether from
exhaustion or inhibition, I'm unsure. But during canon law
session I began to evolve a theory that class is a violation
of the natural law on the grounds of frustrating the intellectual
faculties, a direct and deliberate interference with the cogni-
tive process. Developed properly, it might make birth-control
controversy look tame, at least in academic circles.

By lunchtime I was reeling about (more than usual) and
betook myself to the infirmarian, who looked appropriately
grieved when I told him I hadn't strength to go on performing

the more elementary human functions and who shot me full
of Vitamin B-12, which he said would pick me up. It did.
More class in the afternoon. Then I turned loose on moral,
covering the first commandment, the highways and by-ways
and interstices of it, before dinner. After dinner I skipped
community recreation, adjourning to my attic hovel, where
I hunted down all possible avenues of escape from the second
commandment. What a mess. Then another fellow and I dis-
cussed hypothetical confessional cases based on these two
commandments, this for an hour and a half. This sort of
moral discussion, by the way, is called a "repetition," and the
people who do it are, logically enough, "repetition partners."
They study together at odd hours during the year and at very
fixed hours before exams, the idea behind the system being that
human nature is frail and when one partner weakens or is
convulsed the other will steam on ahead and thus they will
both be spared a moment's inactivity, a fate worse then flunk-
ing. Repetition is an ancient and venerable custom in the
Society of Jesus. Today it serves mostly as a means of sharing
information and opinion, a way of forcing oneself through
barren tracts of required matter. My repetition partner is fantastic: he reads everything necessary on a required subject and
he has total recall. He's the nearest thing I've seen to a human
IBM. I find repeating with him difficult, our approaches being
so different, but it's good for me to see how the other half
(the half that gets good marks) thinks and besides it is he
who constantly insists that we study together. For me, it's
just another way to lose my mind. I hate it.

At the moment, of course, I'm riding one of those deceptive
waves. You think: "Well, at last I've hit my stride. I'll just
keep this steady pace and have everything under control in
no time." But it's illusion. It's B-12. I'll have a headache or
my eyes will give out or something will intervene, because
I know from experience—dear Lord, from how *many* experiences—that I can't work that hard that long. Why *is* that?
I have the will to. But my body just gives out.

David writes today asking me to be Sub-deacon at his first
Mass in June. I am honored and accept of course. Paul Messer
writes that George is going mad, but not so slowly any more.

And Naomi writes, air mail mind you, to tell me not to start back to work too soon after my disease. She is good. And I have started too soon. And have had a relapse. And will, pray God, not have another.

## Wednesday, 22 January

THIS AFTERNOON Justin and I went for a brief walk and stopped at the farm to see the two young bulls. They are only six months old, black and square, with huge velvet eyes. They stared for the longest time, just looking off in the distance and now and again looking at us. Then one ambled off and scrubbed his neck on the corner of the barn (an Andrew Wyeth barn; the paint all worn away on that corner where they must satisfy their itches all the time) and the other one gave us his young behind and along with it, I suppose, our definitive rejection.

And now, late, I have gobbled up *All's Well That Ends Well*—my treat for a needless and very trying moral repetition all this morning.

## Saturday, 25 January

WHO KNOWS WHAT I will be like at fifty? Or if I'll be able to accept being that? Will I have to look back at years wasted and a life never lived and a whole string of books remarkable only for their unvaried mediocrity? At a priesthood never spent richly, squandered for other people? The thought is terrifying. I begin to see how and why some Jesuits have retired to their rooms, pulled a small segment of reality in behind them, and locked the door forever. God, keep me from that.

Today is Virginia Woolf's birthday. I offered Mass for her this morning and finished her diaries this evening, finished with some regret because I've been stretching the book out as much as possible. How fascinating this closet writing is and how terribly it reveals her suffering as an artist and as a person.

Neurotic, unstable in the extreme, sensitive to every slight; a tortured life. And Godless. Happy in a sick Socratic way, with beauty and truth. God help her.

Historical note: I began this afternoon to whittle away again at my Albee tree; the completed totem is due on June 1. How can you explain that irrational terror before a blank page? In an hour and a half I managed to write one paragraph of less than a page, wrote it over and over. Now I wonder whether it is merely pretentious or a good opening, and I wonder also if perhaps I've written the conclusion and must lead up to it with a running jump from fifty pages back. In any case it isn't snappy and involving as an opener to a long long article ought to be.

## Sunday, 26 January

DURING REPETITION (the Middle Ages' revenge on the present) this morning, my partner bazzooed me half out of my mind on the importance of Catholic grammar school education. Neither of us attended a Catholic grammar school ourselves. He sounded like the organizer of "Young Americans for Ottaviani." And he was appalled at my ignorance of world politics. It's all so provoking the way "honor thy father and thy mother" suddenly involves the morality of voting for a Communist puppet in East Germany. The fundamentalist is a happy man.

Franz Hals' picture of the Fat Cavalier just this second fell off the wall with a great kerplunk. Scared the hell out of me, my nerves today being frayed violin strings. Blame moral theology.

Later. Two passages from Woolf's A Writer's Diary: "My only interest as a writer lies, I begin to see, in some queer individuality; not in strength or passion, or anything startling, but then I say to myself, is not 'some queer individuality' precisely the quality I respect? . . . People with this gift go on sounding long after the melodious vigorous music is banal." Yes. She's talking about "voice," a writer's unique and unmistakable accent, which marks his work *his* and which is the reward for much pain and exploration and failure. A real voice is easily isolated but impossible to define. Elsewhere in her diaries she writes: "It occurs to me, as we drive, how I'm disliked, how I'm laughed at; and I'm rather proud of my intention to take the fence gallantly." Did they, I wonder, laugh at her? God, how awful.

Later. Instead of looking at the facts of creation as we customarily do, what if we suspend the usual method for a moment and consider the possibility of an incarnation before the Incarnation. Fr. Lynch, S.J., suggests this for consideration in our seminar on Theology and the Arts. Suppose God took on man's way of seeing and doing when he created the world just as later he took on human nature when he redeemed the world. Thus he would have created the world according to the way *our* minds know and create; with forms and shapes and time and space and distance; with matter and with—how wonderful a concept of Gus Weigel—waste. The excess and profligacy of creation: billions of years, rock fissures becoming rivers and condensation of gases becoming oceans (how's my physics?), the long long evolving process, the infinite amount of matter consumed and over millenia worked patiently into the perfect fabrication of a finger bone. This backhanded approach to the creative mind and God's creative process has the merit, I think, of demonstrating his overwhelming love for us at least as thoroughly as the Garden of Eden does. A beautiful little speculation.

## Monday, 27 January

I HEARD THE most incredible thing. One of our priests, saying Mass yesterday in a parish church, discovered there was no wine in the sacristy and sent the altar boy to fetch some from the rectory. The boy went to the house, and finding nobody in evidence there and knowing the priest was waiting to begin Mass, he let himself in, went directly to the kitchen refrigerator, where the wine is usually kept, filled the cruet, and returned red-cheeked and bright-eyed to the sacristy. At Mass the priest noticed the wine was unusually strong, but thought

no more of it until after Mass when the boy was explaining
the difficulty he had had in getting the wine; it again crossed
the priest's mind that the wine was unusual. He checked what
remained in the cruet against the bottle the boy had evidently
grabbed in his haste and discovered that he had used Heub-
lein's Manhattan Cocktail Mix to say Mass and hence very
probably had not said Mass at all. Furthermore he had broken
his fast with the Manhattan and could not say the next Mass
for which he had been scheduled. Memo for the future—
never, never trust an altar boy.

## Tuesday, 28 January

CLASS BEGINS IN three minutes. Canon law. The professor talks
like those singing chipmunk records that were so popular
about five years ago.

Fr. Rector returned my note this morning with an okay.
Incredible. He has given me permission for summer studies for
three days or more in New York during the Easter vacation
(to do research on the contemporary theater), and for my own
censors—two men to whom I can bring my poems directly and
from whom I can get them without weeks and weeks of waiting
and worry. Noble concessions. I am touched and very grateful,
so I wrote him a little note telling him so.

Encouraged by Fr. Rector's largesse, I wrote Dr. Ianni at
the U.S. Department of Education, asking if he knows of a
travel grant that could take me to Oxford this summer, there
to thrash happily among the leaves and bicycles and poets. I
met Dr. Ianni last summer at Boston College, where he was
addressing Religious Superiors on the Herod Complex or something of that nature. I recall his being entertained by my
chatter about formation in the Society of Jesus and he opened
his talk by unfurling one of my pennants: "The main problem
with Religious Superiors is that after a while they get to think
they are." If I could land some kind of travel grant, the scholarship to Oxford from the Institute of International Education
would take care of all other expenses and a summer in Europe

would cost my Superiors nothing. It's all a bit far-out though, I fear.

Later. More Albee today. The stomach quakes. Eight or nine hours' writing has produced only two pages. And that snappy introduction remains singularly unsnappy. Why do people write? Why do they do this to themselves?

Fr. Dulles was superb this afternoon. After presenting a bewildering array of opinions on the nature of Christ's risen body, on its physical and spiritual characteristics, and particularly on whether or not it was visible to all men and to what degree recognizable as the Christ, he concluded: "At any rate, we can be fairly sure that he didn't have to go around hiding under bushes." And then he gave that wonderful, winning, shy grin.

### Friday, 31 January

I STEAL FIFTEEN minutes before afternoon class for this moral jokebook. Jim Bowes and I went for a walk out beyond Ma Zepp's grocery store to investigate the abandoned Methodist church and the cemetery behind it. Jim is a New York man in my year; whereas my interest in the graveyard was perhaps bizarre, his was antiquarian. Fine man. Anyway, the church windows are broken and inside there are neither pews nor any of the ornaments which must once, I suppose, have made it at least a bit churchy. Flower baskets all bruised and dust-covered lay about and old wooden boxes and a cardboard carton marked Campbell's Soup. It smelled unused but not musty or close as you'd expect. Behind the church there are some surprisingly recent gravestones, and some wonderful old ones too—the kind with verses written for the occasion by a bereaved but inspired mother. One of them is delightful, even if a little ghoulish. We could barely make out the inscription and the last word of each line we deciphered by braille. It goes:

> Weep not for little Clyde
> His gentle spirit fled—
> Sleeping sweetly with the angels

Among the silent dead.
BY HIS MOTHER.

Clyde Eugene Parsley
d. 1888; 5 yrs., 2 mo., 11 days.

Isn't that something?

And on the way home we saw a funny-looking basset hound that almost got itself run over by running down the center of the road while looking back over his shoulder at us. And a wonderful goat that kept making goat noises as we went past. And upon entering the house we were hailed from the cellar by one of Ours who was lifting weights while listening to a Bach fugue. It was a full afternoon.

I'm somewhat amused and really a little disheartened to discover that I find it impossible in writing critical pieces to let the personal and the subjective enter in. Consequently my writing is not only impersonal, it's thoroughly dull. Scientific and dull: the reaction to three years of philosophy during which even my slow mind divined that what was cleverly or even pleasantly said was not going to be taken seriously. God became "the ultimate principle of being" and one would sooner be discovered making disreputable noises at Mass than writing a scholarly article that revealed any trace of individuality. Despite my lamentations, though, the Albee piece is beginning to show promise.

## Saturday, 1 February

ALL YESTERDAY AFTERNOON and evening I sweated over Revelation. Literally. And more people getting sick with that flu or whatever it is.

All these men so terribly intent upon self are professedly, by vows and ten years of visible commitment, more interested in Christ. Existentially, what greater proof do you have for the credibility of Revelation?

## Monday, 3 February

AND SO AGAIN I am sick, this time with intestinal flu. Fever all Saturday night, all Sunday. Hallucinations. Conversations that last for hours—awake or sleeping, it's all the same. It makes me fear losing my mind. How could you continue living? I begin to understand why Virginia Woolf, feeling yet another siege of madness upon her and fearing that this one might be permanent, left her husband a note and walked— I can just see with what calm resolve—out into the water of the stream behind their house and there drowned herself.

## Friday, 7 February

MY FIRST DAY with any strength. I don't know how anyone creates anything meaningful out of sickness. When I get sick, everything goes: the body, the mind, the will ever to face reality again. However, to work.

There are two extraordinary passages in Virginia Woolf's *Between the Acts*. I copy out the first because of its horrific writing.

> There, crouched in the grass, curled in an olive green ring, was a snake. Dead? No, choked with a toad in its mouth. The snake was unable to swallow; the toad was unable to die. A spasm made the ribs contract; blood oozed. It was birth the wrong way round —a monstrous inversion. So, raising his foot, he stamped on them. The mass crushed and slithered. The white canvas on his tennis shoes was bloodstained and sticky. But it was his action. Action relieved him. He strode to the barn, with blood on his shoes.

This is her symbol, I am sure, of the world as she saw it at the height of World War II.

And I copy out the second passage because it makes one wonder if perhaps *Who's Afraid of Virginia Woolf?* is not merely an elaborate gloss on Virginia Woolf's last book and especially on this paragraph, Albee's protestations notwithstanding.

Left alone together for the first time that day, they were silent. Alone, enmity was bared; also love. Before they slept, they must fight; after they had fought, they would embrace. From that embrace another life might be born. But first they must fight, as the dog fox fights with the vixen, in the heart of darkness, in the fields of night.

· · ·

Then the curtain rose. They spoke.

I wonder if I should do a little paper for *Critic* or *Commonweal* drawing parallels in terms of character, character relations, and theme between Virginia Woolf and *Who's Afraid of Virginia Woolf?* This is a marvelous discovery and it's kind of a shame to waste it in *Thought*, where nobody will ever read it. You don't read *Thought*. You may perhaps buy it, but you certainly don't read it.

### Saturday, 8 February

Dr. Ianni of the Department of Education wrote that there are several different possibilities for a travel grant and he invited me to spend a few days at his home with his wife and family while he lines up appointments for me with various people who shower grants on the worthy poor. He also asked me to phone him, which I did, and I assured him—since he seems eager to give me a grant—that I can't accept it without first consulting my Superiors and therefore it might be better to hold off until I discover whether or not they'll let me accept. This, I suppose, reaches new heights of shoddiness in the manner of asking favors. But he was very understanding and good and said to come to his office anyway and we'll discuss it. So I have a date with him on Tuesday next. How do I get into these things?

### Sunday, 9 February

5:50 in the morning. It just occured to me that Fr. Dulles said last night in confession after I had dumped my laundry bag of sins and peccadillos, "Try to enter with great joy and thanksgiving into the spirit of these holidays now." (We have no classes until Friday.) Isn't that a wonderful thing to say. I wonder why I'm astonished by it. Wonderful.

### Tuesday, 11 February

"AND HIS NAME shall be called 'Wonderful.'" Isaiah, 9:6. It is snowing, thick wet snow in great swirling eddies, and so the trip to Washington has been postponed. In a way I'm glad. I had sort of dreaded popping in on Dr. Ianni in my search for monies. Another *crise* deferred.

I finished the rough draft of the Albee article. It's so long I fear *Thought* will want to back out of publishing it. Understandably, too. Fifteen thousand words is long for any magazine. How I've worked on this thing: the hours and hours of thought that didn't stop even at bedtime, the hasty notes scribbled on yellow cards and allowed to steep in my mind like rice in water, the ideas of other people that I let float in my pudding like raisins until they became my own. And the blood, drop by drop, with which I wrote the damthing. Why do I say that, why do all writers say that, I wonder: they write with their blood? Self-dramatizing, probably, or the need to have people recognize that "this may not look like much, Buster, but respect it because it's *me*." Defensive. Prohibitive. And, I think, inexcusable.

Later. We had a movie tonight, *This Sporting Life*, an awful thing with some very good acting. I am so tired of these English suffering-bum movies with their self-sensitive and inarticulate anthropoids punching walls and kicking tables in their desire to express tenderness. They have no claim on my time. Nor do the people who make these films. Sillitoe and Osborne and—in a way, though the genre is different—Pinter tire me to death with their shouting about waste of the human soul while at the same time they implicitly canonize their hero-bums for evading responsibility. Coming out of the film, Joe Towle was fumbling for words and I told him: "Express yourself, Joe. Kick a chair . . . or scratch." Sick.

### Ash Wednesday, 12 February

HERE I SIT AT 8:15 in the morning having contemplated
Fr. Linehan's injunction to "greater feeling of humanity within
the family of the Church and within the Woodstock family."
I sit like a dodo, thinking of ashes and fasting and futile
literary criticism and the importance of prayer in my life (I
*never* pray enough) and I grow a little sour on humanity.
I guess we always expect from humanity something just a little
better, a little more consistent with our redeemed nature. At
least we expect it from others. As for us, ah, well we . . .

### Thursday, 13 February

So MANY PEOPLE have written me letters about the Kennedy
poem in February *Atlantic*. Strange. It's not a particularly
good poem. I like only the last line. And the words "in ways
we do not ripely understand." The rest of it is not so good,
not so good at all.

### Tuesday, 18 February

YESTERDAY I FINISHED typing the Albee paper. It's not bad,
I think; there are some pages at the end that badly need
development, but otherwise it's a creditable piece of writing.

*Critic* came yesterday with my poem "Tapestry"; I have
mixed feelings about it. And *Queen's Work* showed up with a
whole bundle of poems and mine one of the better ones. Even
the title is keen—"Trains and Roosters and Everything"—and
some lines in it are razored: the train skreeks and grundles,
we wake from the night of our impatience, purpling two
thousand years of silence. Good.

Paul Messer, S.J., popped in yesterday from Boston College
High, down here for a debating tournament at Georgetown.
My cubic in this dingy attic staggers him. Paul is good; he
was alive and full of hell and it was summer to see him.

## Wednesday, 19 February

A SKATING HOLIDAY TODAY—ruined by snow, wet and heavy. And of course Harry the Sweep has had a field day: his whole store of conversation is replenished, reinventoried, displayed in gaudy colors whenever these greater cataclysms occur—snow, rain, sunshine. Hail, I imagine, would set him up for a week. Harry is improbable, wandered into Woodstock from a barge in Baltimore about three years ago and has been sweeping the fourth floor corridor ever since. He is like Melchizedek, without visible parentage. Nobody has ever heard him talk about anything except the weather, and that without cease. Twenty times a day: "Nice day today. Yes, sir. Gettin' a little colder." Remarkably, I think he's happy.

All morning I've been writing letters, trying to catch up on some of the mail that has kept piling and piling, like Harry's weather commentaries, since January. (At this moment Harry is right outside my room telling someone, who seems to have little comment in return, about his younger days in the Yukon. The Yukon. That would explain it.) Where was I? Writing letters. So I wrote Joe Jennings, whom I taught at Fairfield Prep, about the poem he had sent for criticism. I told him he writes best when he dramatizes least. Young people, young poets, never realize that. Existence itself is dramatic enough. A leaf, a stone: they are. Don't shout; don't underline; don't tell me how the bullet sounded how the blood spurted how you thought you'd die—just show me the wound. If your experience was really a shocker, I'll see, I'll know it.

Dear God, Harry's back telling Mariano Santiago (who is from the Philippines and experiencing snow for the first time) that it is snowing again. "March will take care of it. Yes, sir. March winds. Blow it right away. The wind, you know. Yessir, snowing again." By my fourth year here, I'll be hiding in my room, scrunched beneath the bed in flight from weather commentary. I'll read with a flashlight.

Later. I've been watching the fish bin, a huge tank on the second floor that holds five hundred pounds of water. There's a shark who is neurotic; he stands on his head all day in the corner of the tank. And a wonderful fish who, as you watch him, puffs himself up like a great balloon—all red like a monsignor. And kissing fish—two of them, white and pink—who go around kissing the glass walls of the tank: either that's their way of feeding or else they've got problems. The Scholastic fish is black, lies at the bottom of the tank all day, lives only on refuse, and comes alive at night; and he looks depressed.

Midnight. Just finished Katherine Ann Porter's *Pale Horse, Pale Rider*; marvelous insight and linguistic precision. And an incredible grasp on the real.

## *Thursday, 20 February*

FR. PROVINCIAL WRITES regarding my request to accept a travel grant to Oxford this summer: "It seems to me that it would be better not to plan on any foreign travel during the summer, although I appreciate the interest of Dr. Francis Ianni and his recognition of your ability." That's all. *Roma locuta est, causa finita est.* I informed Dr. Ianni and thanked him for his great generosity. I am disappointed, of course. Some day Superiors will look at things differently. Some day.

I wrote *Thought* a while ago explaining that I had completed the article on Albee and was wondering if the rates they paid would be sufficient to defray the cost of having somebody retype the thing for me. They replied today saying they would give me fifty bound copies of my article. Now what on earth am I to do with fifty bound copies? I don't want to see the thing again at all, let alone have fifty copies of it. Most distressing though is their comment "if the article is accepted." I've been under the impression it *was* accepted. I've got a good mind to send it elsewhere, *Tulane Drama Review* or *American Studies*. Jesuit publications get my goat; they operate on the presumption that to publish someone is to do him a favor. Forget it. Perhaps what I ought to do is keep the essay, write two more on Williams and Miller respectively, and offer the lot to Doubleday as a little book of essays on contemporary dramatists. Petulance is the springboard to accomplishment. Scarcely, however, one of the Christian virtues.

## Sunday, 23 February

I've BEEN TO Washington again—lovely wide streets and white buildings and awful slummy areas only three minutes distant. We had an experience of the Waugh-man, 1964. The post office was closed for business although people were swarming in, out, and about. Bill McKenna stopped by a little colored man who stood at a sign marked "Information" and asked him some trivial question about mailing a package. The man was grand, monolithic in his importance at being able to incapacitate two clerics merely by his refusal or inability (he kept his informational status secret) to divulge the requested intelligence. I was highly amused, and Bill was, of course, furious. The man beamed, beatific in his joy. He stood there saying over and over, "We're closed today. We can't tell you anything today." We left him glowing at his single-handed preservation of the integrity of the United States postal system. How amused God must be.

Later. The Christian life cannot be lived against a clock or a ruler. The point of our lives is not that we be found whole and unsullied at the end of them; the point is that we live them fully and richly *in* Christ *for* others. And you can't do that, you can't live at all, unless you rejoice in St. Paul's freedom from the law. Freedom from the pseudoimportance of self. Now if only I could live that.

## Monday, 24 February

Here's something silly. I was talking to some friends last night after recreation had officially ended when a sub-superior swooped in like Captain Marvel and told us we all must say a culpa. It is ninety-seven years since I've said a culpa. Culpa: you kneel down in front of the community in the refectory during dinner and proclaim: "Reverend Fathers and dear Brothers in Christ, I say to you my culpa for all my faults and negligences in the observance of our holy rule and in particular for [whatever the fault] and for the same Holy Obedience has imposed upon me the slight obligation of declaring to you my fault and of saying one Hail Mary." In short, it's a public penance; every religious order has something corresponding to the culpa; eventually everyone gets around to saying one. Well, as I knelt there today waiting my turn, Lucifer whispered in my ear in one long whisper:

> Reverend Fathers, dearest Brothers,
> For this my fault and all my others
> I say to you my culpa.
> I *did* prolong the hoopla
> Beyond allotted time.
> For this pernicious crime—
> Albeit ordinary—
> I now say one Hail Mary.

Prudence won out, of course, and I didn't say the rhymed variant. And thus I lost my chance to be remembered forever in the oral tradition of the Society of Jesus.

I've just finished the first two books of Evelyn Waugh's trilogy—*Men at Arms, Officers and Gentlemen,* and *End of the Battle.* The books are fascinating, written with great humor and at least as much depth and insight (I almost wrote with Freudian perspicacity "sinsight") as *Brideshead Revisited.* I can't imagine why the trilogy was reviewed so indifferently when it appeared. Waugh wasn't *in* at the moment, I suppose. God, how that kills me: that a work is measured not by its worth but by how fashionable its author happens at that time to be.

Here's one of my favorite lines ever. From *Men at Arms:* "Guy's Uncle Peregrine, a bore of international repute whose dread presence could empty the room in any centre of civilization—Uncle Peregrine was considered *molto simpatico.*" A bore of international repute: think of it.

### Thursday, 27 February

NAOMI TELLS ME Doubleday will submit my book for this
year's Lamont Award. So my deadline moves from September 1
to June 1; earlier because the book has to be with the Lamont
people by June 1. This will be my third time up for the
award, three different books. Three times a loser? I hope not.
In fact, I think not. I'm going to win the damthing. For three
reasons: (1) since Dan Berrigan won it, the Lamont Award
is the only kind of recognition Jesuits accept as a sign of
merit (and *yes* I do want to be accepted by my own); (2) I
owe it to Naomi; (3) the book isn't half bad and deserves to
win. Arrogant. You'll get yours.

Naomi must be a very remarkable woman. She writes me
about every three days, wonderful letters full of genuine concern and affection. Married, no children—past the age, she
says. I'm a bit frightened to meet her. I'll be a disappointment, of course, dull and muddied, with my whining voice
and overcompensating jabber. Enough of this. All roads seem
to lead to self-scrutiny. It's morbid. It's another of pride's
masks.

Evening. Inspiration in the Scriptures—in what sense, in
what manner are they inspired? How has God's word been
written by man's hand?—occupies most of my time these days.
Inevitably I'm reminded of my philosophy years when I
wanted to major in aesthetics, to probe about in the areas
of divine and poetic inspiration—as if I were able. At that time
I did a good deal of reading in the Old Testament, especially
Isaiah and Jeremiah and the Psalms. Out of the reading grew
*Picnic in Babylon,* a book of poems that was really one long
long poem with detachable parts. Modestly, it attempted to
span salvation history from Moses to John the Evangelist.
A truly dreadful book, it performed the airy feat of being
frivolous and dull at the same time. I submitted it to Sheed
and they offered to buy the title but not the book. The concept of the book is good, I think. Perhaps when I've finished
theology, I'll be better able to actualize the idea.

### Friday, 28 February

AGAIN AND AGAIN I'm struck by the moral miracle of the Church in general and the Society of Jesus in particular. Here are all these brilliant men giving their lives freely, nothing withheld, to a Church which from the fifth century has ruthlessly crushed initiative, intelligence, enterprise. In the century following Trent, Lutherans and Calvinists and Catholics were claiming for the Vulgate an inspiration and inerrancy that extended down to points of grammar and style; when a poor Franciscan consulted some Jewish scholars in search of a possibly superior Hebrew text of the Bible, he was denounced as a Judaizer. Then there is the incident of Pope Benedict XIV and his suppression of the Malabar rites. And indeed the suppression of the Society of Jesus in the late eighteenth century. And the countless Jesuit stories of human superiors frustrating what certainly appears to be the progress of the Church and the will of the Holy Spirit. Yet they come—eager free spirits intent upon giving their lives to God in the Society of Jesus. They go to classes which are dull; they obey totally if not unquestioningly; they give themselves. I can imagine no greater testimony to the divine nature of Christ's holy Church and the inspired origin of our Society. We are men and therefore fools and bunglers. No wonder Christ said: "Without me you can do nothing."

### Sunday, 1 March

8:30 A.M.; A LONG MOODY breakfast mulling over the Lenten Mind. We present Christ as somebody who came to earth and got beat up. We keep concentrating on this as if it were a finality in itself, as if we were personally and primarily responsible, forgetting that Christ's death on the cross is part of God's universal salvific plan and is Christ's total gift of himself to the Father. We *are* responsible, but not in an isolated action that occurred twenty centuries before we were born. Christ's death and our responsibility for it is around us every day. We do not kill him; we reject him; we are more humane, we like to think. But look at the Jews of Auschwitz, the insane of St. Elizabeth's, the poor of the Tennessee hill counties, the morally destitute of the Beverly Hills counties: Christ goes begging for our love and does not get it. I was hungry and you fed me? Naked and you clothed me? No. I was hungry and naked and you formed a committee. It is easier, we find, to concentrate on the death of somebody who lived two thousand years ago.

For meaning and relevance we substitute ritual or quasi-ritual. Each year we spend forty days pretending Jesus is going to die; we go hungry and grow—despite ourselves—angry; we *prepare* for what is going to take place. But it *has*, dammit, it has taken place. Christ has died and redeemed us and has risen from the dead. We are new and alive. Love should be our concern now (read St. Paul) and instead we mope around and bewail our sins, which have killed our Savior. Well I have more to bewail than anybody, of that I'm certain, but I'm tired of bewailing and I'm tired of going hungry and growing angry, and I'm tired of pretending Christ is going to die. I am forgiven my sins and the bridegroom *is* among us. Lent as we now observe it as a medieval hangover; we have drunk too much Roman wine. The carnival days bear me out: carnival, farewell to meat, so gorge yourself and orgy yourself for tomorrow we diet. One last fling. Sick. Tumescent.

We commemorate the death of Christ as if it were our destruction rather than our salvation. Liturgy, yes. Have some sort of token Lent, a week perhaps, and have the beautiful Masses and the symbolic ritual; but why these externals which are, if not meaningless, at least so anachronistic as to be alienating? I'm thinking of fasting, the morbid attitudes we put on as casually as purple vestments, the excessive gloom and pseudoreverence (eyes down, whispering) of Holy Week. I don't mean liturgy. But the sick self-conscious Lenten Mind has to go and the Christ-conscious joy of a positive Christianity has to come. The cross is meaningless without the Resurrection.

Later. On the other hand, there is the current tendency to concentrate only on Easter, only on the risen Christ. We are saved. We are good. This is the *Worship* tendency; it hasn't yet filtered down to the popular Catholic mind. This spiritual cakes-and-ale attitude inculcates a false optimism just as destructive as the Lenten Mind. It encourages complacency. It is milder. It satisfies.

Well, what is it I want? Something of awareness, something of relevancy, something larger than self—whether self-damnation or self-salvation. The hard bone of Christianity is what I want. The eye of bones that sees both the Lenten Mind and the Easter Syndrome as exaggerations and hence as betrayals; they fly the issue, they evade involvement in Christ today. Now. This I think is the value of Existentialism and Absurdism and the plays of somebody like Albee: they bring us back to issues. Man is suffering and Christ is lost in him. There are problems to which only Christianity is the answer. Absurdity points the question and there is no answer forthcoming. We have it. The relation must be made between the absurdities of existence and the coherence of Christianity, between Lent and Christ suffering in our contemporaries, between Easter and Christ showing us our ultimate triumph. Lent and Easter are not merely personal experiences. They reassert the divine economy of salvation. It is criminal, therefore, to reduce Lent to self-reproach and Easter to self-complacency. Forgive me, I preach . . . and it is I who most need the sermon.

## Monday, 2 March

PROUST SAYS in *The Captive:* "People who learn some accurate detail of another person's life at once deduce consequences which are not accurate, and see in the newly discovered fact an explanation of things that have no connection with it whatsoever." Go, Proust, go.

## Thursday, 5 March

EARLY MORNING. A terrific wind howled all night. I woke and thought of Emily Brontë walking the moors during electrical storms, drenched to the skin, thinking. This morning the snow

is gone. But the wind still rushes through the gaps between
my window and the frame. I like the sound. And in the corridor two men are frantically refurbishing one of the little
chapels and making a noise you couldn't believe. I don't like
the sound.

## Friday, 6 March

A POEM out of St. Paul. And rather acceptable too, I think.

### The Imperfect Eye

I saw tonight that he is on my side,
the lion. For the first time, I saw it.
And by God all the furniture got up

and danced (that hulking desk
a creditable tango) and I, though not much
on my feet, waltzed through Judah

like a Crazy-priest. Sometimes joy
is like that, coming quick as dandelions
springing to attention while the sun

shudders still—a little—from the melting
winter. Anyway here I was with lions
to account for and that desk

and questionable antics all along
(indignities of sun and dandelions
while our bones still creak with Lent)

and I thought God, what now, until
again I heard the music of the dance
again I waltzed through Judah.

"I something fear my father's wrath" no more.

## Saturday, 7 March

LET ME just stop all the noise. For five minutes, just stop. How
can anyone exist, let alone pray, in this chaos: books to read,
poems to type and send out, my book to type and have cen-

sored, theology to review, letters, the journal, so much, so
much. And then Proust and Virginia Woolf and the book I
must write on Albee. And prayer to be made. When will I
ever begin to pray? *Really* to pray. Without the noise. Without
mind reeling and tongue flapping and head swirling so that
God couldn't possibly get through without first clubbing me
into insensibility. So be quiet. Give your tongue a rest.

### *Laetare Sunday, 8 March*

FINISHED ANOTHER Woolf book, *Mrs. Dalloway*, this morning.
Really an extraordinary book: it presents the same world seen
by the sane and by the insane. I copy out one of Mrs. Dalloway's reflections. "Death was defiance. Death was an attempt
to communicate; people feeling the impossibility of reaching
the centre which, mystically, evaded them; closeness drew
apart; rapture faded, one was alone. There was an embrace in
death." I wonder if my great fondness for Virginia Woolf is
explained by the fact that she uses even more semicolons
than I do.

I've been pursuing Karl Rahner and John McKenzie on inspiration in the Scriptures. They proceed in much the same
way, examining inspiration as the concrete experience of God
rather than as the frightful anthropomorphic notion of God
dictating to an uncomfortable human secretary. The best
theology always sits comfortably with common sense.

### *Monday, 9 March*

MIDNIGHT. I've been working on inspiration since ten. The
mind rushes and, lunging for an idea, stubs its toe and stumbles
on a corner of Latin or a block of philosophy. Eyes squiggle.
And then the stomach starts . . . two cougars are fighting it
out down there for the privilege of devouring my liver.

The wind is going oooooh, oooooohf at my window the way
Wally Kane used to breathe during asthma season. Oh, go to
bed.

## Tuesday, 10 March

HARPER'S will publish my poem "An Investigation into the Nature, Function, and Attendant Circumstances of Radiators" and has paid me eighty dollars for it. Eighty, count them. To celebrate I shall put on an extra push and finish typing *Spider* tomorrow.

## Thursday, 12 March

IN EDITING *Eye of the Spider* (I see a black cover with white scraggly print), I've dropped nineteen poems and "A Solemne Musick," added fifteen of my best poems written since I first submitted the book a year ago, completely revised "Nathaniel" by taking out the Eliot embarrassments (though you can still hear Eliot breathing every line), partially revised several others. Changed commas. Introduced periods. Put spread-out poems on one page instead of two. Got the manuscript down to seventy-four pages, excluding table of contents, etc. Now I'll have it Xeroxed for the censors and, providing the house doesn't burn down, I'll have the manuscript off to Doubleday by the end of March.

I feel splendidly fulfilled for, besides finishing the hunky work on *Spider*, I also destroyed around five or six hundred typed, carbon, mimeo copies of poems that have been clogging my shelves for the last six years. I am literarily clean.

Don Matthews forced a copy of John Updike's *The Centaur* on me, so I've had to read the damn book. *Centaur* reveals such insight into the little things that make people themselves; it froths with self-conscious and pretentious exhibitions in language; it sludges with mythological horse droppings. Updike must suffer from my vice—only a sledge hammer could compel him to read what he has written without the subjective glow of approval that masks the thing from him. He is so preoccupied with the way somebody picks his nose or scratches a scab that he fails to acknowledge the soul and its province. He hasn't really advanced beyond the psychology of *Thérèse*

*Racquin.* I don't know who would be more offended by that statement, Zola or Updike.

## Friday the 13th, March

I AM FEELING a complete clod again. Too much self, too much work going in all directions, too much Lent. What a heretic I am—and what a hypocrite. Trying after all these years to bludgeon my way to sanctity, trying to strong-arm the Holy Spirit into smothering me with grace and at the same time kidding myself (nobody else; I don't kid anybody but myself) into thinking that I am "waiting on God." How patient he is with me.

## Saturday, 14 March

IT IS EXPECTATION that makes life possible. Is this true? Well, it sounds true.

## Monday, 16 March

CHAOS.

I finally got around to answering Pauline's letter. Months ago Pauline wrote me a long and delightfully reminiscent letter about when we were kids and played in the sandbank and went swimming at Hillside Beach and wrought hell with our bicycles on the big hill where they were putting up houses. The nostalgia did me good. Pauline recalls me in a much kinder light than I recall myself; I seem to remember me as self-centered and generally insufferable. I was especially pleased to hear that I once gave Pauline some of my bookplates with the scroll where you write your name; I wasn't very givey in those days. And she mentioned Thornton Burgess' animal books. See how we escape from chaos into memory.

It's good to be getting around to letters at last. All my letter-time seems to go to high school girls who are editors of their

yearbooks and who want to reprint my Kennedy poem surrounded by hearts and daisy chains, and it never seems to cross
their minds that this is going to cause me anything but exquisite delight. They always conclude: write soon, we have a
deadline. Meanwhile my parents go unanswered and Naomi
worries that I've run off and all my friends think I've died,
been shipped away in the hull of a steamer for Tangier.

Van Doren says: "The shortness of breath in Shakespeare's
later verse was a sign of seriousness and power." Implications
for my own verse, riddled now with an abrupt gaspiness? If
this is the end of my line, do I just choke to death poetically
over the next few years? Or do I revert to the old Romantic
pitch? Gooey. Or maybe go on to something very plain? Prose?
We'll go under that bridge when we get to it.

Later. At the workman's Mass yesterday one of the kitchen
workers suddenly surprised me by reading the Gospel in English
to the congregation. With his rich Negro voice and his halting
reading of St. John's ecstatic prose, he was marvelous. He
stumbled a bit and read every "Thou" as "Thy"—"but Thy
says," etc. I was overwhelmed with the rightness of it; his reading was completely unaffected, no pretensions, no masking the
inadequacies of voice or diction or collocation. I was touched
by the man's simplicity, his complete honesty before God. He
may swipe hams every week from the kitchen for all I know,
but he is naked clean beautiful before God. I thought of the
time before I entered the Society when, making a retreat at
the Passionist monastery in Springfield, I saw a doctor and a
lawyer get so panicky during a public recitation of the rosary
that they forgot the Hail Mary and the priest had to finish
the prayers for them. How our pretensions strangle us; how
hopelessly difficult they make our approach to God.

One last thing. Bob Fitz and I went for a walk yesterday
afternoon and down by that crazy wooden bridge we discovered
a car, sideways, its front end hanging off one side of the bridge,
its back end off the other. It *is* a narrow bridge. Our own fire
department stood by curious and vaguely amused, while police
took photographs of the damage and of the car's location on
the bridge; meanwhile the two former occupants of the car were
in a drink-fuzzy state, one protesting they had been side-

swiped by somebody who passed them on the bridge, the other claiming they had been charged by an elephant coming down the hill from the college. The car looked considerably the worse for the experience, but the gentlemen themselves looked impervious to all damage. They were relieved to have escaped the elephant.

## Tuesday, 17 March

MARY SHELLEY remarks in her journal for 6 October 1816: "Here's a cat eating roses; she'll turn into a woman; when beasts eat these roses they turn into men and women." Marianne Moore could make a superb poem out of this.

I wrote a poem today. During afternoon class. An awful awful class on apostolic succession. The poem is twenty-eight lines, completed in less than an hour—which is something of a record for me. Justly, it's called "Apostolic Succession."

## Saturday, 21 March

I LOOKED over part of this journal today. There is very little that would have to be censored before publication. I'm going to keep at it for the next few years and see what happens. I keep out things that would be offensive to the Society or to individual Jesuits; there's a great deal here that would be damning to me.

## Tuesday, 24 March

YESTERDAY I read to Jim Bowes a description of Elizabeth Taylor's reception in Boston. She was mobbed, it seems, had her clothes torn, her back wrenched, her face pushed against a wall, and some of her hair torn out. Jim listened attentively and asked: "Good heavens, why did they do it? Was she trying to get into Church or something?"

Fr. Bill Lynch gave me some good advice on my Albee

paper yesterday. For an article it should be cut down to fifty pages at most. He also suggested a short book of maybe one hundred fifty pages, not necessarily about Albee alone, not necessarily on playwrights: just some unifying motif from the contemporary theater. Despair? The search for meaning? God, it's a swamp.

Later. What is this crazy compulsion to write, to record every thought that saunters through the back alleys of my brain? I shall never understand it. I strap myself to the typewriter for hours and hours and of course nobody cares whether or not I write, nor indeed should they. Then why do it?

Much later. Don Hinfey says that as a poet I give a good virtuoso performance, my range of technique is fine, but there is no consuming passion, no fire. Is he right? I think he is. I had fire once but it died of a little awareness. Now everything is problematical; everything considerable from five different angles. The fire gets trampled out this way. Perhaps in twenty years, when things begin to simplify?

### Thursday, 2 April

So I'M HOME from New York. I met Naomi, that's the most significant thing. She is a Dominican tertiary, shamelessly spiritual, a business woman of frightening directness and effectiveness; and she is beautiful. I had expected at least beauty of soul, but she is radiantly lovely as well. She glows. We attended Mass together and chanting of the Office at the Dominican church, St. Vincent Ferrer. I have never met anyone who so overwhelmed me with personal sanctity.

New York was freezing cold the whole three days. But it was diverting to be out among people who are concerned about something other than fulfilling the will of God (let's be honest; life lived intensely and with the spiritual strain we bring to it is tiring), among people who are crazy in more singular ways than we here, among that vast army of ladies with orange hair and mink coats and that other army of dark-suited and dark-tied gentlemen who never allow themselves the indulgence of a personal opinion. It was so diverting in fact that I didn't

mind having worn my summer suit and thus disposed myself
to the arctic blasts of Eighty-third Street.

The Doubleday experience was good. They are going to
rush ahead with my book so that it should appear by fall; they
called *Thought*, who agreed to publish "A Solemne Musick"
in the summer issue so that the copyright difficulties can be
cleared before the book's appearance; they were cordial and
gracious and impressed me with their family-ness.

I saw some wonderful shows: *Dylan*, with Alec Guinness,
which was a much better play than the reviews would lead
you to believe; *The Chinese Prime Minister*, with Margaret
Leighton, which I saw only because of her and which she made
worth seeing; *High Spirits*, with Bea Lillie and Tammy Grimes
—marvelous. I took Naomi to see *Dylan* and she liked it as
much as I, so I'm glad.

And what else? Oh yes, Naomi's dog, Ambrose, is fat and
wuggly and we got on fine right from the start. Ambrose is
my first Corgi.

All day Tuesday Naomi and I worked on *Eye of the Spider*,
going through it poem by poem, line by line. "A Solemne
Musick" is back in the book, three poems are out altogether,
a number of others marked for very minor revision. The book
is awfully long, a problem we never did tackle. She's amazing.
She never seems to tire. When I got droopy, she'd chat away,
telling me interesting stories about Merton, whom she knew
for years and years when she was his agent.

This morning I stopped by Doubleday to say good-bye and,
like a clown, forgot my bag at the door of a fifteenth-floor
office. I remembered it when I was three blocks away and
rushing to catch my train. Then the Chaplin chase began. I
didn't remember where I had last had it, couldn't find it in
the elevator, couldn't remember which elevator I had taken
(there are several), couldn't remember in what offices I had
been, finally found it in a corridor. There it was: a fat black
headless pig. I would have kicked it a memorable one except
I was so glad to see it. And I managed to catch my train.

## Saturday, 4 April

MY PARENTS are here visiting me. We caroused modestly last night at their motel, after which I worked on the book as I did again this morning. Mother and Dad are dallying now so that I can finish work on the manuscript—and this after their seven-hour drive to see me. That's thoughtfulness carried to the level of fine art. God seems to make parents a breed by themselves. The phone is ringing; they must be here now.

Later. Tonight I find awaiting me a letter from Naomi saying nobody at Doubleday likes the title of *Spider*. I like it. Well, I *am* gloomy. She says it sounds like a gloomboat. What should I call it? These leap to mind: *In the City of Wonder, Voice of Honeycomb, The Eyes of Morning, The Eye of Bones, A Lasting City, Shores of Light*. All of them awful. Besides I think there's a book of criticism called *Shores of Light*. How about *In the City of Wonder* or *The Eyes of Morning*. They're all bad, aren't they? Typical poetry titles. No imagination. Blah. Naomi recommends *Flowering Sudden*, which she likes because of my poem of that name; I hate it; it sounds like a cake mix—no yeast necessary, just add water, stir, place on the radiator. Yesterday everything was so clear and now it's all complicated.

## Sunday, 5 April

*Eye of the Spider*, or whatever it's going to be called, is at last in the mail to Doubleday. I hope never to see it again. How about *Strong as Death* for a title, from Solomon's Canticle: "Love is strong as death and jealousy is cruel as the grave"? Beautiful. But it sounds gloomy. Stygian. I don't know.

Mother and Dad left this noon, mystifying me once more with their gentleness and their generosity and their uncomplicated loving. Where in hell did they get me?

Midnight. We underestimate the significance of our consent. We are what God made us. In accepting that, and all that it implies, there lies great sanctity. Consent.

### Wednesday, 8 April

I'VE DECIDED pretty much on *The Eyes of Morning* for a title; positive, joyful. I had also considered *The Trees Clap Hands*, which has its merits, but I think I prefer *The Eyes of Morning*. What a liar I am. I hate *all* those titles.

Rain again today and a runny nose and depression thick as—what; what is thick?

Later. I've just finished John Osborne's *Luther*. It's not so great a play, though there are some splendid stage bits with Tetzel and with Martin on the day of his first Mass. Perhaps we could produce it here next year; it would be only right and just for me to play Martin.

The theater is so ready for a smashing play. When I think how much tripe is selling at ten dollars a ticket, I get ill. Think, only think of the influence for good if some Jesuit could turn out plays—good ones, not necessarily deathless ones. And contemporary things, not studies in "life of saint." I'm convinced there is room for any first-rate play, whatever the creed or code or cult of its author.

I submitted the book of poems this evening for censorship by the Society of Jesus. Here is the real test: for me, for the poems, for the censors.

### Thursday, 9 April

Now I HAVE everything. Leo Fahey sent me an orange sweatshirt in an immense package; despite the impossible size of the parcel, despite the fact that I haven't seen Leo in eight months, instantly I knew what was inside. The orangest sweatshirt in the whole world. I haven't worn it yet, I shall save it for some very great occasion. Meanwhile I'm hiding out in my room with this dreadful cold, unable to face people, nerves like naked wires.

## Friday, 10 April

WHY NOT WRITE a play? The idea has been windmilling in my mind for some months. I've written four and they've been, all of them, easier to do than most poems. And there's no reason why this has to be outstanding: *any* play by an author whose I.Q. is above fifty is going to be better than customary Broadway fare.

Today in class it occurred to me that Edmund Campion's trial offers excellent possibilities. It's been done of course hundreds of times—St. Joan, Thomas More, etc., but always the focal point is expediency versus sanctity. It occurs to me that I might dramatize my own *crise:* the last temptation is to normality. Campion isolated in youth, in Jesuit life, in England—unconvinced that anyone could ever love him, uncertain he has ever loved anyone or anything. Invent for him a childhood trauma. Cure it with his castration: that which destroys and heals at the same time. His physical castration must be only emblematic of a spiritual castration—the dead self dissevered, the sick self-man cut away, and the wounded incomplete lover is now prepared to embrace humanity and in humanity, Christ. Make him all will and let his will dominate his character which is at heart romantic. (My own?) He could have been a great writer or teacher. Make him timid and frightened as a child, alone and unsure in the Society, doubtful and triumphant with the practical and reasonable Elizabeth. The focal point then becomes his struggle, not with God, but with himself; his truimph is his awareness that he *can* be loved. Goes singing to the scaffold. Is this corn? Or good?

Later. For no reason it pops into my head that theology is not really at all abstract. Or rather ought not to be abstract. It must begin with a fact. A fact I know about God or his Church and whatever follows from that. (That ain't what they've been telling us, Dad.)

### Saturday, 11 April

A WONDERFUL LINE, a possible theme for the Campion play, in Mary McCarthy's *The Company She Keeps:* "He could not bear to succeed in his own personality, any more than an unattractive woman can bear to be loved for herself."

The book of poems is to be called *Quick as Dandelions,* a phrase from "The Imperfect Eye." So that's settled.

Fr. Weigel's little textbook on the Act of Faith is fascinating —a stew of scholastic jargon and Gus's own existential growl. I don't care much for the jargon, but I can hear Gus in the growl and I like that. I'm afraid from here on in Gus gets rather short shrift: the hour for practicality has sounded. Canon law exam is in ten days, moral exam is ten days after that, and then we face the June dogma nightmare.

### Sunday, 12 April

MARY MCCARTHY's *The Company She Keeps* is amazing: a Catholic conscience trying desperately to escape itself. The result is some brilliant writing and some glaring confession. "You stood to him in the relation of Man to God, embraced in an eternal neurotic mystery compounded out of His infinite goodness and your guilt." It takes arrogance and a degree of courage to say something like that; and great hurt. How very disappointed in God she must feel.

One of the stories, "The Genial Host," is a scarcely concealed allegory of her theology, with its talk of Pflaumen's Jewish-Christian "microcosm" in which ordinary rules of politeness are dispensed with, of his meal at which everyone studiously ignores the host, of his dark and hairy body "like a member of some early barbarous tribe" upon which had been superimposed "an additional person, a comfortable, cigar-smoking, sentimental family man." He is guilty, moreover, of having removed all risk from social life: "Every time you accepted one of his invitations you entered into a conspiracy

with him to hide the fact that he was a foolish, dull man
whom nobody had much use for. She loads on the details. He
is somewhat under thirty-five. His room is furnished in an
adapted monastic style. His bed is "narrow with a monk's cloth
cover." Moreover each of Pflaumen's guests is selected "for his
allegorical possibilities" so that his dinners are presented as
morality plays. It is Pflaumen who gives each of his friends his
own identity card, Pflaumen who always is offended if "two of
them should meet in his absence." And finally: "He was like
an $x$ that you can never drop out of an equation no matter
how many times you multiply it or add to it this side of infinity. All at once you saw how he could be generous and
humble and look predatory at the same time . . . he wanted
part of your life."

"The Genial Host"—even the title is perfect—is a frightening and frightened picture of a very unpleasant God. For so
short a story, it conveys successfully an elaborately reasoned
and hopeless theology. An incredibly negative view of life. Her
Catholicism is like a ripe scar on a white and pampered body.
I must pray for her.

## Monday, 13 April

YESTERDAY AFTERNOON Jim Linehan and I took a walk to a
farm he knew about, where we asked the people who owned
it if we might look around. It was great. We spent over an
hour investigating rabbit hutches, duck pens, and a wonderful
group of pheasants who didn't seem notably resigned to farm
life. We also saw some lambs, newborn ones with their
mothers. They look so patient and innocent and interested.
They'd like to get to know you. I wonder why people don't
keep pet lambs the way they keep dogs or kitties.

I think of the time when, teaching an advanced placement
section at Fairfield, I gave the kids a Latin assignment that
consisted in kneeling down next to a kitty ("If you don't have
one, borrow a neighbor's") and listening to the purr. It caused
all sorts of alarm among the parents, but a few students, for

the first time in their lives, became vividly aware of a life
other than their own . . . a lesson, it seems to me, as significant
as anything in Cicero.

## Wednesday, 15 April

No POEMS in the last seventeen years. No desire to write them;
no ability even if I had the desire.

This morning as I was going downstairs for coffee, I ran
into one of our Brothers attired in habit thrown over his
pajamas and clearly on his way to the infirmary. He was
mooing. Like a cow, mooing. Great morose moos. I wonder
what kind of sickness makes you moo.

## Thursday, 16 April

WHILE THE ACT OF FAITH is struggling for equal time with
canon law (God of truth versus God of law; compatible?),
I'm squandering hours on Campion. The difficulty I've met
in my earlier plays has been something like this: how do you
fill in two hours of talk unless you have something vital to
the character to talk about? Nothing can happen unless you
know your character as you know the shape of your nose.
It's not a question of plot because the character *contains* the
plot; what he *is* determines to a large extent what will happen
in the play.

The solution, I suppose, for a nonwriter who insists nonetheless upon writing is to fragment himself, put on stage
splinters of his own character, or what he believes to be his own
character. And so the only crisis I could construct for Campion
would be the particular and lifelong struggle to accept self, to
love self, since he sees himself as essentially incapable of being
loved. Not because he was that way, but because I am that
way. And, in view of what actually happened to him, I could
make his triumph an ironic one: that only when he is castrated
does he fully accept his manhood, only when he is abandoned
by court, etc., does he feel loved by Christ, only when he is

led to execution does he begin to live. Too pat? Too easy? Maybe it would just be a crashing bore.

And Elizabeth, think of it, saying as she slammed the door on everything in England: "I would give my soul to rule England for fifty years." She ruled for forty-seven.


### Friday, 17 April

NAOMI WRITES that I must submit another typed copy of *Quick as Dandelions*, this one for the Lamont Award people. I cannot, will not, type another copy of that damned thing ( I must have typed each of those poems twenty or thirty times by now), so I asked Naomi if she'd find a clever typist and send me the bill. And apart from censorship, no minor consideration, the book problems seem to be at an end.


### Sunday, 19 April

"THE JUST, like sandalwood, perfume the ax that strikes them." Is this a quote from somewhere? Perhaps it will grow into a poem. Perhaps it is related to "the dancing tree" that keeps popping up in my mind.

Two writing things I must decide. The Campion play: I'll have to shelve it until some future time, summer maybe. And the Albee paper: a book such as Fr. Lynch suggested? Or shall I wait until Albee produces a few more plays and then give him a book of his own? If Superiors give me the summer free for writing, I could really tear into one of these projects. Or could I? I feel so tired when I approach the typewriter that I can't really look forward to a summer abandoned with the infernal machine. And what will I be like in June?

Later. While working on canon law cases and while enjoying—imagine—text analysis of Vatican I, I'm reading John Updike's *Pigeon Feathers*. Astonishing how the same characters recur in these little stories. I wonder if he is capable of creating real characters or are all his people merely pale images of his mother, father, grandmother, grandfather? I'm told that the town of Alton in *The Centaur* is really Reading, Pennsylvania. No wonder Updike waxes florid so often; compensation for Reading.

### Monday, 20 April

IT's BEEN sort of a frantic day with four classes and hours of study on canon law. Then a Sister I know wrote me about her spiritual director, who sounds dreadful and unsympathetic and as much like a divinely commissioned hairshirt as I can imagine. Surely he could not happen to anybody by chance. God meant it. And yet I wonder how much of the misdirection and heartlessness and stupidity we must put up with is really intended by God and how much we men inflict on other men and casually blame God. I don't know what to tell Sister except what I've just said. It's strange how we never know what to say in the presence of a suffering that isn't our own.

*Poetry* returned some nice poems today. Which reminds me, I began toying with sandalwood during moral class today. "The Dancing Tree" comes back to mind, something like that. Maybe the continuity of Christ's passion in the lives of his saints—even the trivial ones, the little Brueghel ones with hoops and codpieces and puppy dogs yapping at their heels. He loves us. And all the trees clap hands.

### Wednesday, 22 April

I HAVE just made a poor showing in canon law exam. Kicked the easy questions. Well, God is glorified even in my stupidity.

More transportation problems on my trip to Washington to have dinner with Dr. Ianni tomorrow. I can go in to Gwyn Oaks Junction in the morning on the eight o'clock bus, take a forty-minute bus to the Baltimore train station, take a train to Washington—and this for a three o'clock appointment. I *maybe* can return with the Sodality group that leaves Georgetown at ten-thirty; maybe not. Dear God, how has the Society of Jesus survived the incredible inefficiency and waste of your chosen superiors? My stomach rages when I think of the time thrown away, the waiting, and always the uncertainty.

Karl Rahner says: "But in the commandments of human superiors we find nothing but a human will, and thus, instead of making us free, they take away freedom, unless we obey them out of love for you." There's the answer to my complaint. My stomach, however, still feels exactly the same.

## Thursday, 23 April

*Quick as Dandelions* manuscript arrived from New York yesterday typed on two different machines. Few things are centered. Many errors. It's a fright. I shall have it done over altogether. There is an agency in Washington that types by the hour. I meet Dr. Ianni today; feel like death upon wires, bones in a sack.

## Saturday, 25 April

THURSDAY'S DINNER with Dr. Ianni was an incredible affair. It appears that Ianni was holding some kind of Department of Education meeting; how I came to be there is a mystery. Harry Levin the psychologist, Wade Robinson of Harvard Education, and a fellow from Stanford in mathematics, and I. I have never felt quite so out of my depth before. They were all restless, all dynamic, all going somewhere. I'm not sure, having observed them at close range, that I want to go somewhere. I kept wondering: whom do you love, for whom have you ever squandered yourself, whom have you called back to life? I'm not sure they, any of them, could have answered. Or even understood. In fact, they would have thought me quite mad. As it happened we talked about religion—a curious indefinite form of religion—and that safer topic, literature, much of the night. I don't think I made a fool of myself, which is a blessing.

Dr. Ianni and his son left the party and drove me back to Georgetown to catch the "maybe" Sodality ride. On the way he asked me to work with the Advisory Board on English Literature for the U. S. Department of Education. Honest. I refused outright, of course, with all manner of protest about unworthiness and ineptness and the pursuit of theology, which takes all my time. Now that the shock has passed, I'm feeling rather pleased. It's nice to be asked to be on an advisory board, *any* advisory board.

### Monday, 27 April

SOME FACTS. Fr. Burke, the New England prefect of studies, says yes I may go to Boston College and write for the summer. The Boston College Grad School Newsletter has me and my book all over the front page. I passed canon law, not gloriously it is true, but passed all the same. I'm up to my neck in moral; exam will be on 9 May. What else? Oh, my book cover is to be glossy white with yellow *Quick as Dandelions* . . . all very well, but is yellow on white visible? Long book. About one hundred pages. These are facts. True ones, maybe.

The agency in Washington estimates the cost of typing *Dandelions* at about one hundred dollars. The trip there was absolutely Kafkan: I couldn't find the place, I was late for my meeting with Ianni, so when the lady explained that the typing was difficult and poetry was a very hard thing to type, especially this poetry whose lines were all indented funny, I just said yes, yes, how much? And when she said a hundred dollars, I was too sick and tired and sweaty and discouraged to say no. Because if I said no, who could I get to type it? And it has to be done quickly. So there we are.

Later. I phoned the typing agency and asked them to send back the manuscript untyped. They've already done fifteen pages, will charge me fifteen dollars. Better that than a hundred. I can't in conscience throw money around like that.

Naomi writes that Robert Fitzgerald, poet and critic, has read my poems and likes them very much. That's a break. Tell people. Tell people.

## Tuesday, 28 April

WE ARE ENGAGED in making the spring triduum. Thus far, it makes last summer's retreat look like an intellectual banquet. The director is a Billy Graham for the underachiever. Except that Graham usually has some intellectual substance. This chap—I leave him mercifully nameless—whooped and swooped about the altar, shouted in a voice that began too loud by many decibels and which grew constantly more loud and more ludicrous. He had two huge magnetic boards to which he kept attaching little red and green signs; visual aids, you understand. He dove under and circled about these boards, hopped up and down the sanctuary step, darted at us waving his hands. Once, seized for a moment by some overpowering truth, he turned his back to us in meditation. He also had two immense drawing slates on which he performed for us—free hand! Like that, with an exclamation point. A truly incredible performance. I am not going back; I'll make my triduum in the privacy of my room.

A new poem is forming: "The gods of blood drink bowls of milk and roses . . . the soul's relation to itself . . . something." And Rahner's statement about Christ: "You are forever in the process of Your coming."

## Wednesday, 29 April

ON THIS BLESSED twenty-ninth of April, Fr. Rector informs me that the censors have given approval for the publication of *Quick as Dandelions*. No changes necessary. None even recommended. *Deo Gratias.*

## Saturday, 2 May

DO YOU SUPPOSE you could work out a proof for the existence of God from—not the order—the absurdity of things in the cosmos? The waste, human and spiritual, the senseless destruction of people and things can be explained only by Someone who will bring it about that all things shall be well and indeed all manner of thing shall be well. Car accidents, flash fires, rumbles, abortions and stillbirths, children who die of cancer and old men who cannot die at all, murders, rapes, the Boston Strangler, the President's assassination; poetry killed with drugs, theater emasculated with homosexuality, novel eaten up with success, industry dehumanized by money; creative talent squandered, simplicity shipwrecked, spirituality trampled in the stampede for things; suicides, genocides, hydrogen stockpiles that will eventually destroy the universe: you can't explain the unspeakable without God's saving Word. You can't. St. Thomas's five ways and St. Anselm's a priori arguments may be fine, but I've never understood them really, and I *do* understand the horrors of contemporary existence. Mine isn't a very rational approach to the problem of philosophically proving God's existence; it probably isn't even an intelligent approach; it gives me more conviction than the others, though, and I think it's not solely an emotional conviction either.

## Sunday, 3 May

LIFE AT WOODSTOCK is a little bit frantic during May. People are beginning to tense up and tempers are a mite shorter than a month ago.

As for me, I remain steadily the same—nasty. I finished reviewing moral today, everything from human acts through conscience, law, virtue, sin, commandments, sacraments. Though nearly prostrate from the push, my customary posture before exams, I now have an opportunity to review everything once more and thus save myself from disgrace on *one* exam this year.

A new poem. "On Hearing of a Former Student Stabbed in a Rumble" was inspired by just that: five boys were stabbed at a party that turned into a nightmare; one was stabbed fifty-one times in the chest and of course died from the wounds.

> So at last you hold still, your angry bones
> no longer rattle as you stalk, your tongue
> has ceased its clatter.

I don't know who the boys were or indeed if they were all from Boston College High: the story reached me seventh hand. But right away I thought of a fellow I did teach to whom this would most likely have happened. I wrote the poem in something short of an hour. A good poem, I think. And the other poems, the sandalwood and the milk and roses, float somewhere on the horizon.

I am typing *Quick as Dandelions* at the rate of fifteen pages a day, pausing only to curse at every third page. I hate the damned book.

## Ascension Thursday, 7 May

SINCE THAT TERRIBLE canon law debacle, moral theology obsesses me. All my worktime goes on the intricacies of sin. Poems have become desperation moves of the subconscious, a last ditch attempt to assert the existence of something, anything, besides positive moral science.

Sleepless nights—these many—I've been reading Edith Sitwell's *The Outcasts*, a nice little work, repetitive and grandiose sometimes, but essentially strong and individual. Only ten poems for a book, and not long poems either: the indulgence of fame.

## Tuesday, 12 May

SATURDAY'S ORAL EXAM in moral theology was poor. The questions were uninteresting, my answers uninspired, my presence of mind deplorable. I passed, certainly, but with no great credit and with very little to feel satisfied about. The exam has the single merit of being *over*.

So now I've begun racing through ecclesiology, skimming the book to see what the course was about. One does get tired of this steeplechase.

*Thought* sent galleys for "A Solemne Musick" yesterday; there must be a hundred printing errors. Fierce. I tremble to think of proofreading the whole of *Dandelions*.

### Thursday, 14 May

Fʀ. Pʀᴏᴠɪɴᴄɪᴀʟ has sent his *imprimi potest* for *Quick as Dandelions,* sort of his official confirmation of the censors' approval. We're shooting the rapids with a formidable show of facility these days. Now only June fifth and the dogma exam stand between me and mental liberty.

Jim Donnelly, a second year man, wrote a song whose first verse has been echoing in my head all week:

> You call from afar,
> And I dash to the basement—
> I grab my guitar
> And I rush to the scene.
> So stop counting sheep
> For I stand at your casement
> To sing you to sleep
> With the Brooklyn Beguine.

There's a touch of genius in the exquisite combining of basement, guitar, and casement. Jim is unquestionably the world's cleverest Hebrew scholar.

### Saturday, 16 May

Uᴘ ᴀᴛ ꜰɪᴠᴇ this morning, slightly giddy with the unwonted hour, and then a wonderful morning with the Gospels of Luke and John. Review is progressing fairly well, and despite the panic which I can never seem to sidestep, I'm rather enjoying it. Yesterday as I was finishing some of Fr. Fitzmyer's notes (the unbelievable amassing of details), I felt a great dark butterfly inside my head. He was fluttering wildly, trying to get out. I expected black gore to come shooting out of both ears. I lay down for ten minutes and, feeling better, charged back to Fitzmyer and his stranglehold on the truth.

I wrote a poem this afternoon. "The Dwarf." It is dreadful.

### Thursday, 21 May

WALKING TO THE Methodist graveyard today, I was amazed at the noise of the bees systematically emptying the pollen from long rows of syringas. Maybe they aren't syringas, but they're lovely anyway, with huge white blossoms falling in clusters like very delicate bunches of grapes. Beautiful things. And the humming. (I sound now like that poet Fr. Gallen describes who used to go out on the lawn and stare at a pine tree for an hour, returning home with a double rupture; he identified with the pine tree, according to Fr. G., though I fail to see how a pine tree can bring on the disastrous physical defects imputed to it by Fr. Gallen.) At the graveyard itself I was most taken by the stones of Garver and Myers. Benjamin L. Garver's memorial is intriguing for a number of reasons: he was only eighteen when he died, the spelling of *mortal* and *Christ* and *savior* is curious, and the workmanship is identified as that of J. Pfefler of Reisterstown.

> Friends and physicians could not save
> This mortle body from the grave
> Nor can the grave confine me here
> When christ my saviour shall appear.

> BY HIS PARENTS AND SISTER.

Dorsey G. Myers' inscription has a real Elizabethan ring to it; I wonder, in fact, if it might not be an ancient inscription which Dorsey's family just transcribed.

> Though parted here, the hope is given
> That we shall meet again in heaven.
> Dear friend, who live to mourn and weep
> Behold the tomb wherein I sleep;
> Prepare for death, for you must die
> And be entombed as well as I.

He seems to have left out the "cursed be he who shifts my bones" part. It's a delightful place; makes me want to write myself a grave inscription with blessings and warnings and maledictions.

Meanwhile back at the manse I've taken up residence in a new room on the second floor. It's not a very desirable room, but on the other hand it's not a garret either. Since I'm number fifty-two in seniority in first year and since we are preceded in room choice by both second and third years, I'm fortunate to get any room at all on the second floor. The room itself could be fixed up rather nicely with new paint on the walls and new finish on the floor and a sensible furniture arrangement. I don't have a sensible furniture arrangement. Everything that has to do with my writing is crammed into one corner—bookcase, typing table, desk, file cabinet. That one corner, you see, spreads out to include most of the room. I've hung a couple of paintings, my own, put together while in the process of moving. One is called "Opus Number One with Spraygun and Hypodermic." I sprayed a big chunk of cardboard with white enamel, squirted red ink on it from an old hypodermic needle thrown out by the infirmary, more paint, more ink, tossed on some pencil sharpener shavings, sprayed some black paint over them, and voilà—"Opus Number One with Spraygun and Hypodermic." Two of the men have asked if they might hang it in their respective rooms. When I explained that the picture was only a joke, they weren't at all sure I was joking about joking or just joking.

I am unreasonably happy these days considering my exam is only two weeks away.

### Friday, 22 May

I'M ALL DIZZY and tired from reading half the night—Brian Moore's The Lonely Passion of Judith Hearne. A splendid novel, it is full of rare insight into the terrors of alone. I must write Moore a note; we spent a day together a couple of years ago at the Boston College Writer's Conference. An amiable and admirable chap.

Later. Midnight in fact. It is impossible to move two feet in my new room without a truly horrendous skreeking of the floorboards. I don't mind, but what about the poor soul who lives downstairs? He must feel he's living in Camp Kafka.

## Tuesday, 26 May

THE CHAP NEXT DOOR has a recorder—Elizabethan, not tape—
and he plays it at eleven each night. Isn't that unusual.

I finished J. F. Powers' *Morte D'Urban* this morning after
spending almost all yesterday reading it. I had become so filled
with theology that nothing more would go in, so I took the
day off. So today I'm fresh, pretty much, and back on the
work schedule again. But before I begin work, I must copy
this passage. Fr. Urban is thinking of the kind of men the
Clementines will be dealing with in North Side Chicago—
"worldly executives who liked it for its atmosphere, neurotics
engaged in the lively arts, retired crooks and politicians, and
the womenfolk belonging to all these—not exactly a family
audience. Perhaps it *was* a job for the Jesuits. . . ." That's
marvelous. There are a couple of other things like that, but
to bed, to bed.

## Wednesday, 27 May

NAOMI WROTE yesterday that one of the several reproduced
copies of my book now circulating among writers and editors
fell into the hands of Howard Moss, poetry editor of *The
New Yorker*. He was enough taken with the poems to phone
Naomi and ask if he might consider them for publication. She
explained that much of the book had already been published
or at least committed to certain periodicals and that there
were copyright difficulties with all the remaining poems (I
don't know why that should be, but apparently when you
publish a book of poems you've *got* to have copyright difficulties), but he remained nonetheless interested and asked
her to ask me to contact him or at least to send him some
poems. So I'm elated, sent him a bundle of thirteen yesterday.
It was probably gross to send such a packet and so quickly
too, but I felt it better to let him choose what he liked out
of a great number since it's clear from past rejections that my
idea of what *The New Yorker* wants is not a very sound one.

How agreeable to be asked for poems by the most *in* magazine.

The weather is beautiful. Full summer: the air heavy with bees and butterflies, a light breeze across the pool; and in the house, hayfever people coughing and wheezing half the night away.

### Thursday, 28 May

I AWOKE THIS MORNING very late—six-thirty—with the room spinning and my head flopping about as if my neck were broken. I waited for everything to come to a halt, but nothing did; even in chapel I couldn't get my bearings, couldn't even walk straight on my way to the altar. So I left chapel immediately after Communion, nauseated and very dizzy and a little frightened. I thought, because my head was full of Scriptural proofs and Church document numbers, O God, this is the beginning of a breakdown. Or maybe I'm simply losing my mind. I was frozen except for my forehead, which was blazing. So I went to bed and felt worse until I finally fell asleep; I woke at eleven feeling infinitely better. Though I look as if my face has been run over by a caterpillar tractor and though I'm still somewhat shaken by the experience, at least I have a grip on reality now and the nausea has left me.

I dislike recording all my quasi-illnesses in this journal. The impression given is that I'm the world's prize hypochondriac or else awfully prone to sickness and accidents and God's just vengeance. Actually this has been my most disastrous health year ever: my hypochondriacal tendencies have been more than matched by verifiable ills. It's impossible for me to work as hard as I have been without some kind of collapse setting in. So I mope about now thinking of 5 June and freedom.

### Sunday, 31 May

THIS MORNING I took my notes on the Act of Faith outdoors —anything to break the monotony of endless days spent in my room going over and over the same old business. In front of the library I ran into Fr. Sanders, a hundred and seventy years old and deaf as that proverbial post, but so delightful and chipper. (Only somebody one hundred and seventy years old can properly be denominated "chipper.") He stopped me, asked my name, then cupped his ear while I repeated it two or three times. Then he asked me to spell it. So here I am in front of the library shouting John L apostrophe H, when down swoops a bluejay who alights if you please on my head and proceeds to flap both his wings wildly against my ears while I continue to spell and the bird flaps and shrieks and Fr. Sanders reels backward shouting "Glory be to God." I am most pleased about my conduct. I go on spelling straight to the end of my name. The bird flies away. Fr. Sanders applauds. This doesn't indicate I'm remaining cool during exams; it indicates rather what I have come to expect as common experience. Even the birds.

Later. I began the second volume of Sigrid Undset's *The Master of Hestviken* today. Marvelous.

## Thursday, 4 June

I BEGAN VOLUME THREE of *Hestviken* at one this morning. No writing, no typing, no letters; just review, a little escape reading, and a random glance at theology. The mind bulges. There is a huge wet cat asleep in my head.

Tomorrow the exam.

## Saturday, 6 June

YESTERDAY'S EXAM was quite successful. Fr. O'Connor and Fr. Dulles examined me on inspiration and faith. I did reasonably well. For a change.

During dinner I had to leave the refectory to—as Victorian novels used to put it—get violently ill. Nerves, I suppose, and a queer lunch of unhappy salmon. Sick for the rest of the evening. Blinding headache. The whole bit. A hideous day.

### Sunday, 7 June

WORK THIS YEAR has taken ten years off my life. No, not the work but the worry about work. And I regret the loss of those ten years; I'm just beginning to discover living can be fun.

Later. Merton in *Life and Holiness* says: "In all things, the Christian spirit is a spirit of love, not a spirit of violence in defense of absolutism and power." This is a truism, I suppose, but I like the ring of it. Dogmatics have always frightened me—the people who legislate the casting out of motes while they themselves stumble blindly behind that beam.

Still later. Does the religious life really involve a frightening commitment to uncertainty or do I merely imagine it?

### Sunday, 14 June

PRIESTS TODAY. All those men who earlier this morning were just other Jesuit Scholastics are now fulfilled in a way which makes coherence stutter. The ordination ceremony is beautiful anyway, but because I daily get closer to my own ordination in both time and desire, I found today's surpassingly beautiful. The parents of the new priests shook me up a little with their white unbreakable joy and with their selflessness, which somehow seemed particularly in evidence as they stood about with their new priest-sons. And I found myself wishing terribly, wishing with a great ache in my stomach, to be ordained soon; partly because of the great happiness ordination brings to everybody who has helped raise and teach and train the priest, but mostly because I want to belong completely and irrevocably to Christ Jesus. Forever.

### Monday, 15 June

FIRST MASSES this morning began in a bit of confusion what with rain and anxiety and the willingness of everybody to cooperate, which resulted of course in people tripping over each other. But now it is done: every priest has said his first Mass, though of course actually his first Mass is the concelebration he performs with the Bishop immediately following the ordination ceremony, and every parent has gone away happy, and every guest has driven home rejoicing—except the one who bumped his fender on the hydrant. And I sit in my room prostrate, too tired to do anything but read Shirley Ann Grau's *The Black Prince*, which isn't as good as I expected. I shall sleep now for the next twenty years.

## Friday, 19 June

THINK ON IT, only think. Here I am in Boston and it's marvelous. The flight up was a little funny. The plane, scheduled for 8:05, was periodically announced at 8:45, 9:35, 9:55, and 10:10. It took off at 10:10. Meanwhile I bought Mary McCarthy's *The Groves of Academe* and read half of it, a delight I punctuated with periodic nervous trips to the men's room.

David Morrissy and Paul Messer met me at Logan Airport, took me to dinner, and then David and I went to the Arts Festival in the Boston Common. We saw some fine paintings and a number of grotesque ones. At night Leo Fahey showed up and we talked some more. It is such a treat to see my friends. And they *like* me. What do we make of the mystery of that?

## Monday, 22 June

I AM ON THE TRAIN for New York. I hate trains, but if you have to be on one, it's nice to be on one bound for New York. Besides these four hours will serve admirably to record a few things about David's first solemn Mass.

The singing was in a modest way a howl. The least offensive was my own, I think, because although I sang twice as fast as I should have and although my voice leaves much to be desired, still I belted it out strong and certain; few things put an audience at ease so much as self-assuredness. My knees beat out a Bengalese tattoo and I thought I might well swallow my tongue in that gargling process that passes for risings and fallings of the voice; my tongue in fact got caught in my teeth (which seemed constantly in the way as if singing were the operation of a blissfully disembodied tongue), but I forged on right through errors and misreadings and warbled irrelevancies and secretly congratulated myself on being somewhat of a liturgical Elvis Presley. The Deacon's singing was slow and weak and I guess accurate, though I confess my attention was absorbed more in trying to hold the book for him without shaking than in listening to what was perhaps the only correct rendition of the day. David wisely chose to sing *recto tono*, a mode of song well adapted to his one note, which he sometimes hit on pitch. The choir, which in any case was something less than celestial, went to pieces in the face of *recto tono*, their responses before the Preface for instance being more an inglorious rout than an invocation of the divine.

Rubrics were unfortunate. Whatever small glory I acquired in my sung Epistle was sacrificed altogether in my random stumblings about the altar. The seventeen hours of rehearsal with those ancient rubric sheets I borrowed from Justin proved to be not much help. Only a schematic idea of what was happening generally (Gloria, Epistle, Gospel, Credo, etc.) kept me from wandering off to the sacristy in total retreat. I was awful, but because I bowed reverently before each new error, nobody much noticed. David was fine, but then again his charm and affability could carry him through anything; social difficulties lie down and roll over dead in his presence.

The reception afterward was fascinating. I somehow ended up with a little old lady who sang and twittered in my ear like an ancient but lively bird. She was marvelous, one of those non-Catholic ladies who know every priest in the city of Boston, who remain unmarried but who spend all their days in a restrained roguish flirtation—not with people but with life. And yet in their own way they are fulfilled and happy. Their skirmishes with reality as they hover on the periphery of existence give them the illusion that theirs is an exciting life; and for all I know it may be. She was happy that I listened, and I was glad to listen really. While she was telling me of her terrible siege of pneumonia two years ago—"and the pain right here, you wouldn't believe it, I just couldn't get my breath at all; the doctor, he said it was one of the worst cases he'd ever seen, the congestion you know, and I breathed like this, hughf, hughf"—I keep thinking how important it was for her to be telling this to somebody who knew nothing about it and who cared. And that made me care, I think, so I spent several hours with her and took her up to David finally for his blessing. She was lovely; faded and brittle and kind.

There was one thing, a little incident that cut deep into my awareness with its humanity and its hopelessness; the sort of incident Henry James would make a novel from, the sort of incident Virginia Woolf would drop casually into a paragraph like a berry in a pie. Before the Mass we stopped briefly at the house of one of David's old friends and this fellow's mother said: "David, can *we* come to your reception?" But David was talking to somebody else so she repeated: "David, can *we* come to your reception?" It was a sort of mock-pitiful request containing and not concealing the girlish wish of assurance that not only might she come but that the party would not really be one without her. The moment when the request might have been handled as a joke, as a "cute" exchange between people who like one another (so long as David could manage a return both witty and reassuring to her), passed and at that awful juncture she repeated her request once again, this time awkwardly and vaguely conscious of the wrongness of the situation. Her daughter who was up until then very pleasant and charming suddenly spun on her and snarled: "Stop saying that, Mother. Of course you can come, we've been invited." And while the mother stumbled through an apologetic: "I know, I was only trying . . . I only meant . . ." I could see the towers crumble and the flag on fire and all her city walls go down and down until in a minute her whole bright day lay at her feet in ashes. She smiled radiantly and thanked David for coming to see them before the Mass. And I felt all sick at my stomach.

*Friday, 26 June*

I HAVE JUST finished proofreading *Quick as Dandelions*. But I'll start at the beginning.

As soon as I reached here on Monday, I whipped off to the box office and was so lucky as to pick up a row B cancellation to Burton's *Hamlet*. He is a great Hamlet up until the disastrous play scene, which itself was bad and after which Burton was really poor. I got the impression that either Burton had confused Hamlet's "readiness is all" attitude with "to hell with everything" or else, more practically, Miss Taylor showed up backstage and a row was in progress. Or perhaps he was unwell. In any case the last third of the production is poor and the reason is principally Burton. Donald Madden, who I saw several years ago play Hamlet at the Phoenix, did a better over-all job. Though, to be fair, I suppose there is nobody today in theater with the vocal and physical and I suspect intellectual equipment to surpass Burton's performance. But Walter Kerr is right; Burton plays Hamlet with everything you could ask except feeling. And a Hamlet without feeling is a fine body and a brilliant mind without a soul; sour. I was disappointed.

On Tuesday I picked up my *Dandelions* galleys at Doubleday, lunched with a friend, and arrived in the Village fifteen minutes late for an appointment with Albee's secretary. Albee himself is out of the country, writing I think. I bought the secretary, a clean-cut and efficient young man, a couple of drinks in some crazy pub and pumped him for information as decorously as possible without putting him in a situation where he'd have to betray Albee's confidence or the secrecy natural to his job. I was interested to learn that he had typed the last act of *Who's Afraid of Virginia Woolf?* as it came hot off the Albee mind.

He took me back to Albee's apartment, where I shamelessly nosed about, looking at everything and making mental notes. The staircase, for instance, was put in by Albee himself; it is a spiral thing made of wood and, because of the weakness of the downstairs floor, it is suspended from the roof of the building. The bottom step rests firmly on the air. I can think of no more perfect symbol for Albee's orientation to reality. As you enter there is a huge bar and adjoining living room and office and kitchenette and, I suppose, bathroom. Upstairs is larger, with two bedrooms, bath, kitchen, office, living room. The apartment is filled with curios and assorted art goodies: a harpsichord, two Picassos, a Rouault, any number of uncelebrated paintings and sculptures, a life-sized wooden torso that comes apart (used in medical schools aeons ago) which Albee allows nobody but himself to disassemble and which, sporting a pair of sunglasses, stands beside a sofa in the living room. And his books: as I suspected he reads the existentialists and absurdists and an incredible pile of junk. It was a small collection, certainly not over a thousand volumes, but he perhaps keeps others elsewhere. Anyway I was more impressed by his good taste in furnishings than by the splendor of his library. It was a marvelous exploration—after which I rushed back to Fordham and corrected galleys until the little hours of Wednesday.

On Wednesday this journal came into serious being. Naomi proposed a contract to be signed now, for which I'm to receive a thousand dollars, advance. Then in four years a journal is to be delivered to Doubleday. And they'll publish it. Incredible, isn't it. There are two drawbacks: she wants the journal to be more autobiography than diary, something I don't much approve, and she wants me to sign the contract now, something I suspect Superiors would not approve. So what do I do? I told her I would think about it.

Yesterday I proofread *Quick at Dandelions* one more time and discovered a few errors that I may have missed the first time through. Distress. Anxiety. And then who came in but Ned Lynch, who took me to dinner, expensively, at Jim Downey's Steak House. What a good man he is, Ned, and how fond I am of him. He is still walking on the clouds of his ordination two weeks ago. After dinner we went to see Frank Gilroy's *The Subject Was Roses,* a good, understated play about the family in-fighting of an Irish Bronx threesome. The family that stays together decays together. Though weak on plot, it packs a good deal of dramatic impact. It was a very very pleasant evening.

And so I have finished proofreading that book—I've come

to like it again now that I needn't look at it except to admire its cover—and am free. Off to see LeRoi Jones' *Dutchman* this evening.

## Sunday, 28 June

I'M ON THE train for Boston. I hate trains, and if you have to be on one, it's especially sad to be on one leaving New York. However, it gives me a chance to blast *Dutchman*. It is a foul play, not a play at all really, but one of those powerful skits that talented young people write for themselves to show off their abilities. Very histrionic and all that. Words I've never heard on stage and only rarely off stage. So of course I expected to meet a mouse. And Jones is. A tiny little man who reminds me of James Baldwin. Quiet, soft-spoken, painfully shy, he seemed more eager to get away from me than anybody I've met in a long time. Albee's secretary, who arranged the meeting, had apparently told everybody backstage that I'm doing a book on the contemporary theater; probably scared the hell out of them. Anyway, back to *Dutchman*. I don't know that I'd agree with *The New Yorker* in saying it is clear evidence of "a most promising playright." He is shocking, yes, but so is a trip through a public lavatory if you go in a group of one hundred, and somebody in a loud voice and with a great deal of emotional involvement reads the graffiti at you and describes the accompanying illustrations. *Dutchman* lies somewhere between good drama and rest-room graffiti; and not terribly near good drama. I doubt Jones can create a real play.

## Wednesday, 1 July

BOSTON COLLEGE. I find the best way to settle into a new place is to read a book there, so I've just completed Mary McCarthy's *The Groves of Academe*, which I began in the Baltimore airport, waiting for that foolish plane. It's a splendid book. I like McCarthy more and more. Her subtlety in

*Academe* is so involuted and her satire so astringent that I found myself reading more and more slowly and laughing out loud very frequently. That's unusual, to laugh out loud. Look at this devastating sally on English teachers: "Van Tour interrupted excitedly. 'Catholics are not free either,' he protested with heat. Like many teachers of English, he was not able to think very clearly and responded, like a conditioned watchdog, to certain sets of words which he found vaguely inimical." And she says those terrible things that make you ache for her, like: "The more ambitious teachers, as everywhere, vied for the better students, partly because these were more interesting and also easier to teach, partly because of vanity, and partly from the more insidious egotism of the Potter's Hand, the desire to shape and mold the better-than-common clay and breathe one's own ghostly life into it—the teacher's besetting temptation, God's sin, which Christ perhaps redeemed." What can one *do* for Mary McCarthy, I wonder, and why does she inspire such concern—not for her writing but for herself?

*Friday, 3 July*

THIS SUMMER will be valuable for prayer if for nothing else. I have no excuses now: there are no deadlines, no writing commitment, no exams hovering here at Boston College. I have the entire summer free to write. I have begun the prayer-part well enough with Merton and Schillebeeckx, but my difficulties have never been chiefly with beginnings. I keep no time schedule, make no attempt to get in my hour's minimum of meditation; that's depressing and negative and takes all the spontaneity out of prayer. I just read quietly until I feel moved to pray and then I do, though to be truthful I feel as many movements to clean my desk or dash off a quick letter as I do to pray. But nobody ever said prayer was supposed to be easy. Only Jesuit novices think that.

Reading Merton's first little meditation in *Thoughts in Solitude*, I felt inclined to assess my spiritual status; that old temptation still skulks about my darker recesses. From an analysis of the spiritual status—always an appalling ordeal—

we proceed directly to discouragement, and after a period of
feeling grim and grimy, we move on to distraction and dis-
interest: the attempt to forget what appears to be guilt, to
escape from accusations leveled by nobody but the self. The
Puritan is in my blood, taking pleasure in acknowledging the
clean sweep of the burnt village, in admitting that no progress
is possible. God, what a tortured psyche we create for ourselves. What explains it, I wonder. Novitiate emphasis on
personal faults, the old negative concentration on spiritual
truancy and the ponderous peccadillo? Whatever explains it,
nothing excuses it. But I will escape it—this Puritan syndrome
—even if I have to live the rest of my life half suspecting
I am damned. And today I begin my escape by refusing to
give in to morbid speculation on how bad I am because I
do not pray enough.

Midnight. One lives constantly in hope of the miracle of
re-creation.

## Saturday, 4 July

THE PROVINCIAL'S secretary just phoned to congratulate me
on "A Solemne Musick" in the new *Thought*. Seems they
prefaced the poem with a note that is most laudatory. I've
never heard of a periodical doing that before. I'm off to the
library to look at it.

## Thursday, 9 July

THAT POEM OF the last several months is done, all one hundred and eighteen lines of it. It's all there, too, the gods of
blood who drink only their crazy bowls of milk and roses, the
sandalwood business, the animals "wearing on the fuzzy face
the heart's cartography." I hope it's good. "The Masked Ball"
is mostly about metaphysics—of the mind, the heart, the soul.
Funny how it took me all these months to worry it into shape
and yet I did most of the actual writing in the last two days.

Rain today. Vile trying to get down to the dining hall.

I got soaked and feel like pneumonia. "All things conspire unto good for those who love God."

Later. I finished Waugh's *End of the Battle* this evening. I'm convinced that this trilogy is Waugh's major work, a really brilliant study of war and disillusion and the improbable workings of God's grace. There is a wonderful passage on prayer; the main character has been praying and becomes aware all at once of his overriding apathy. "That emptiness had been with him for years now, even in his days of enthusiasm and activity in the Halberdiers. Enthusiasm and activity were not enough. God required more than that. He had commanded all men to *ask*." The trilogy is permeated with this kind of awareness, a recognition that the state of man is not just "nature" but nature that has been saved from itself, nature that has been graced. This awareness is rare enough in contemporary literature, more rare by reason of Waugh's being a first-rate stylist (that dirty word) and a novelist of unlimited imaginative invention. He is great. And so is his trilogy.

## Tuesday, 21 July

THIS MORNING I finished the first draft of the new Albee article, "The Last Illusion," in some ways a digest of the long *Thought* piece but with many improvements. I've cut out altogether the detailed accounts of the contents of the early plays, reduced each to a paragraph. And I've expanded the critique of *Who's Afraid of Virginia Woolf?* With a good deal more work the article should be quite acceptable, I think. It's a pity I've promised it to *Thought*; I suspect it would be quite salable to a moneyed magazine.

I've been reading *A Moveable Feast*, Hemingway's fictionalized memories of Paris in the twenties when famous types were rubbing elbows and martini glasses and turning out things like *The Great Gatsby* and *The Making of an American* and *The Sun Also Rises* and an American chap named T. S. Eliot was working in an English bank while writing poetry in his spare time. It's an interesting book because of the people it deals with; because of the sniggery and inverted way it deals

with them, however, it is a vicious book, a terrible thing. The
style is artificial early Hemingway and the content is pepped-
up Hedda Hopper. A vile book. Its clearest picture is not of
Ford Maddox Ford or Fitzgerald or Gertrude Stein but of
Hemingway himself, an aging Hemingway saying nasty and
sometimes unprintable things about people who are safely dead
and who never wished him ill. A sad book.

## Friday, 24 July

SUMMER SCHOOL is delicious, with so much time to do everything. I read and read, which is marvelous, and even write a
little and talk an awful lot and pray twice as much as usual
and half as much as I ought.

Today I shall finish Muriel Spark's *The Ballad of Peckham
Rye*, a delight, one of those books you keep wanting to run
and share with somebody. And tomorrow I shall visit the
parents in South Hadley and on Sunday I shall finish typing
"The Last Illusion" and on Monday rework for publication
an old paper on Allen Tate's *The Fathers* and on Wednesday
begin my treatment of Albee's *The Ballad of the Sad Cafe*,
which I shall finish writing by 5 August. And then I shall have
redeemed my summer.

## Monday, 27 July

Do YOU KNOW what's wonderful? This is wonderful: that all
my plans fall apart with nobody to lay the blame on but myself
and just the same I'm not discouraged. Sunday I went out
all day to Joe Devlin's house, where we had a delicious dinner
and a long evening's carouse, and this morning I was completely shot and couldn't type, and this afternoon I'm taking
Paul Messer to see *Tom Jones* and then to dinner because he's
working too hard and will collapse unless I force him out. So
that effectively takes care of all my talk about typing "The
Last Illusion" and reworking the Tate piece and charging
away at the *Sad Cafe*. While I was home on Saturday, though,

I did manage to buy and quick-read Albee's play. So I will get
the thing written by the time I leave B.C.

Later. Naomi writes about the journal, saying she likes it
but there's not enough me in it, not enough personal stuff.
(I did suppress some passages in the pages I sent her.)
She still does not know how my day is made up, how much
I pray and study and carry on. She says: "I still after reading
this (first hundred pages) don't know what you do every day
beyond the fact that you don't like getting up in the morning,
that you thought a great deal about the Albee project, which
makes me feel horrible for not being more encouraging, and
that you went for walks on occasion and played handball."
Well, that's all I *do*. She's right. But I can't invent things.
Thinking and walks and handball: that's *it*. The notion of a
very personal journal gives me the willies. This one seems
already too naked and I don't like walking around naked in
a room full of clothed people. I'm not like Merton, you know;
I have to go on living with people, teaching, studying, etc.,
*after* the damned journal appears in print. I've declined signing
a contract just now.

### Saturday, 1 August

I FINISHED A new poem this morning. It's called "The Measure"
and is distinguished by its manner of composition—I dashed
it off in about ten minutes, all but one word somewhere near
the beginning. Finding that word and then making all the
changes the new word inevitably involved took me a little over
four hours. I finished the poem at three this morning. I like
the beginning:

> have done have
> done with me
> your body is rare
> with music
>
> and my mind hums
> its subtle cadence

and I like the ending too:

and end of harmony
I choose my eyes
and the immensity
of air.

### Sunday, 2 August

I'M FEELING SCURVY about wasting time this summer so I've spent the morning engaged in that kind of busy work that makes you feel you're accomplishing a lot even though way inside you know you're really not doing much of anything. I wrote six letters this morning requesting permission to accept Fr. Frank Sweeney's invitation to give a poetry reading at Boston College on 2 December and telling various Superiors where I'll be spending villa. So much tape. And then I finished *The Sibyl,* a tour-de-force by Lagerkvist, absorbing, insightful, of rather limited appeal. I read his *The Dwarf* earlier the summer with more enjoyment, I think. Lagerkvist has a flawless dramatic eye; you could film some terrific movies from his stuff. Funny Hollywood hasn't snapped up his novels. And then I worked on my new book of poems, tentatively entitled *That Mortal Knot.** I planned and plotted and revised. I discover that with my good poems, which for some reason or other did not fit into *Dandelions,* and with the old "Being Born and a Few Consequences" and the new "The Masked Ball" I have about half the book done. I should finish it in mid-1965, though if things go very well I might finish some time in January. So I'm all hopped up with the excitement of planning, rather worse than the excitement of composing and certainly less profitable. My nerves are all out at the end of my fingers and squeaky doors send me into paroxysms; I actually chased around the campus looking for a can of 3-in-One oil to lubricate the door of the room next to mine. Frantic. Pardon me while I go jump out the window.

* Later entitled *Rubrics for a Revolution.*

## Monday, 3 August

ALMOST ALL RELIGIOUS orders have what's known as a villa. That's a term covering both the vacation-rest period and the place where you spend that period. Our villa house is an old hotel on Lake Sunapee in New Hampshire. I love the place, the boating and swimming and sunning, but especially being there with the great men of the Society, and some not so great, all relaxing together. Beer in the evening. Singing. Cookouts and parties and like that. It's great and it restores you to a primal vigor you never really had in the first place.

Well I'm taking my shattered nerves and bitten fingernails off to villa on Wednesday and I am not going to read or write or anything. I'm going to pull myself together and prepare my soul to face second-year theology.

# II

# THE LONG JOURNEY

AUGUST 1964–AUGUST 1965

## Monday, 31 August

WOODSTOCK AGAIN. Our annual retreat begins this evening, and although I have high hopes it will be my best retreat ever, I think I won't record anything about it in the journal. The temptation will be, I imagine, to let these pages in on the story of "what's really going on." And then I'll find myself writing things that ought never to be written and making myself ashamed. On the other hand it might be a good thing to embarrass myself a little.

For the past weeks I've been mending my soul at villa. The remarkable thing about villa, and indeed the week that preceded it, was that I worked almost continually on *That Mortal Knot*, writing at a rather fevered pitch and then rewriting just when I thought I had finished a piece, so that I managed to complete the section on the priesthood, polish up the section on falling in love heart-first, and organize the rest of the book pretty well. The plan is this: *Mortal Knot* is to be the autobiography of any religious; it will have eight sections, each of which will be a group of poems interrelated with each other and with the other sections of the book. The relations will be loose enough so that the poems can be read independently but tight enough so that the book will be a whole, a little chronicle of being born, falling in love, growing up to an awareness of other people, falling in love in a different way, vocation, early facility of the religious life, later horrors of the religious life, ordination, afterthoughts. It strikes me, fevered as I am with enthusiasm right now, as quite a good book.

So villa mended my soul and left me physically frazzled. I was more tired when I left than when I arrived. But I had a good chunk of my next book written and tucked beneath my wing. This terrific writing fluency explains, I suppose, the awful nervousness and sense of frustration I experienced for such a time at the end of July; I kept worrying that I wasn't getting much done and that I was wasting my time, or rather the Society's time. It was that awful waiting period, that March we must all survive before we can understand April.

I managed to leave villa early and visit Fairfield University for a few days where I saw David and renewed acquaintance with Don Maloney, a Jesuit from California. David wasn't well, had a virus of some sort, but again he overwhelmed me with his generosity, his spontaneous Christian charity. What a beautiful thing a life is when it's lived. Really lived. I served David's Mass and we had several long talks. Our friendship deepens with time: cost helps, the cost of doing what you'd rather not or of giving what you'd like for yourself. Cost and time.

Then I hopped home to South Hadley and visited my parents for a couple of days. That was great. They are so happy together, still very much in love after all these years. It is not the years but the *shared* years that have turned a simple marriage into an almost selfless concern for the other's happiness. They praise one another, not always with words, with respect and affection. One of them must die and leave the other, to survive how?

They've promised to bring each a painting for me to hang in my room at Woodstock, on loan to my gallery. I am terrifically proud of their work, of Dad's, which is precise and polished, of Mother's, which is not precise and which has a primitive painterly charm as nice as anything I've seen in a long long time. Not primitive à la Grandma Moses; primitive in a very sophisticated but untutored way—if these concepts aren't mutually exclusive. Do you follow?

Now off to dinner and then retreat. My Woodstock friends gave me a very warm welcome this afternoon; I was touched and grateful. It's nice to be back here . . . I think. The new first year seems a nice crowd. God help them; first year.

## Retreat, 1964

I'M GOING TO RECORD occasional retreat thoughts, some mine, some Fr. Peters', some quotations from Scripture. Like so.

We think of prayer as an ascetical exercise. It is a privilege we have. God does the work. He speaks.

We have distorted God into someone who hates violators of the sixth and ninth commandments. We do not know him. He is the God of the humble and the poor in spirit; he hates pride and hypocrisy.

Psalm 103: He knows our frame, remembers we are dust.

We must always remember that in prayer we are constantly moving toward surprise. The surprise of encounter, I suppose.

. . . God whose name is love and whose irresistible passion is to be merciful . . .

The heritage of post-Renaissance, post-Reformation man is to be scattered, disharmonious. We no longer hear God. No longer see him. We have lost the faculty of wonder. Nor do we love mystery; we barely tolerate it. Faith has become a scandal and yet without the darkness of faith we can never learn to read God's handwriting.

Prayer equals meditation equals thinking: not true. Prayer is not thinking. It is what happens beyond and above thinking. God teaches us to pray in prayer.

Our past is not merely past; it is a part of us, one area of a life continuum. So our future is something more than merely what will be. The *fact* of eternal life is a reality, a dimension we must consider to be every bit as real as our past. And so (1) no matter what happens, God is present, guiding and caring; (2) whatever my life may be, I must strive to be a source of blessing for others; (3) I must be attached and involved in life since it is a great happiness, one of God's choicest blessings.

## Wednesday, 2 September

I DON'T UNDERSTAND what happens to me. We're on the second day of retreat and I'm suddenly wondering *why* I want to live a life of blind obedience in the Society of Jesus. Now, don't misunderstand. I'm not saying that I find myself tempted to leave the Society; I just wonder why, after ten years a Jesuit, I feel I must be one. I've examined this before of course (God knows how many, many times), but being so close to the irrevocable step of ordination, I owe it to the Society if not to myself to be very clear on what I'm doing here. Why a Jesuit? To be happy? No, I'm not particularly happy as a Jesuit. Would I be happier as a layman with a wife and family? I don't think so. I suspect I'm one of those people (maybe all people feel this way) who are not intended by God to be especially happy in this world. No matter. I can wait until the next.

Then what is bothering me? Is it that I feel I have some responsibility to my poetic talent? No. I solved that difficulty long since. That particular responsibility falls upon the Society seeing that I'm not my own master. It's my paltry gift to God through the mystery of obedience. He doesn't need poets; should he need me as a poet, he can always bend Superiors' arms to get whatever he wants. He's certainly bent *mine* whenever he's wanted. And if Superiors tell me not to write, I won't write. If they tell me not to publish, that would be hard, but I would obey. So it isn't the frustration of my writing ability that has me all upset.

Would I, as a non-Jesuit, be a better person, a better artist? I think so. In what way, though, a better person? Now we're getting to the point and I start backing off from it. Well, I'd be more normal emotionally and psychologically, though not—I think—more patient or more generous or more honest than I am now. Am I honest? I don't know. Pretty near, though. I try never to pass myself off as more than I am, though I do make the opposite error of trying to pretend I'm less than I am. But to return to the original question: in what way would I be a better man? Oh God. I suspect that in the world I would become the completed self that people are generally meant to be. I would have a wife and children, I would love and be loved and be completed by another person in a way no Society relationship can accomplish. What I sacrifice by remaining a Jesuit is precisely this, my completed self. Is any man justified in sacrificing this? I think so . . . for a higher motive: to be a better Christian, a better servant of Christ's people. For in giving up the opportunity to become my total self, ironically I can live more completely for others, give my love more lavishly, belong to others selflessly. I sacrifice what I might become for myself in order to give my incompleted self to many many others, for the love of Christ. A man is justified in doing this.

But why as a Jesuit? (I'm supposed to be meditating now on sin; instead of asking for compunction I'm asking understanding.) A priest, yes, but why be a Jesuit surrounded by inflexible rules and attitudes and this incomprehensible medieval concept of obedience? My only answer is that this is part of the mystery of fact, I am a Jesuit—for me, irrevocably a Jesuit—and I must be a saint this way, crazily, with all the difficulties the Society has already thrown up and all the future ones it can and will throw up against me and topple down on me and maybe crush me, out of concern for me, not out of spite. And that's that: it is my way and I can't explain why it should be because in so many respects (writing especially; how can you write anything with an executioner in the next room?) it is absurd and incomprehensible. I suppose it sounds funny for me to answer myself with recourse to mystery. Yet isn't that what fact always leads to? The soul's relation to itself is wombed in mystery. I love God and I love the Society. I am tempted to pray that the former protect me from the good intentions of the latter.

An hour of prayer here.

I feel much better now having written this. And suddenly it occurs to me that perhaps Christ is telling me in his own obscure way that writing is prayer for me and I am not to worry myself to death as I always have for not praying enough. Surely all my poetry is merely the objectification of my deepest thoughts and aspirations toward God. And don't think I'm going to start writing poems during meditation and try to kid myself that I'm praying. If thought is not meditation then poetry falls even farther short of prayer. But writing is a way of praying for me; not a substitute, a way. And I'm not just reworking the old formula that you can by a proper intention make anything a source of merit and grace; I'm saying it is a way of prayer. Period.

### MORE RETREAT GOODIES

GOD REVEALS US to ourselves. He tells us how he wants us to be present in him, in what way.

Let us be honest. Death is a terrible thing; we leave life, love, friendship, all the joys of creation that God gives with an open hand. Life is an immense gift and we do wrong to diminish it. Death is terrible, but eternal life is a fact and that is wonderful.

Psalm 131 was sung on the journey to Jerusalem, symbol of our own journey through deserts. Praise is such an easy form of worship.

Death and judgment are *facts*. Do you know what that means?

To know and accept myself does not mean acknowledging only my sins, failings, potential for evil. It means seeing that essentially, at least in desire, I am a good man. My trying to be a good man is testified to by this my eleventh year as a Jesuit. I condemn myself with too great ease.

Psalm 95: If today you hear his voice, harden not your heart. The brittleness of the mystery of faith.

It is God who was cast out of the Garden of Paradise; history is a record of his attempts to win back our love.

Christ cursed the fig tree for bearing no fruit at a time when it could not be expected to bear fruit. What does this mean?

Christ is both the image and the revelation of his Father. Contemplation of the Trinity then implies involvement in the human family. The shape of mystery is always an appeal to love him more; there is no love without involvement. God always works with secondary causes.

## Monday, 7 September

I MUST CONTENT myself with prayer that is not arid so much as blank, negative, nonbeing. I must not expect—I do not *want*—those superficial and dangerous consolations of prayer:

peace that borders precipitously on complacency, satisfaction at having "put in my time," ease of conscience at being comfortably saved. They are too easy, too delusive. My salvation, my hobbling sanctity, will consist it seems in learning to live with myself on Christ's terms—accepting my gross failures and my dissatisfaction and my restlessness in prayer as that which God intends for me, being careful to keep in touch, however, with the Holy Spirit. The prayer of quiet too easily tapers off into one long snooze.

## Wednesday, 9 September

WELL, RETREAT IS over and I guess it was a good one. I don't know that I'm any better for having made it. I'm more settled anyway; I suppose that's progress. Of a sort.

## Sunday, 13 September

CLASSES BEGAN YESTERDAY. Christology looks as if it will be interesting; moral theology will be as deadly as ever; I dare not think of canon law.

Conrad's "The Secret Sharer" is the first Conrad I've been able to force myself to read. I liked it. There's an added dimension of terror lurking behind the simplest statements until the entire action seems some terrible commentary on the nature of being a man. I even dreamed about it.

I have officially inaugurated the school year. I have cleaned my desk. A clean desk doesn't help me to work better; it merely reminds me that I ought to.

## Monday, 14 September

*Quick as Dandelions* did not get the Lamont Award. Naomi wrote this morning that the Lamont people, when they return your manuscript, never give any information other than that you failed to win the award. I learned that I had lost on the last day of villa but I was too busy then packing and arranging for transportation to get upset about it; now I have time, however, and am thoroughly disappointed. There is one consolation. I've picked up little book squibs from William Stafford, Edward Weeks, Robert Fitzgerald, Thomas Merton, Archibald MacLeish. And I've sold another poem to *Atlantic*, "On Hearing of a Former Student Stabbed in a Rumble." Specious consolations, perhaps, but the only ones I have at the moment and so I prize them. The little blurbs are not nearly so satisfying as I would have liked. Weeks, for instance, told Naomi that he thinks I'm one of the best young poets in the country, but he authorized her to use only "Fr. L'Heureux has something to say and says it well and boldly," which seems a pretty shabby recommendation for somebody you consider one of the best young poets in the country. And Fitzgerald, who was supposed to have swooned and wept and all that when he read my stuff, says merely: "Lots of original, gay and some quite beautiful things . . . beautifully formed." Blah. I begin to prefer the folly and fanaticism of Yvor Winters, who once said that "Adelaide Crapsey is not only certainly an immortal poet but has long been one of the most famous poets of our century."

One last word. I read today Muriel Spark's *The Comforters*. It is a good book and a clever one, perhaps too clever for its own good, becoming so completely a tour de force that it blunts the knife edge of the Spark wit. Although, on further thought, I can't imagine what could ever deaden the Spark wit. In any event, there is a remarkable passage about Christianity spoken by a young lady who has been harangued by a pack of Catholics lamenting the persecution of Catholics by governments, businesses, individuals. She says: "The demands of the Christian religion are exorbitant, they are outrageous. Christians who don't realize that from the start are not faithful. They are dishonest; their teachers are talking in their sleep. 'Love one another . . . brethren, beloved . . . your brother, neighbours, love, love, love,—do they know what they are saying?" So think about *that* one.

## Friday, 18 September

WORKING ALONG BEAUTIFULLY at the new book of poems.
Maybe I'll call it *Rubrics for a Revolution. That Mortal Knot*
is a good enough summary title but it doesn't make you wonder if you heard correctly; it doesn't tease the imagination.

Later. I bought Jim Linehan a Bible for his ordination
and only yesterday he discovered it is highly defective. I wrote
to the Thomas More Bookshop, where I purchased it, and
while I was writing, Justin wandered in, read the letter, and
urged me to include it in the journal. So I will, because it
is a silly letter and hits me off rather well: slightly mad but
with a method. Here it is.

Dear St. Thomas More:

I am very unhappy. The inclosed Sainte Bible which I bought
at your lovely store is somewhat less than useful. I wonder what
can be done about it.

If you check the pagination, as I did not when I purchased it,
you will find it goes along nicely up to page 1230 where it suddenly
jumps to page 1327. Then a little later you go from 1358 to 1263.
As you can see, this leaves quite a chunk missing. What *is* there
is kind of mixed up.

Were it my Bible I would just curse and carry on; unfortunately
it was an ordination gift for a priest friend who asks if I can
return it and get one with more conventional pagination. He's
using it, you see, for textual work and the missing pages would
be a help.

So what do you think? Can you send me another Sainte Bible
where the pages all go in one direction? I should be most grateful.
It's neither right nor just that one have great chunks of Matthew
missing from so expensive a Bible. It suddenly occurs to me that
of course I don't have the sales slip. Faith. That's the thing.

Yours faithfully,

## Saturday, 19 September

CHRISTOLOGY ALONG THE lines of Schillebeeckx and Rahner is
far more interesting and relevant than the textbooky sort of

approach we follow in class. Scholastic terms are necessary, I suppose, and render dogma clearer than any degree of intuitional speculation could, but I can't help feeling that the price of clarity is excessively high and that our invariable precision is purchased at a heavy cost to nuanced truth. We live in terror of heresy. I don't see why we can't risk a little hypothetical heresy for the benefit of discussion. I'm not saying teach it; I'm saying discuss it . . . among ourselves . . . as theologians. But no, we aim always at absolute precision and absolute orthodoxy and in doing so we rob mystery of its richness and orthodoxy of its excitement. Because the truth about Jesus Christ ought always to be exciting, we are obliged, it seems to me, to ask ourselves why it is not. The answer lies somewhere between the way in which the truth is investigated and the way in which it is presented. The richness of ambiguity has not always been appreciated by the Scholastic mind.

Well, have done. I like Christology and that's a break. It's nice that God arranges each year to throw me a biscuit I can chew on while the rest of the meal goes by. Last year it was apologetics and revelation and inspiration—a good-sized biscuit. This year it will be Christology and redemption, I guess. Thank you, God. I need something.

I've read some books in the last few days: Forster's *Where Angels Fear to Tread* is superb; Thomas Mann's *The Black Swan* isn't. It aims at so many levels of meaning that it fails to meet the first requirement of a novel: it's not interesting. There are all sorts of ambivalences between art and nature, the lover of art and the lover of nature, the power of mind over matter. There is even a mythic current undercutting the whole thing; the story of Dido and Aeneas and Anna courses just below the action, point for point, like the Jason myth in Allen Tate's *The Fathers*. But alas, so what? Nothing ever comes of the story because the characters are not real, their dialogue is as foolish as it is pretentious, it is impossible to care about them. But the best thing I've read recently is Forster's *A Room With a View*, the kind of writing that would happen if the spirits of Jane Austen and Virginia Woolf somehow got locked within one body. Mann doesn't seem to like women. Forster clearly does. I like women . . . do you suppose that explains my delight in Forster? He's so well bred he almost suffocates me at times. Maybe I just like snobs? Well, so long as I like *somebody* I'm still in the human race.

## Monday, 21 September

Acceding to Naomi's request, I'm going to give a thump by thump description of my typical Sunday here at Woodstock; in time I'll work up to class days and the other unbelievable excitements we have.

Sunday. I had gone to bed at midnight, having taken a tranquilizer and read Mary McCarthy's *The Oasis* in the hope that a combination of the two might induce sleep. It didn't. I was still awake and hopping about at twelve-thirty, dropping off at last sometime in the wee hours, awaking glue-eyed and semiconscious at five-thirty. After six o'clock Mass, I brought myself round with a cup of coffee and then walked about the grounds meditating until twenty to eight. Then breakfast. From eight till ten I worked uninterruptedly on theology, reviewing and taking notes on the moral and canon law we've been exposed to thus far this year.

Coffee break and jabber (I was crass about liturgy and cruel about one of our recent classes; the men laughed, which of course led me on) from ten to ten-twenty. I washed socks for a few minutes. I chatted with a fellow who dropped by to ask me to go for a walk with him after lunch. Then I wrote until noon; that is, I proofread and corrected the journal entries I had written during the summer. During this time there was an all too familiar knock at the door, one of the gabbier brethren whose incessant chatter about himself and his room decorations and the rich people he knows is therapeutic neither to himself nor to me. So I played possum and didn't answer. Selfish maybe. I've rarely ever done this sort of thing before; preservation of my sanity forces me to it. I don't really give a damn, you see, who has or has not got pickled oak paneling in his drawing room. At noon I shaved. Then fifteen minutes, examination of conscience, which showed me, among other edifying facts, that I had done a good bit of work, been uncharitable at least three times, had made a couple of people happy, had been attended constantly by God's continued kindness—his grace to which I had only sometimes responded. Lunch.

At one I was ready to go for that walk, but because the chap was twenty minutes late, I continued with *The Oasis*, which isn't very interesting, being only another Utopia story without real characters and with an ax wielded in all directions. The chap is in first year, an apparently solid and stable young man, who proceeded to do something of a war dance all about me—literally—as we walked and who burst periodically into little shouts and bird calls and whoops bordering first ecstasy and then dementia. I was utterly at a loss how to react. Finally I asked the fellow if he were unwell and he assured me he gets "silly" like this periodically. Silly! At any good asylum they'd clap him into a tight white coat. We returned home at three, he a little more in possession of himself, I completely shattered.

I read the Sunday papers until four. Marty Palmer mentioned (he was reading News of the Week section) that Goldwater and Humphrey wooing the farmer reminded him of nothing so much as Goneril and Regan at the birthday party. Marty should be writing a political column for *The New York Times*. More *Oasis* until around five when I fell asleep; Benediction at quarter to six; dinner. Joe Towle, splendid man, and I walked during evening recreation, after which I finished *The Oasis*—the least inspired of any McCarthy book I've read—and wrote letters. There was a haustus (a recreation session with beer and potato chips and ice cream that we have about twice a month; it is *not* typical fare) at nine and I had a couple of beers with Ned Lynch, who told me about his weekend call at a home for abandoned and/or misguided kids. And I got off some little uglies to a faculty member who joined us.

Examination of conscience and points for the next morning's meditation from ten to ten-thirty. (I pass over what I learned from this evening's examination as too depressing to commit to paper.) Washed, and then read Rahner for fifteen minutes. Then to bed. Up again because unable to sleep, I began reading

Julian Green's *Moira*, which I pursued until about midnight. The stars were out and I was not comforted to think that when I should wake the next morning the same stars would still be out and I would feel that I had never gone to bed at all.

With this for a typical Sunday (except that yesterday I spent more time than usual on my spiritual duties), Naomi can scarcely expect something more exciting than a report of study, prayer, and a walk. If that's the case, of course, what justification do I have for keeping a journal in the first place?

It's Monday now, canon law period, which I have not bothered to attend. Nor did I attend moral. I'm feeling just a little bit guilty, slighting obedience this way; I don't feel at all guilty about missing class. There is a meeting that we must all attend at five-thirty this evening; rumor says that class will be made optional, in which case I shall have been merely anticipating the mind of Superiors by remaining in my room this morning. Rationalization.

Later. Class is optional from here on in. I am tempted to disbelieve. Join me now in a brisk run-through of the *Te Deum*.

## Tuesday, 22 September

*Thought* writes, returning my Albee article. At the promptings of my censors and driven by my personal greed for wealth and rapid publication, late this summer I wrote *Thought* and explained that I had this neat little thirty-page article, which used a good ten pages of their longer article, and would they mind if I withdrew the long one from publication. Their response this morning is frosty, as well it ought to be, and I suddenly realize the grossness and stupidity of my request. I dashed off a note of apology and thanks; it would have been wiser never to have withdrawn the article. Now I have made an enemy of *Thought* and will perhaps never be able to place the shorter article in another periodical. *When* will I learn? Tell me. When?

Later. I had a fine talk with a young priest after dinner tonight. We sat in the refectory until the workmen had finished setting up the tables for breakfast, locked up, asked us to put off the lights, and left. We were talking about spiritual formation in the Society of Jesus. This priest reinforced my belief that the way of prayer for me is predominantly through my work and that my work is writing. It is almost impossible to rise at five-thirty, pray for an hour, Mass, two examinations of conscience that last fifteen minutes each, spiritual reading, rosary, Breviary for anywhere from a half hour to a full one— and then, only then, take on a full day's work as teacher or research director or God knows what, coupled with the priestly apostolate of seeing people and talking to them and of bringing Christ into their lives by hearing confessions, giving instructions, sermons, retreats, etc. Almost impossible. I certainly can't do it. I write for a few hours each day—on the good days. Not write like at a typewriter, but think-write at least, which consumes psychic energy all over the place and which in the end is just as productive as if I were seated at a machine batting away at the unresisting keys. Given the time problem, your working day must be suffused with Christ. He is not something you tack on to the free periods. He is in you and with you at every second. And if he isn't, then it seems to me that your work isn't worth a hell of a lot. And if he is with you all that time, with you when you don't want to be doing this work, when you'd rather be in bed or alone brooding somewhere, if he is with you all that time, then your work is a prayer and a good one. A better one, it seems to me, than if you do as some priests I know do: just announce that you are unavailable and spend the time seeking the relaxation that makes you more fit to say your Mass with the proper devotion and to make your full hour meditation each morning without dozing off during it. For whom are you working then? Christ? I wonder. I think I prefer to burn myself up in fifty years for Christ than to live a comfortable ninety years for Christ-and-me. Ours is the comfortable age. It will fry.

We talked about being happy in Christ's service and we agreed that few of us really are. But happiness is not the point. We so often think that happiness in God's service is somehow equivalent to some sort of success, that it's God's imprimatur on the evidence of our lives. And it isn't. Christ never called men to follow him and be happy on this earth, as far as I remember from my imperfect acquaintance with Scripture. He spoke about yokes and burdens and all that. Talking with this priest makes me glad I'm not especially happy. Though I'm not *un*happy either. I'm just restless. With a holy restlessness . . . I hope.

## Friday, 25 September

I FLEE TO THE typewriter for distraction. Our new optional class system has resulted for me in such an onslaught of study and reading and writing that I am all muzzy in the head and feel like I did when Gus Schmidt inadvertently whacked the base of my skull. So I flee here, though lately I dislike the journal, dislike writing it; perhaps that's because I do it now at the machine whereas in ancient days I scribbled in my spidery hand. It might be better to return to the notebook, which made me feel pleasantly Dickensian.

I notice a tendency lately (perhaps it's been there all along) to write in the journal insinuations and sometimes even admissions of great terrors that lie down deep within me. About what I will become in the Society of Jesus (writer? would-be celebrity who bores everyone to death with his tales of prestigious writers who are his friends? alcoholic? egomaniac?); about my talent (do I really have any? am I handling it properly? developing or just endlessly repeating myself?); about why I am writing so much (to get attention? to say something? or is it as I suspect some deeper drive that can't be handily identified and categorized?); about my survival as a person (will the combined tensions of being both Jesuit and writer finally exhaust me? will that exhaustion mean a nervous breakdown? a heart condition that puts me on my back for the rest of my uninteresting life? madness?). Things like that. They're not all spelled out in the journal. Which is kind of a shame because even if I were to excise them before anybody sees them, even Naomi, I could undoubtedly learn a great deal about myself while writing and excising. Fortunately, it grows close to Litany time and I must away.

## Saturday, 26 September

KARL RAHNER'S *Mary, Mother of the Lord* is superb. He is the first theologian I've discovered who says something meaningful to me about Mary: that she is important because she is the perfect Christian. He explains that Christianity in its purest form is the acceptance into our lives of the saving and loving power of the triune God who has come to us as man in Jesus Christ; Mary is the archetypal Christian because she, as no other, accepted Christ, received him into her womb and brought him forth for the salvation of the world. Beautiful and sensible. There is no saccharine in this. Rahner always makes good sense.

## Sunday, 27 September

IT OCCURRED TO ME at lunch today that half the people in religion are desperately trying to find out who they are and the other half are just as desperately fleeing that same knowledge.

## Monday, 28 September

I'VE SENT MY albatross, "The Last Illusion," to *The New Yorker* in the unfounded hope that they'll be so delighted at the occasional witties that they'll overlook the permeating theological viewpoint. In scholastic jargon: that they will buy my substantial orthodoxy for the bemusement of my accidental heresy. What do you think? No. They'll send it flopping back, dead and gloppy like a fish on a wharf. I'll send it to *Show* next and *Yale Review*, neither of whom will take it, and then I'll go like the prodigal son to *Thought*, humiliating myself by asking if they want it—back. And they will put a ring on my finger and wine upon the table and lead out for slaughter the fatted L'Heureux.

It's raining. A nice even steady determined rain whose tappity-tap I woke to this morning and which has kept on perseveringly all the day. I'm delighted, not having seen rain in a long time. Thanks for the rain.

I'm writing the journal in longhand again. I hate writing by hand: it's difficult at best, but then I get crampy in my fingers and forearm and can never seem to set anything down quite the way it was in my brain. But handwriting does give you that illusion of leisure, which prompts you to mention the rain. And rain should be mentioned. Not always, but many times.

## Tuesday, 29 September

RED INK. Maybe I should have the journal printed in the colors in which it was written. A comic book for the senile.

Fr. Provincial of New England was here for his annual visitation and told me I would be teaching in one of our colleges, English literature, as soon as I finish studies. He asked me to investigate colleges for a Ph.D. program, urged that I look into Yale. This is the first time any Superior has ever spoken to me about my future in the Society, and I must say it makes me feel good all over . . . despite the rain.

Later. At recreation tonight Ned was preening himself on getting a fan letter and I knew immediately that it was from Tugboat Annie. Last weekend he conducted a triduum for sixty high school girls at a nearby parish and, in telling me about some of the funny things that happened and some of the memorable folk he met, he told me of a freshman girl who looked like a fullback for the Giants and who talked like Tugboat Annie but who was an awfully nice kid. So she wrote him today, still excited about the triduum, still ecstatic —I imagine—over Ned. I'd love to see him with kids. He's infinitely tolerant, and crazy about kids anyway, so he must be good. How do you explain Ned? He lives blessedly above all pettiness. Suddenly I laugh, remembering that last week he caught three mice in his bedroom—he lives directly over the kitchen and they commute—and flushed them down the toilet. What a hilarious way to dispose of excess mice. Let's all drink to Ned. Hear. Hear.

### Wednesday, 30 September

RAIN FOR THE third day; a sufficiency of rain. Beaverish, I finished my preliminary survey of Christology this morning in a commendable show of fidelity to the theological enterprise. The new nonclass schedule allows time for real study and thus far I've used it for study. Still, I worry. Virtue in this world flourishes only a brief hour.

Incredible. The Government Information Service wrote me some time ago requesting reprint permission for "Death of a Man." Since it is for a French brochure, they wanted to print a translated version also; naturally, I reserved the right to approve the final translation. Things waxed more complicated until yesterday when a secretary from the Information Service phoned me four times during which—and this is the point of the story—our Woodstock switchboard operater managed to secure for God knows what reason not only the name of the party calling, what they wanted, why they wanted it, but the further more engaging facts that they were calling from an unlisted phone whose number cannot be given out, that it costs them nothing to call, that they are publishing the brochure in Africa, that the publication deadline in Abidjan is some time in October; she incidentally managed to find out that the woman calling had never met me and therefore helpfully described me as resembling Bobby Kennedy except I keep my hair neater. Our operator should have a job with the C.I.A.

Later. While I was reading V. Woolf's *To the Lighthouse* this afternoon, it came to me that most of the sensitivity I have to people's unexpressed (and perhaps inexpressible) feelings comes from my reading. I read, I suspect, with a writer's eye, which tends automatically to notice reactions and those more subtle reactions to reactions. Which explains in some degree why I like Virginia Woolf so much; this is her special province: sensitivity colliding with sensibility to generate illumination or generate at least a terrible sense of awareness. The irrational, perhaps more accurately the suprarational, wanders freely in this Woolf territory.

And I have a new poem, "The Swan"—five poems for Virginia Woolf. It's about the word and madness and that frightening awareness of self. Not much of it is the result of my reading in or about V.W.; it is more nearly the product of my fears, grotesque ones, about losing my mind. The excessive poetry production of August-September is laying its little ax to the roots of my nervous system. All is calm now, though, thank God.

## Thursday, 1 October

Rain. A gucky day, clearing in the afternoon but never really very pleasant. Weather is beginning to hang heavy; if we can't have sunshine, we ought at least to have haustus.

I'm nibbling away like a provident mouse at *To the Lighthouse*, plunging like a great hungry boar into the pages of *A Writer's Diary*, where she speaks of *Lighthouse*. I find it fantastic that anyone can write a novel, more so that anyone of the Woolf temperament could write a novel, and positively astonishing that she could produce the intricacies of *Mrs. Dalloway* or *The Waves* or *To the Lighthouse*. I hang my head in the presence of such genius.

## Friday, 2 October

It is five minutes past Thursday midnight, 1964. I must begin to live now. I must stop this compulsive reading and writing and occasional study and talk talk talk. I must pack a lunch, go for a long walk with somebody, and listen to them. I must go to Baltimore and make believe I am Pete DuBrul exulting in traffic, people, store windows. I'll notice the color of buses, shapes of buildings, books in display cases, expressions on people's faces—happys and grumps. I'll search for something very funny I can write about in my journal and something very human that will make me more human. And I must do this so that when I'm told I have only one month left to live, I won't have to look back with regret at having been busy about so many things that, in my rush, living was the one thing I overlooked.

Morning. The need to think and pray and be alone.

Late night. I wrote a couple of long letters today, illustrations of how I fail to communicate with others. Letters, phooey. Reality takes on a new face in being reproduced. I tell David about what I've been doing and feeling and somehow the *fact* itself becomes different.

## Sunday, 4 October

RAIN NOW FOR days and days, though yesterday afternoon was nice enough to allow Justin and me to walk long long, discussing aesthetics. A poem, Justin says, is a step toward definition—never finally achieved of course and never an absolute. I wrote a poem about that, or about something, called "Isomorphism." It begins: "No x is y. Of course not/with that extra leg and all." The poem is rather a dud, though.

Later. Tonight I'm depressed. A little social *crise* at table (wherein I told somebody who had been picking picking picking at me all during dinner that he was a thorny character) cast its nasty gloom over the whole evening. I feel hateful and ugly and gah.

## Monday, 5 October

*Quick as Dandelions* arrived a while ago and I am astounded at my surprise and delight. I guess I never really expected to . . .

## Wednesday, 7 October

I WONDER WHAT it was that I never expected to . . . ? Someone must have come in and interrupted me. I suppose I never really expected to see it in print. It's quite lovely, a glossy white cover with strong black print: clean. I like it. Even though it does have too many poems and they're packed in together uncomfortably (an oversolicitous mother cramming a lunchbag with apples and cookies and awful things). They need air; I ought to have insisted on omitting ten poems and kept the free pages for breathing. Well, next book.

### Sunday, 11 October

AT THE SUGGESTION of a little article in *Time* magazine, I am trying to make my handwriting more legible by closing loops and opening letters and thinking upright. If anything, my writing is worse—the scrawl of a man with a very sore finger. And now away to the verses.

Later. I shouldn't admit it, I suppose, but *That Mortal Knot* is for the most part done. I'm not exactly sure how it all happened except that in the last few months I've done little work other than on the book. Everything seems to have fallen together with a minimum of anguish. If I up and die within the next month or so, the book can go to press the way it is. I imagine, though, that both Naomi and I will have a great many insertions and deletions before the thing actually reaches print.

### Tuesday, 13 October

ST. PAUL OVER and over again urges his theme of cosmic renewal: all things dying and being re-created in Christ Jesus. Transition from death to life by a process of re-creation. For St. John, cosmic renewal is a matter of illumination: a rebirth to a life of enlightened knowledge of God. Paul sees all things of the first creation as dead until Christ creates them new; John sees all things as darkened until they are reborn to the light of Christ. Metaphors, yes, but these two ways of looking at Christ and creation imply acute differences in their respective doctrines of sin, law, justification, principalities of evil. The result is not contradiction but complement, the incredible richness of the Christian life.

### Wednesday, 14 October

NAOMI'S AUTOBIOGRAPHY came yesterday noon. *More Than Sentinels* is a fine performance: profound and personally touching and genuinely funny. I've laughed out loud at many passages and run next door to read Joe Towle others that were penetrating or illuminating or wonderfully human. Naomi has the rare art of writing sentences that carry her voice. She speaks on every page; the irony, the sincerity, the tough-minded awareness of truth bounces out at you. Easily as good as Merton's journal *The Sign of Jonas,* Naomi's *More Than Sentinels* renders my own journal at least unnecessary and very probably impertinent.

Fr. Frank Sweeney, S.J., sends today an advertisement for my poetry reading and Naomi sends word that she will probably be at Boston College to attend it. Dear God, I never considered *that* possibility. I don't know why, but I like to do these things on the sly, sans parents, sans editor, sans anybody I fear to disappoint. Actually Naomi won't be disappointed no matter how I perform, yet I somehow dread her being there. What I dread really is having her see me surrounded by admiring students I taught in high school. Now why should that bother me? It would please most people. I must be very strange, v. strange. Well, I shall write her and tell her to come if she possibly can since I will be delighted. And the amazing thing is that on the lecture night I will.

During noon examination of conscience I was harassed by all manner of distraction, but mostly worries about what new direction my poems should take. I have come to think of the second book of poems as finished, you see, and am already beset by the fear that I will begin repeating myself. The third book must be an advance over the second, just as this one is an advance over *Dandelions.* It is, isn't it?

Well, I was thinking that I should employ a whole new field of image, that I recur too spontaneously to masks and cold and animals in my first two books. Immediately, of course, the problem arises that you don't just select a field of images and begin thinking in terms of them or, more accurately, experiencing in terms of them. You don't superimpose images on a "poem idea." Just as the inner logic of each poem compels its own structure, its own outward form, similarly the inner logic (form, strictly speaking) of each poem generates its own images. Not all the firm intentions in the world can change that. What I ought to do, I suppose, is simply stop writing for a while and see what happens. But that's hard since I have at this moment a snappy long poem percolating in my psyche, a bit far down yet, but due to come up before too long. It's about Deborah or whoever it was driving a stake through that guy's head in the Book of Judges, and about our tendency to become what we attack, and about the nature of South Hadley. What is the poem trying to say? I haven't the foggiest. Given the poem's birth-nudges, however, it seems foolish to sign off writing poetry and wait for new image patterns to gather. But honestly and coldly it might be better to wait. My third book must be different and better. (Suddenly across my mind flashes the possibility that Naomi may hate my second book. Then what?)

## Saturday, 17 October

SEVEN TWENTY-FIVE in the morning and I've just finished meditation, a series of uninteresting distractions. I can never decide on mornings like this whether God wants me to put out more effort or just resign myself to the discomfort of being me—even at prayer. Since I couldn't use last night's spiritual exhortation, a beautiful presentation of that good old clock-punching spirituality, I used *More Than Sentinels*. Sorry to say it didn't help. One thought, Naomi's, did pass through my mind though—gratitude. When you give something to God he always returns it, and in an improved condition. My life, for instance, in return for which he's given me the possibility of living it, fully living it, and on to which he's tacked my little gift for writing. A better thing than the original gift? You bet, in view of the fact that my life was a pretty shabby gift in the first place. Writing may yet justify or at least excuse my existence. May bring happiness to some people, may even bring Christ to some others. I hope. So I spent a little time this morning trying to express gratitude for this gift of living and writing and I asked help to use it to its utmost for God's holy and mysterious purposes and the next thing I knew I was wandering off lost in Xanadu. I am grateful, with a cold unfeeling purely intellectual gratitude: inadequacy, thy name is L'Heureux.

Later. I'll tell you about my day, fairly typical, I guess. Rose at five-thirty, having retired sometime after midnight, and flopped off foggily to Mass. Coffee (to fight sleepy nature) followed by meditation and journal entry. (You've noticed I describe a typical day only when I can tell you I got through required prayers; sneak.) Breakfast of rather interesting dropped eggs. I wanted a second one but bypassed it partly for mortification and partly because I eat too much for somebody who gets so little exercise. Laundry day today so I had to mark those clothes where my name was beginning to succumb to the acid our well-intentioned laundry uses. Then I went for a short walk in the rain and said my rosary; I like to walk alone in the morning, I like to walk in the rain. Christology occupied me for the next hour and a half with its not very fascinating problem of two wills and two operations, human and divine, in one and the same person of Christ. I suppose I learned something, but I'd be hard put to tell you what. Christology surrendered to the blandishments of one of the newly ordained who harangued us on the possibility of an existential ethic; since I was half asleep from my early pursuit of wisdom and since the word "existential" acts on my nerves like a razor blade on glass and since the chap swooped about in a gaseous world of heady abstractions, I turned him right off like a leaky faucet. Heard scarcely a word the man said. Fierce. If I had me in class, there'd be hell to pay. I typed poems from my new book until noon examination of conscience and wept because I received no mail.

Rain after lunch gave me the opportunity to read the paper and discover that Khrushchev did not resign but was rather jet propelled from his chair of authority. Then I read Naomi's book, spent an hour in the library rummaging through biographies and autobiographies, tried to snooze a little and didn't succeed, and began writing this a half hour ago. It's now four-thirty and I will spend the rest of the afternoon (ha, a likely story) reading in Christology—reading as opposed to studying. Studying is sort of lethal. My life is fascinating, isn't it? Don't you think young men everywhere will come running to join? The adventure. The romance. The advancing senility.

Later. Much later in fact. It's really tomorrow but since I've committed myself to recording one day, I'll finish up.

Immediately after writing that I'd spend the remainder of the afternoon reading Christology, I snatched pen and notebook (such constancy of purpose) and recorded the following four gobbets of information and anxiety:

(1) All the birds going south use our beech trees as a motel. Squawking all day long, even in the rain. I love it.

(2) Finished Naomi's *More Than Sentinels*. Splendid book.

(3) I've given way a bit to my Book of Judges poem; eleven lines written. I'm deliberately making it wait, holding off as much as I can.

(4) If this journal is to reflect the making of a priest, shouldn't there be some sign of growth, of the operations of grace, of *something* more than my backsliding and my hideous preoccupation with self? It makes the Society of Jesus look bad, ordaining a glom and all. What the journal does reveal is my neurotic obsession with becoming a writer when it ought to reveal the growth of a soul in grace and desire—or at least in self-knowledge and hence in an awareness of where that self stands in relation to Christ. What shall I do? Not junk the journal necessarily; *it* isn't at fault. I *could* write pious goodies about what's going on in my soul—except really not much is going on there and . . . I'll think of it tomorrow.

Well, I finished writing those four little paragraphs with the awareness of a ferocious migraine hovering somewhere in the dank recesses of my skull: too much introspection, too much tension while I work. The work never gets to me; it's the intensity, the tightened nerve system I bring to the work. So I wandered about the house looking for someone to talk to but not really wanting to talk. Drifted into chapel for a half hour or more, prayed so much more attentively than this morning, then read *Kenyon Review* for a short while before dinner.

Dinner and recreation until seven-thirty, after which I finished Philip Young's delightful Hemingway piece in the current *Kenyon*, talked to a couple of people who dropped by my room, and finally did succeed in reading Rahner on Christ's knowledge and self-awareness. Points and examination of conscience from nine-thirty till ten. Walked outside briefly, since the rain had stopped. Read *Saturday Review* and *Jubilee* until eleven-thirty, went and got a glass of milk, then read half of Pirandello's play *At the Exit.* Off to bed a little after midnight. Somehow I have the feeling of a lot of time wasted, but writing the day out this way, I can't discover how I wasted it. A typical day, uneventful, unimpressive.

## Tuesday, 20 October

WHILE READING *To the Lighthouse* this morning I came upon that extraordinary passage near the end where the child James is watching his father read: "James kept dreading the moment when he would look up and speak sharply to him about something or other. . . . And if he does, James thought, then I shall take a knife and strike him to the heart." I was reminded of something similar told me recently by a Jesuit undergoing psychiatric care; his boyhood relations with his family were filled with all kinds of unspoken tensions. Suddenly I thought of my own psychic repressions. From the age of ten to sixteen I was an intensely unhappy and constantly worried boy, desperate to avoid the obligations of manhood. At a time when Freud would say I should have been identifying with my father, I was withdrawing from the human race altogether. I can be grateful, I suppose, that at least I wasn't identifying with my mother; that way lies Oscar Wilde. Withdrawal is not a healthy progress. What a terrible thing to spend six of your most important years unconsciously wishing you weren't. The only glad spot I remember in all that time is my overwhelming love for Adria Holmes. She did not love me in return—my first conscious encounter with love and rejection. There is no pain, I think, quite so total as this first loss.

Nine days pass and I stumble on this and read it. Is what it says true? Was I really so unhappy? Certainly never consciously. Yet, I wonder.

## Friday, 23 October

I'M DEPRESSED BECAUSE somebody tonight told me a little anecdote illustrating that one of my fellow Jesuits dislikes me rather intensely. Isn't that humiliating? Not that he dislikes me, but that I'm depressed over it. I'm not terribly fond of him myself, so there's no reason why his dislike for me should matter, apart from the fact that we manifest our feelings in sardonic cracks that can't be very edifying for the brethren. I'll offer Mass for him tomorrow and pray not to dislike him or, if that's not possible, at least not to think of him.

The *Beloit Poetry Journal* has bought my lengthy "Being Born and a Few Consequences." I'm elated because *Beloit* is a snazzy journal and because "Being Born" is the first section of my next book. Which, by the bye, I finished typing yesterday and which is entitled *Rubrics for a Revolution*. Snappy title. Publishing my first chapter so quickly is like getting an advance imprimatur; I feel warm all over.

Ever since *Dandelions* arrived, it has lain hidden at the back and bottom of my closet. Nobody knows I have a copy. In fact, I lie to inquirers, saying no, it hasn't come yet. I *am* a little peculiar, I guess. Well, today I dug the weed up and really looked at it for the first time. It's quite beautiful. Too crowded. And a ghastly spacing error in "Gardens." But my original impressions are confirmed: it's a handsome book. Now if I can survive the reactions of fellow Jesuits, I'll be o.k. It's like getting used to your face; once *you*'ve accepted it, other people's reactions don't matter so much.

## Saturday, 24 October

MISTRESS ANNE BRADSTREET, gentlewoman of New England, 1612–1672, writes in "Meditations Divine and Morall": "There is no object that we see; no action that we doe; no good that we injoy; no evill that we feele or fear, but we may make some spirituall advantage of all." Great lady.

## Sunday, 25 October

AUDEN SAYS SOMEWHERE that when he is among scientists, he often feels like a shabby curate in a salon full of dukes. I, on the other hand, being a shabby curate to start with, often feel like a disinherited duke in a laboratory full of computers. Not often; just sometimes. But at those times I feel that my IBM card has been folded, written on, stapled, and mutilated.

This afternoon, while looking for something else, I stumbled into a note I had written during a course on Pope sometime during the late 1950s. It is amusing. "We do not think of Alexander Pope as great or magnanimous; he was unquestionably maladjusted to society, bitter, small, spiteful. That is the privilege of the artist. Only the critic can afford to sit back and peck at the foibles and idiosyncrasies of genius. Generally the artist is too occupied with creation to do much self-evaluation. That his genius should cost him the title of 'perfect normality' is understandable. The two are not compatible. Every artist is queer to some degree." Listen to the tone: I sound like Moses giving a performance of the Ten Commandments. Reading the note now, I can't help wondering in which direction I was working: trying to excuse my foibles by a plea of genius or—more likely—trying to appear a genius because of my too evident foibles. In any case the note is funny and a little bit sad.

### Thursday, 29 October

I was thirty on Monday. A bit pitiful, I suppose, but it was the happiest birthday I can remember; pitiful because if the happiness of a birthday matters to you at the age of thirty, your future encounters with reality ought to be rather bruising. Nonetheless, it was dandy.

Five different priests said Mass for me and as many fellow Jesuits remembered me at the Mass they attended. Cards of course. And gifts: candy bars, cheese, (yes, cheese), an orange and green and white striped shirt that would scare the hell out of a zebra, a book, a leather box good for holding nothing identifiable, a rubber statue of The Phantom (apparently one of the current television monsters), and from David what was supposed to be a Steuben glass giraffe (price $135.00) but which turned out to be a broken glass pitcher of some kind—with a note that said "O dammit, I dropped it." Well, all this has made me very happy. Not because people gave me things and paid attention to me, but because they— quite a few actually—like me. For somebody who sees himself as so pitifully unlovable as I see myself, that means a lot. So I went to bed happy twice over: I did smashingly in the canon law exam. Hee hee hee, he cackled.

Georgetown has asked me unofficially to be Poet in Residence next summer. It means participating in the Writers' Conference, giving a reading or two, reading and criticizing some student poetry now and again, and receiving as my just reward a comely bundle of cash. I doubt I'll take the offer, but it's nice to be asked.

I whipped off some requested criticisms to two aspiring poets today. I find I get more dogmatic the more outrageous the poems are. Too bad. But they must learn that poetry is not concerned with being profound but with being true. One true thing. Just one. But no, they go ripping around the provinces of metaphysics and epistemology brandishing their crazy abstract words like clubs, beating truth to death. And just end up blah. Anybody, any poet at least, has an immense world he can create by reason of the fact that it is his. It's so futile to try to be Robert Frost or Dylan Thomas, to have the experiences and the ideas of Eliot or Lowell. (Ideas especially betray the phony; poems aren't ideas.) Write about what you *know*, not know epistemologically, but know from intuition and experience in the very fiber of your bones. And no one listens.

I have a new brief poem, "Dawn," written during a day's break from the long Book of Judges-South Hadley poem I began a few weeks ago and which shows no sign of ending yet. It's something about violence and survival and what? what?—I can't find the words.

I am in love with Christ Jesus. No apologies.

## Thursday, 5 November

FOR THE PAST few days I've done nothing but work at my long poem. I finished yesterday in one of those terrible prolonged composition sessions that leave me with hot ears, a sleepless night, and a headache for the next couple days. I got everything in: South Hadley, the Book of Judges, violence and survival, even Aunt Anne's encounter with the pressure cooker. I'm not sure how you'd describe what the poem is about, but you could approach a description in terms of violence and survival and the sickness at the heart of all things mortal. I wonder if this is my best work . . . it certainly is my most outrageous.

I dropped the long poem "The Concert: Oratorio for a Season of Wrath" at the censors at lunch hour and was astonished this afternoon when Fr. O'Connell came to my place with the poem and said: "I really dig this one, daddy." Dig. But he did like it and that makes me awfully happy because he's never said before that he liked anything of mine— not even my book. This means, unquestionably, that nobody else in the civilized world will be able to stand it.

### Saturday, 7 November

*Quick as Dandelions* was officially published yesterday. The *Times* and *Tribune* carried little notices confessing the fact. No reviews of course. Major incident of the day: I waited on table.

### Sunday, 8 November

THERE IS A haustus "in honor of John L'Heureux's *Quick as Dandelions*" in an hour. God help me. I am tight as a drum with terror. All day I've been fair game, shot down with well-intentioned but nonetheless shattering inquiries. People keep asking things like how much money I'll get, if the book is selling (the very concept: a book of poetry selling), why there were no reviews in today's paper. Worse than this, though, is the chap who grabs your hand and pumps it and shouts and beats you on the back as if you had just won the two-hundred-yard dash. You don't know where to look or what to say and nothing comes to mind except obscenities; awful. And then there are the real insults: the few who stand distant, looking, smiling their benign condescension and making remarks behind their hands to someone who immediately shifts his eyes from you. That makes me sad. Well, we'll get through it. I can survive anything. If the situation gets very embarrassing tonight (some have threatened to applaud me, others to demand a reading of the poems), I shall calmly stroll to the nearest window, open it, and jump out.

### Monday, 9 November

JOHN KENNEDY's memento card sits on my bookcase arrowing me now and again. Amazing how things that lie at that level can pain you so long.

I survived Sunday haustus. The Captain Marvel sub-superior was at the door, urging us to leave exactly on the stroke of ten. God must be pleased with his punctuality.

### Wednesday, 11 November

MY BOSTON COLLEGE poetry reading has become more and more complicated. Originally it was scheduled during the middle of our Woodstock triduum, so I had the date for the reading changed. Almost at once the dates for the triduum were changed so that once again the reading fell in the middle. After much checking and letter writing and seven hundred permissions, I am now being allowed to go to Boston on 3 December and remain there until the tenth, making triduum with the Boston College scholastics, recording some of my poems for the Harvard library, and incidentally giving the one-hour reading—the original reason for the trip. Sometimes red tape can be used to strangle you and sometimes to wrap you a lovely present.

Merton says somewhere: "Prayer and love are learned in the hour when prayer has become impossible and your heart has turned to stone."

*Sunday, 22 November*

THE FIRST ANNIVERSARY of John Kennedy's assassination. There was a poignant memorial program on television for an hour this evening. I caught the last half of it, which left me in ruins. I went to chapel and stayed there for some time, praying for Jack, his wife and children, and for this poor truthless world, which could not tolerate within itself the kind of principle Kennedy stood for. I am not trying to make him a saint or a martyr; I have no proof that he was bristling with honor or integrity, but he certainly defended these as ideals and, for most of us, embodied these ideals in his own magnificent person.

*Thursday, 26 November*

HAPPY THANKSGIVING.

*Saturday, 28 November*

THUS FAR I've seen only three reviews of *Dandelions,* all of them disappointing. The Boston *Herald* carried a very small piece by Edward Wagenknecht, who found me "with a somewhat sardonic temperament (despite his uncommonly agreeable appearance in the photograph included)." The second review, from some paper in Ohio, was lifted in large part from the book jacket. And the third was a vile column in the Boston *Pilot,* Catholic newspaper naturally, saying that first books of poetry are always tentative affairs, and although there are some excellent poems in this collection, chances are if you threw away the junk you'd have damned little left. Thus far the book reviews. Grief.

On the other hand I've had some nice letters from other poets, from a few Jesuits, and best of all from complete strangers. The editor of *Beloit Poetry Journal* wrote me a most enthusiastic letter, I hear good things from X. J. Kennedy via

Naomi, Doubleday continues to take advertisements in lush magazines. So I rejoice.

I read my poems last night at the convent of the School Sisters of Notre Dame in Baltimore. Wonderful evening; I am embarrassed to discover I'm still such a shameless ham. Jim Linehan recorded the reading and so we have my incredible voice preserved for posterity. It has always been a source of wonder to me that anybody could abide my voice at all, let alone for an hour. Irritating, monotonous, it rattles around in my throat and nasal passages and becomes increasingly unpleasant by reason of my clipped pronunciation which makes everything I say sound affected. Well, I'm stuck with the voice and I fear my audiences will be also.

What else? *The Catholic Review*, Baltimore paper, sent two fine fellows out to interview me the other day: tape recorder, photographer, the whole bit. It was a fine interview. None of those stupid questions that are impossible to answer without sounding as if you're speaking from the Chair of Peter; none of those other questions that pry into your personal relations with the Society of Jesus. I enjoyed myself once I shed my initial discomfiture. Thomas Murn, the interviewer, managed to put me at ease and to flatter me with his familiarity with my poems. That is flattering, you know, when somebody knows your book so well that he can flip open to a given poem with as much speed and accuracy as yourself. I hope he reviews *Dandelions* for the paper; I should come off well, I think.

If my well doesn't run dry, I should like to bring out *Rubrics* in early '66 and my third book sometime during my last year of theology; my fourth will be written during tertianship. If the well does run dry, I'll be relieved of that burden and can go on to less taxing things. To the spiritual life, for instance.

I've been working like one possessed during the past many weeks on canon law and moral theology and the intricacies of Christology and soteriology. I rather enjoy theology, even though it so often goes dry as deserts as you stumble from mirage to sandstorm. Without a camel. At the moment I'm reading Schillebeeckx' *Mary, Mother of the Redemption* which helps to keep theology within some practical focus for me. He mentions over and over again that the greatness of Mary lies especially in her surrender to incomprehensible mystery, the mystery of her own life and particularly of the life of her son. To deprive her of her incredible faith is to deprive her at once of her greatness and her suffering. I find this approach especially immediate because, I suppose, of my own need for faith. My own life is not a little mysterious to me.

## Sunday, 29 November

FR. MURRAY talked to us last night about his experiences at Vatican Council II. Being an official *peritus* and the principal framer of the Church-State decree, he was in a most advantageous position to see and report on what transpires behind the scenes. It was quite a good talk, a revealing talk. Cardinal Ottaviani, it turns out, is not the villain he's always painted; another Cardinal, former darling of the American Bishops, *is* the villain he's never painted. The in-fighting was always most gentlemanly as, I imagine, a jeweled dagger is gentlemanly. No switch blades. No brass knuckles.

He had some funny things to say: descriptions of the several committees appointed, adjusted, readjusted to view and review the document on Church-State; descriptions of the witty Bishop who kept coining bawdy limericks about his conservative opponents, descriptions of the opposition, best typified by Ireland's Bishop Brown, whom Fr. Murray referred to as slightly more unsinkable than his cousin Molly.

Fr. Murray is an extraordinary man. Feeling that the Council has accomplished during this session more than even the most sanguine had dared to hope, he feels nonetheless that over the clear and definitive work of the Council there broods the fog and the ambiguity of that most mysterious character Pope Paul VI. And yet Father adds at once that perhaps the irresoluteness of the Pope, his unwillingness or his inability to commit himself to a position on the power of the Bishops among innumerable other things, is precisely what the Holy Spirit wishes in his vicar at this time. The Church at the moment is in a state of massive upheaval; perhaps a strong hand and a definite line of attack are the very things that should *not* be felt just now; and so Pope Paul's temporizing becomes not the fallibility of an uncertain man but the infallibility of the Spirit working with the poor human materials he has always chosen for his most mysterious work. I can only guess at the annoyance St. Peter caused in the primitive Church by his shilly-shallying on the question of dietary laws. Pope Paul's problems at the moment are considerably more momentous (though perhaps not so in implications) than the Jewish dietary laws.

We are living in the early days of the new Church. I really believe it. I may yet live to see Mass totally in English, women as deacons, priests as servants not only of God but of people. Exciting. And I wonder . . . is there ever such complete change without the catalyst of revolution?

## Wednesday, 2 December

TOMORROW I FLY to Boston, where I shall regale myself madly, though decorously, with friends and books and Christmas presents. And I shall make a triduum, God help me.

Yesterday, overcome with panic at the amount of work facing me, I sat down and in two hours batted out my liturgy paper. It's the easiest writing I've ever done, probably because for the first time I refused to let myself get tangled in language, in felicities of the well-turned phrase, and just plunged on with ideas, one after the other. Hemingway was a boob in so many ways, but somewhere he says that the way to write is to put down one true sentence and then another and then another, and in that little dictum he's not a boob at all: words seduce, record the facts.

## Monday, 14 December

JET PLANES are beautiful. I realized that for the first time a week ago Thursday as I waited to board my plane for Boston. Enormous silver contraptions with the easy grace of a prima ballerina, they skirted the runway and skimmed off into air with breath-taking self-possession. I marveled that motion controlled can be so disturbing and meaningful. It made me happy the whole flight, which after all was only fifty-five minutes.

David Morrissy met me at Logan and we trundled off together to Park Square, where I stashed my suitcase and incidental paraphernalia. Then we walked: around the State House, down Beacon Hill, the handsome residential areas, the disenchanted Charles Street. It was grand. Dave was in fine fettle, only a little deranged by his having failed to secure somewhere a car that would have facilitated our getting about. I didn't care at all about that, of course, but he did; when New Englanders are determined to be unhappy, there is nothing anyone can do to prevent them. But we were happy nonetheless.

I spent the first night of my eight in Boston with my friends at Weston, seeing lots of people, as many as ten in my room at one time, all of us talking and waving our arms and laughing, laughing. It was a splendid reunion. Then late that night, David and Paul Messer and I had a little party and traded hilarities about life in our respective houses. I think I've chosen the better lot at Woodstock. Forests and moat and all.

Rain for the next couple days and I, like a fool, walked about saving my expensive hat from damage by going bareheaded and contracting a cold, which immediately transformed itself into a species of laryngitis, which in turn threw me into panic lest on the night of my reading I arrive full of good will and hopelessly silent. Then the snow and the cold. I knew I was back in New England.

Triduum was vile. The speaker was old-time declamatory, aimed straight at the heart. I explained to somebody that the poor fellow was wasting his time: "We don't have hearts any more." Jest is a terrible thing. And so was the triduum.

On the last day, no, it was the second day of triduum, I went to Cambridge to purchase a copy of my book; I didn't have one for the reading. Coming back on the subway I ran into Adria Holmes Katz, *the* Adria. She was on her way to Jordan's to buy her baby a stroller. And didn't I go with her. The fine young priest and the lady buying a stroller for somebody's baby. So I wandered off and bought a handsome orange and brown and white stuffed owl as a gift for the baby. The chat with Adria was limited and in *The New Yorker* I suppose it would sound hilarious, but it was terrific to see her and, besides, she invited me to visit on the night of my Harvard recording. I did.

For two days preceding the recording session I treated my clawed throat with great spoons of honey, some terrible suckers, small doses of quite palatable scotch. I arrived at the studio hoarse and vaguely feverous, managing to overcome my physical incapacities by a horrendous act of the will, which for the first time made me grateful for the Jansenistic training of my early Jesuit years. It took us over two hours to get through a forty-minute taped session; the chap was slow and thorough and quite clearly meticulous. He played back for me a couple of the poems, evidently the best reading I've given. I'm eager to hear the recording he will prepare from the master tape. The studio itself was most curious: a three-floor apartment with the performance area on the top floor and the actual machines on the first. The performance area consisted of two or three lavishly furnished salons, silk tapestry furniture, handsome paintings, harpsichord and piano and a welter of microphones. It was the last thing I would have imagined a recording studio would look like.

I repaired immediately after the recording to the Katzes, where I bored Adria and Stanley with an account of the evening. They are a handsome and engaging couple, disconcertingly well informed about everything, and best of all they never make you uncomfortable with their obviously superior educations. Stan teaches history at Harvard; Adria is completing her Ph.D. in philosophy there; they met at Oxford when they were both undergraduates. Life seems easy and full for them, though I'm sure they've had their difficulties and for all I know may still be having them. Their lives seem centered on their baby, Derek; the love squandered among the three of them made me so very happy and I loved them all the more.

The next morning I meditated on celibacy. It is most valuable, I think, when the celibate realizes the beautiful thing he has chosen to give up. He gives visible testimony to the world that he has faith in God's promises, that he has committed himself to a way of life that is contradictory to all our natural desires, that he wishes to give his love lavishly to many many people. Celibates are too often the ingrown toenails on the Mystical Body. They should be not inclosed but open, open to accept and to love the unloved, open to the hundreds of emotional relationships that make a person whole. They give up sex; they cannot give up love. Spending an evening with married people whom you love is the best kind of triduum.

The reading itself was a very touching experience. The room seats about one hundred and twenty and there was a huge overflow audience that lined the sides of the room and even sat up front beside me. Fantastic. They were most responsive too, laughing hilariously at all the funnies, looking appropriately pained at my more hateful poems. Following the reading about a hundred or so came to the reception where everything was confusion and madness, shaking hands with ex-students whose names escaped me, meeting new people who felt they should say something and yet didn't want to keep me from the others I knew, signing copies of my book with the banal "with all good wishes." I loved it.

Extraordinary how many people were at the reading with no proximate excuse. I didn't know them, they didn't know me, they were the wrong age altogether—between thirty and forty. They were some of those people, I guess, who live on the fringe of universities and spend their evenings doing cultural things. Anyway I was pleased to see them.

I cleared out of Boston the next day, flew home to Bleak House, and here I sit now with tears plopping off my typewriter keys.

## Tuesday, 15 December

THE *Catholic Review* interview came in this morning's mail. Tom Murn edited the tape rather well, I think, and the interview is a discussion about what poetry is, how it comes to be, what it tries to do. I sound dogmatic but, thank God, not particularly ignorant. And the article is accompanied by three fine photographs taken by Tom Lorsung. Not flattering, you understand, but nearer to what I look like than any studio portrait represents me; I hope to use the smiling one for the flap of *Rubrics for a Revolution*. Part of my face is in shadow but the old nose and chin stick right out there and seventy-five creases around my smile are evident, every one of them. Real photographs are nice; glamorized ones can be nice too, but you always have to come back to reality eventually and the way you look is an inviolable part of whatever reality you are. If I had a wart, I would want it in my photo.

The mail brought another goodie. Two smashing reviews, diametrically opposed. The Fort Worth *Star-Telegram* says: "John L'Heureux is a Jesuit priest. His verse is a reflection of Jesuitism: Orthodox, 'establishment,' and pretentious, so much so that this reader often thought he was being put on. He wasn't." He then proceeds to draw and quarter me for using "festoony strings of adjectives." The other review is from the *Literary Times*, Chicago. The marvelous chap says warming things about my "robustness of language, humor, originality," and concludes with this mad paragraph: "A poet of passionate temperament and acrobatic wit, L'Heureux in his poetry presents, like the juggler in the tale, a virtuoso performance, which serves as a moving tribute to his God and his religion." Let no one ever say an unkind word about Chicago reviewers. Forgive my quoting reviews of my poor little weed; it is my only child, grew up crippled, was rejected by ten suitors . . . I cannot help rejoice when someone likes it. And as for Fort Worth: I'll read that review for my audiences, follow it with my most outrageous poems, and make a happiness out of my own destruction.

## Thursday, 17 December

I HAVEN'T ENOUGH TIME to do all the worrying I ought to be doing.

## Tuesday, 22 December

I HAVE A COLD and a liturgy exam, both on the same day. I am better prepared to deal with the cold than with the exam. For some miraculous but unidentified reason, panic has not yet seized me.

Guess what. The Woodstock Singers are going to be on Ed Sullivan's Christmas show with much applause and hoopla. Imagine achieving apotheosis in the seminary. Not to mention Christmas in New York.

The Jennings, one of my Fairfield families, wrote yesterday that the Open Book Shop has sold twenty-five copies of *Dandelions* in the past week, which makes it their best-selling book. I suppose every Fairfield boy I taught or even knew vaguely is going to be gifted with the damthing at Christmas. Well, it's good: *Dandelions* is perhaps the only book of poems most of those families have ever bought or ever will buy. My small service to the arts.

## Saturday, 26 December

THE WEATHER is most extraordinary, seventy degrees all yesterday and at least fifty today. And still. Nothing moves. You begin to think you inhabit some strange tropic region where the monsoons are heralded by a deadly calm and the ominous flight of great flapping birds. No such luck of course; it just means more snow.

Christmas eve and Christmas day were rather deadly, as they always are in a house of studies. We reel dizzily from our last exam on the twenty-third and at once begin frantic decorating and cleaning and preparing that goes on a good part of the twenty-fourth, so that by the time of Midnight Mass everybody has on a terrific grouch and only the superabundant graces of Christmas let us get through the night without chewing one another's faces. Eventually somebody is going to decide that decorating should either be done earlier or not at all. Christmas day is always sad for me: everybody goes to such lengths to make it pleasant and that sets up sort of a formal tone—you feel obliged to enjoy yourself under pain of disappointing everybody if you don't. Most of my friends were either out in parishes doing priestly things, or singing at hospitals, or in New York (missionaries visit their families at Christmas), or hiding under Christmas trees somewhere. I spent part of the day reading Bédier's *Tristan and Iseult*, a gesture which is, I suppose, a commentary on Christmas at Woodstock but even more a commentary on me.

On my desk there is a beautiful beautiful tangerine which I shall eat tomorrow.

## *Thursday, 31 December*

THE YEAR 1964 is drawing to a glorious conclusion: I wait on table today, I have a cold, my latest poem is gibberish. Total defeat on the social, personal, intellectual planes. Happy New Year. Here, for the little it's worth, is the poem.

### *The Window*

Ned and I saw cats dancing in the window
and though my watch and clock broke—
both of them—within an hour, I did not mind
so much because the cats were good to look at.
Watches get enough attention anyway.

This morning, timeless, was a footrace and I
ran into myself on the stairwell, stood sick
and wonderless at the same old clutter
of bones and lies. I damned me to my enemies.
A new effective way to pay old debts.

But at the moment of Communion, Christ
lying light upon my tongue, I thought
about the cats and Ned and clocks,
revived the Christian wonder at a dancing toy,
forgave myself—almost—for being me.

Later. Actually, it's not a bad poem at all, is it?

### Saturday, 9 January

A NEW YEAR, a good one, scarred already with a few uglies, but ripe with all sorts of promise.

Some good things first of all. We have no snow yet. That great blizzard we had so long ago tired itself out and melted and we haven't seen snow since. It's mild sweater-weather. I love it. *Catholic World* bought my Avery Dulles poem; *New Frontiers* will publish the long vocation poem, "The Failure"; *Beloit Poetry Journal* has just brought out "Being Born and a Few Consequences." All these things are from *Rubrics*. I've just mailed the whole darned manuscript to Naomi and now wait the fatal word from her. Last one: Mrs. Pecora, that lovely lady from Wisconsin who always writes me alarmingly intelligent letters about my poems, wrote this morning about *Dandelions*, telling me the poems she especially liked, her favorite lines, the parts her young sons liked best. There's a pile of good things for only nine days of the new year.

Now uglies. I flunked the canon law exam; the retake is on 20 January. What's that funny rumble in the pit of your stomach, Mr. L'Heureux? That's an ugly, sir. Another. I've had insomnia for the last three weeks, an agonizing thing that drags me around exhausted all the day and as soon as I hit the sack it begins tickling my heels and plinking my eyes open. Hateful. I've almost begun to plan on it. Last ugly: a spiritual *crise* of unidentified nature, something I can't blame on the canon law disaster—I found out about the flunk just a day ago and the *crise* antedates even the insomnia.

The spiritual difficulty is something I don't really understand. I'm lonely, but that's nothing unusual. I feel lost and unloved and unloving, but that's not particularly unusual either. I have an occasional temptation against faith, an occasional longing for a wife and family to care about and to have care about me, but again there's nothing unusual in that. A failure. I feel somehow a failure (no, not that silly canon law; aside from that; indeed, despite it). Rootless. Useless. A conviction of my total inadequacy hounds me and along with it a terrible longing that is at last, after a month or two, driving me to prayer;

a blind and almost helpless prayer, repeated requests that God will help me to appreciate (if not to understand) that this anguish and this longing is for him, to be with him, to love him. In somebody else, this trial would be a step to a degree of holiness. In me it's just a necessary roadblock, which, causing me to exert myself a bit in the attempt to get over it, keeps me at least from total backsliding—like the terrain in *Alice* where you have to run to stay where you are and run twice as fast if you expect to get anywhere. I flatter myself that this blackness hasn't manifested itself much in my conduct around the house; it has, though, popped out all over in my poems. Check these lines for instance from "Prayer for a New Year":

> We hang upon our Christmas trees everything
> Except each other. An oversight perhaps.

Makes you feel warm and folksy, doesn't it. Well, with God's help and the prayers of all the good people who seem always to be promising them to me, I'll survive this bleak period.

I've had some funny dreams in the past couple of weeks. One was about having my leg amputated above the knee; prophetic: two days later I heard about canon law. The other was about Bette Davis playing the goddess Athena. She was walking along a mountain path a little behind another woman who either threw herself or fell from the cliff and landed splat a good distance down. I hadn't known this was going to happen and recoiled in horror. Miss Davis announced, only mildly distracted: "Dear me, death is such a lying-still-thing." I'd like to have that one explained.

And here's one last good thing, to end cheerily. Dr. Riley Hughes from Georgetown has officially asked me to be Poet in Residence for the year 1965.

### Tuesday, 12 January

SNOW HAS COME with a vengeance. Up to our ears. And I skulk about runny-nosed and tired and ugly. I'm suffering from Vitamin Backlash. You figure it.

*Thursday, 14 January*

RILEY HUGHES and Rocco Porecco are good guys. Visiting them yesterday at Georgetown, where already they are deep in plans for the summer Writers' Conference, I agreed—pending Superiors' approval—to be Poet in Residence. Porecco seemed eager to have me. My duties would be simple enough: one major lecture, one appearance on television being interviewed and swatting banalities around, one week of discussion-lecture with other poets. The rest of the time is mine. They give me board and room and a stipend of two hundred dollars. Could be more impressive, but I'm scarcely in a position to bargain about the petty relevancies of cash. I'm one of those poor you're always going to have with you.

This Poet in Residence business brings up a problem I'm not prepared to deal with, the hyphenated priest problem: how do you mesh the conflicting or at least diverse functions of the scientist and the priest or mathematician-priest or musician-priest or whatever-priest. Fortunately it's an abstract problem, the kind I never answer anyway, preferring ignorance to headaches. In the case of the poet-priest, however, at least as presented by Karl Rahner, the problem is reversed: the perfect priest *is* the perfect poet and vice-versa. Well, you're on shaky ground, Fr. Rahner.

He has a good little essay, "Priest and Poet," in which he says that the finite and the formed, the proportioned and the enclosed, proclaim the infinity of God precisely *through* their good finiteness. It is the poet's job to free these finite things by enabling their infinity to shine through them, to tell the truth by presenting what really *is*. What the poet effects through words, Rahner says, the priest effects through the Word. Thus the perfect one becomes the perfect other. A nice neat solution, to be sure, but I think it's a bit too neat for its own good. It just doesn't work.

For the priest-poet to be realized, there must be a point of intersection between the charisms of priest, of poet. That intersection is absolutely essential. But it seems to me the poet is rarely if ever called to the priesthood. He tends to be egocentric, morbidly self-concerned, with a dedication to words and writing that precludes the larger dedication to any cause. (I'm doing myself out of business.) I sometimes think that the psychic force of a poet flows on a different plane and in a different direction. The psychic force of a priest should bend upward, but the poet's bends inward. I don't see, therefore, how a poet can be a priest without becoming—in his conduct at least—a benign schizophrenic. And I don't see how the poet who is a priest can castigate a world gone mad with self-indulgence . . . and isn't that the poet's oldest office, to flay the hide of illusion from the complacently mediocre? The priest has to love that world gone mad, he must love it with the care of Christ. Finally there is the contemporary mode of writing. The most valuable poetic focus, it seems to me, is irony. Irony is two-edged and can cut even the contemporary mind. Irony is more than a disembarrassing gesture; it's a confession of concern under the mask of humor, a symptom that all the heart's children are not yet snugly tucked abed. But the mocking tones of irony aren't suited to the priest's voice, which ought to be one of love. So I don't see how the same man can be both a significant poet and at the same time a dedicated priest.

I imagine that, when a genuine poet becomes a priest, he ceases to function as a poet. For one thing he has less personal need for poetry; creating and making new with Christ can, I imagine, easily supplant the agony and dissatisfaction of those isolate hours with the smoking lamp and the bitten pencil. I should imagine also that when a priest becomes a poet (an unlikely event), he functions only minimally as a priest. And this for the two reasons I mentioned before: the poet sees everything in relation to himself and as a priest he cannot do this; the emotional strain and the ironic voice of a contemporary work of art drive the poet in any direction but prayer and prayer must be the priest's daily bread.

But here I am trying to parse mystery and you can never do that. Undoubtedly the real cause for the rarity of priest-poet is something much deeper, much less definable. Maybe it is that, having discovered Christ at a profound level, the priest-poet has no need to free things and to tell the truth about them. Maybe it is enough for him to contemplate what he sees. Maybe his poetry is love.

## Friday, 15 January

I HAVEN'T ice skated in four or five years. This morning after a crazy insomniac night I pursued St. Paul on his second missionary journey, attended another debilitating Fitzmyer class, and decided I would probably not survive till lunch without some sudden and violent change of scene. I grabbed my skates and whipped off to the frozen swimming pool. Naturally nobody was there; good people are studying during study hours. I skimmed about tentatively for a short while, then did a little jump, then a more complex one, then finally a great swooping arc and twist and jump like a possessed gazelle; whomp; I threw my neck out or pinched a nerve or something. The pain is terrific, and aside from heat packs applied at great nuisance to the infirmary, there seems no relief from it. The infirmarian gave me a bunch of pills designed to relax the muscles and dull the pain. Nice try, pills. So I sit with a cashmere scarf (70 percent cashmere) swathed about my neck and I wait for the pain quite miraculously to disappear. They were better at that type of cure back in the Apostles' time.

## Friday, 22 January

FOR THE FIRST TIME in a week I have shed my scarf and my blanket and a major portion of the unbelievable pain in my neck; I feel once more able to cause trouble. The infrared lamp and the salves coaxed the pain into submission, but no infrared lamp had quite counted on a canon law retake that sent me into a great panic on Tuesday and a first-class migraine on Wednesday. One of the burdens of being neurotic. I did smashingly this time in the c.l. Small wonder; I studied a full twenty minutes between the initial disaster and the repeat. I *knew* the stuff; I just hadn't indicated I knew it. This time I

went into the exam nice and fresh, with a degree of abandon-
ment bordering the shores of despair. I feel great.

Drowning in self-awareness as I was all last week, I thought
over and over that the world has completely lost respect for
two things: charity and pain. It doesn't believe in charity; it
kills pain. Admittedly some charity is hard to believe in (as
when it is a mask for self-indulgence or a weapon for inflicting
pain) and some pain should be killed (self-evident), but things
have come to a pitch where if you do something for somebody
and cause yourself considerable inconvenience thereby you
are automatically suspected of either ulterior motives or hidden
masochistic tendencies. And if you don't take a Bayer Break
at the least threat of throat-tickle or conscience-twitter, you are
failing in your obligation to preserve life and to care for the
secure future of your family. Pain does that: makes you aware
of its value. Up to a point it is a nuisance; then there is a
secondary stage where the only possible activity is prayer; beyond that lies a region of spun silk where the pain envelops
the personality completely and you become what you suffer—
no rational procedure is possible, there is only waiting. A valuable experience. I am grateful for it. The backlash is really
funny: today, with only slight pains, I feel on top of everything.
Bring on those tigers, baby.

Scripture is marvelous. St. Paul isn't really opening new
territories to me, but he is enabling me to explore them with
a great deal more intelligence and perspicacity than I ever
could before. We've just begun Galatians, the first of Paul's
letters to unfold his doctrine of freedom of the Christian
and enslavement by Law. It's a shaking thing: "It is evident
that no man is justified before God by the Law" (3:11); and
"For freedom Christ has set us free; stand fast therefore and
do not submit again to a yoke of slavery" (5:1). That's for
me. Now if I can only begin to *live* it.

There is still no news from *Atlantic* on "The Masked Ball,"
though today marks the fourth month they've had the poem.
There is no news from Naomi on *Rubrics* either. In fact there
is no news about anything. Ours is a quiet life. Too damned
quiet.

Later. Fr. Walter Ciszek, S.J., spoke to us for an hour this

evening. Hearing him, I was able to understand how he survived twenty-three years in and out of Russian jails and work
camps. He is simple beyond belief. Arrested by the Russians
early in 1940, he was interrogated for five years before being
sentenced. He was variously accused of being a spy for Germany, then for Poland, then for the United States, and finally
for the Vatican—which, if it were not so grim, would be
funny. He was tortured, sentenced finally to fifteen years of
heavy labor, released, and kept under constant close surveil-
lance. While in prison, while in the labor camps, while working as a "free man" in Norilsk, he managed always to function
to some extent as a priest: he baptized, performed marriages,
said Mass, gave Communion. In Norilsk his secret activities
were so well known that strangers coming to town would ask
people on the street how to get to "the church." The Communist purge of religion has not been totally successful.

He is most impressive. He began his talk by saying "the
man who is truly humble and very close to God does not mind
talking about himself. And so I'm going to talk about myself."
Naïveté and a supreme pride are beyond consideration here:
such an opening from a Jesuit necessarily marks him as completely sincere or completely mad. He is not mad. He is
simple as the prophets must have been simple; in fact, as he
was talking I kept thinking of Jonah waiting patiently in the
belly of the whale. Despite his brilliant intellectual background,
he preserves a mind uncluttered by complexities of truth; he
is well taught certainly in suffering and compassion and a
Russian brand of selfless charity. He so obviously loves the
Russian people, so clearly would trade his present life for the
slave-labor conditions of Norilsk. He is, I suppose, a saint and
as such would be a difficult man to live with. He is dogmatic
on things I agree with but his dogmatism on certain touchy
points (the abuses of capitalism, the grandeur of the Russian
peasant) would begin to rub wrongly after a while. His
spirituality, a beautiful thing, is not nearly so profound as it
is intense. "Prayer isn't what you do when they ring the bell
and you go down on your knees. Many times when I was
waiting for trial I couldn't pray at all. Then I discovered that
prayer is your whole life, it is how you are with God, you

want always that he have his own way." You can't get a much more simplified doctrine on conformity to God's will than that one. Life lived, like St. Paul's, in Christ. He was not told until ten minutes before he flew to the United States that he had been traded for a Russian spy, that he would not see his Russian people again. It is as well they gave him no time to consider; he probably would have stayed there among his people. And who could say that might not have been the better thing.

## Monday, 25 January

"IF JUSTIFICATION could be secured through the Law, then Christ died for nothing" (Gal. 2:21). If I weren't such a hardened New England Irish Jansenist, I'd say that St. Paul is going to change my life. Freedom.

## Thursday, 28 January

I AM AWASH with self-sympathy. Early this morning I decided to read Robert Lowell's *For the Union Dead* before getting down to Paul's epistles. Opening at random, I read "The Severed Head" and was knocked cold, blonk, by the ending:

> He left me. While the light began to fail,
> I read my Bible till the page turned black.
> The pitying, brute, doughlike face of Jael
> watched me with sad inertia, as I read—
> Jael hammering and hammering her nail
> through Sisera's idolatrous, nailed head.

There is another line at the end, but I was too numbed to read it because my longest and best poem, "The Concert: Oratorio for a Season of Wrath," begins:

> She gave him milk and incidental comfort,
> a mat for his wintered bones, a cloak
> to hide him from the night. He slept.
> She came to him across the tawny carpet

and drove a tent stake through his brow,
straight through until it rooted in the ground.
So perished Sisera at a woman's hand.
Nothing much has changed; the reedy fiber
of survival springs armed warriors out of stones.

What this proves of course is that both Lowell and I have
read the Book of Judges, but what critic is going to believe
that? I can see the reviews: "Fr. L'Heureux, whose work is
heavily derivative from Lowell in his better poems and from
Adelaide Crapsey in the others . . ." I feel hopelessly defrauded.
Now all I need is a rejection from the *Atlantic* and a solemn
nay from Doubleday.

## Friday, 29 January

THE *Atlantic* wrote yesterday rejecting "The Masked Ball,"
thus bringing a sound kick in the pants to my four months'
expectation. And Naomi wrote too about my book. *Rubrics*
has confused her, or rather I confused her about *Rubrics* in
telling her the sections were interconnected. She asks my indulgence therefore to approach the book in her own time and
in her own way. (Ouch, that's my foot.) Which is o.k. by me,
though I do think that if Doubleday is not going to publish it
at all, they should notify me before many months go by. I've
got to have it published before my ordination. That's settled.

Riley Hughes is my hundredfold. He wrote this morning
telling me that the Writers' Conference is raising my stipend
to two hundred fifty dollars, the fifty extra being "to punish
vagueness," something I am suddenly much in favor of punish-
ing, so long as it's Georgetown's and not my own. I'm delighted. I think I can do this well. It's been so long since I've
felt adequate to meet whatever was being required of me.

## Saturday, 30 January

PAT SULLIVAN went to Washington with Fr. Dulles yesterday,
and while they were in a bookshop, Avery noticed the February

*Catholic World*, with John Courtney Murray's picture on the cover. Flipping through, he mentioned to Pat that there was a poem by John L'Heureux: "Marginal Note in a Theology Text," which is of course about Avery. Pat, reading over Avery's shoulder, recognized immediately who was being described. But Avery, with his face screwed up in a great perplexed question mark, read the poem a second time, grunted, and said: "Well, I don't understand *that.*" I've seen him twice in the corridor and he's given me curious looks; presumes, I suppose, that I've slipped my trolley.

Winston Churchill was buried today. The service is being relayed to the United States television in little spurts all during the day. He was a great man and I ought to say something solemn but the only thing that comes to mind is what happened to me on the night he died, almost a week ago now. I had had insomnia the night before so about eleven-thirty I took a tranquilizer and popped into bed, tenderly lulled by the soft music playing in the room below me. An hour later the music was still playing, louder now and not quite so lulling. All in an itch, I rose and took half a sleeping pill, then pitched back into bed again. Finally hearing on the three-thirty news that Churchill had just died and deciding that I was in some danger of doing likewise unless I got some sleep, I horsed myself downstairs and woke the chap (who of course had fallen asleep with the radio on), assuring him: "Churchill is dead. Can you turn off the radio now?" Groggily, he replied: "I can't hear you. The radio's on." I laughed. It was three forty-five by now and if I hadn't laughed I'd have wept. I was very sad the next day.

## Thursday, 4 February

I AM TIRED to death of studying. Even St. Paul is a terrible drag; imagine what little chance of interesting me poor old moral theology holds. 'Tis the season to take arsenic, fa la la la la, la la la la.

I've been reflecting further on the poet-priest problem: you know, can one person be both. What prompts my reflections is a quotation in a recent issue of *The National Review* about a poetry reading at Columbia University before a mixed audience of several hundred. *The N. R.* quotes the *Columbia Spectator*, a campus paper I guess, in its placid account of Beat poet Allen Ginsberg (author of *Howl, Gasoline;* author and star of the *Beat* movie Pull My Daisy) and his reading. He began by

sitting on a yellow prayer mat, removing his shoes, and singing "Hari Krishna"—a song brought back from India. . . . Ginsberg sang: "Peter Orlovsky will you come out and help me sing to these poor people? Are you in the bathroom?" A man with shoulder-length blond hair and a drooping pocketbook (Orlovsky) appeared briefly and surveyed the audience. Ginsberg read from "The Change" . . . a poem that cannot be completely understood at first hearing, but which is nevertheless very moving and pornographic, in that it produces strong sensations of nausea, heat & desire. Ginsberg's subject is primarily his own body, and its contact with other bodies, and as he read "The Change" he pointed to that section of himself which he happened to be discussing at the time. Peter Orlovsky, who read later, began by taking off all his clothes except for a black pair of bikini underpants. . . . Orlovsky read from a poem published in a New York literary magazine. The poem is built up, extremely cleverly, on love notes typed on a bedside typewriter between Orlovsky and Allen Ginsberg.

How's that, folks? The immediate reaction is either revulsion or amusement. A doleful little performance, it mirrors the landslide of contemporary moral values. Ginsberg and his crowd have sublet the province of the soul in return for kicks; they've exchanged poetry and its discipline for exhibitionism-cum-license. But they've recognized a truth kept hidden for some time now. Poetry does have something to do with life and with living; we may find it hard to accept Beat notions of poetry and even harder to accept their notions of living, yet the fundamental truth remains true no matter who speaks it—if poetry is not quickened by the human voice speaking of an encounter with the real, then it is nothing. We protest (*I* do, certainly) that the experience of Ginsberg can scarcely be considered as an encounter with the real; or if it is the real, it is a reality so distorted by the subjective and the untruthful and the induced schizophrenia of the loveless that it is undeserving of the name of truth. Ginsberg has mistaken activity for art and bravado for performance. He is a hollow man, one more to be censured than pitied. His exhibition at Columbia, however, does have the merit of shocking us into awareness that poetry deals with life and the living, and that only the life lived honestly has value—whether for the poet or for the priest.

I'm going to pursue this a little bit. The function of poetry, one function at least, is to speak truth. So the poet aims always at the identity of word and experience: the poem is significant in proportion to the completeness of its conformity with the original experience and the profundity of that experience which has become the poem. Identity of word and experience. This identity of word and experience must be the priest's as well; on a different and more exalted plane, he must speak the word of Christ. He must experience Christ profoundly, *become* him insofar as this is possible in our limited condition, and express him not only in consecrating and absolving but in every word that passes his lips, in what he *is*. He must as flesh speak the word of Christ to flesh; it must be a living word spoken to a living people in terms they understand, in tones they recognize as love. He must, ultimately, be able to touch a Ginsberg as well as an Eliot; Christ did not come only to the well-washed. I've said the function of the poet is to speak truth; the function of the priest, then, must be to speak Truth. If the poet must become his poem to surrender it, so the priest must become Christ to give him up to a largely Godless mankind.

Of course I'm not a priest yet and perhaps when I am one I shall see that what I'm saying now is mere theorizing from the outside of a situation I am ill-equipped to understand. Still I think it's better to have thought through a problem as best you were able than not to have thought about it at all.

## Tuesday, 9 February

I AM UNDONE. A woman called Michelle Murray has reviewed *Quick as Dandelions* for the *National Catholic Reporter* and she's done it slashingly, calling my poetry lifeless, superficial, reflecting not a profound experience but a stock response. And of course everybody here reads the damned paper and nobody reads any of the papers which gave me noble reviews. Yeah, well the same to you, lady.

Later. It occurred to me as I was undressing for the shower (do you suppose there's an analogy between taking off clothes and coming to face an unrecognized truth?) that maybe she's right. But if she is, what am I going to do about Georgetown? Shall I tell them I can *reside* but I can't *poe?* Or shall I just go there as a poet . . . under false pretenses? And what becomes of my grandiose book plans spanning pretty much the rest of my life? Good heavens, I may have to work instead.

But she may be right. And I must face that unpleasant fact since it's not unlike me, with my somewhat frightening will where things I want are concerned, to have written my poems merely out of a determination to be *some*thing. If that's so, of course, it means that I will never be anything but, at best, a competent craftsman. And I'm not content to be just that; I'd stop writing rather. I'll see how my second book is received. If that also goes unnoticed, I'll publish my third, which will already be prepared for the press by that time, and then have done with the whole soggy operation. And become what? Well, if my neck and back continue to bother me, Superiors can always stick a lightbulb in my ear and use me for a lamp.

## Sunday, 14 February

LATE LAST YEAR or early this year I suddenly realized that there has been no really fine Kennedy poem, doing for the President what Tate has done for the Confederate dead, what Lowell has done for the Union dead. I'm going to try it, even though I can think of few things more difficult to bring off successfully. The public and the political just don't fit my poetry; actually they fit hardly anybody's poetry today because of the personal and highly symbolic stance of contemporary writing. Moreover, grief by its nature is a private thing; turned public, it becomes sentimentality or rhetoric. I'll have to walk a very narrow path.

My first notes, made in the earliest days of January, are suggestions for the poem's structure; since then I've been gathering words and phrases and ideas—casually, though, and with only random notions of where they will eventually fit. This afternoon, while on one of my little solitary walks, I began mulling over the first line, "The king must die." Suddenly I found myself composing lines to follow it, despite my intention of not writing anything until after my course in St. Paul. I came home and wrote them down. Later, putting them in the proper folder, I turned up my first tentative outline and discovered that the fourteen lines I had just written not only fitted perfectly into the proposed poem but also neatly adumbrated what should be its main themes. Fantastic how the subconscious organizes great heaps of data in the apparent absence of intellect. I hope now to put the poem away for another month or two, allow it to ferment at its own pace in the musty cellars of my mind.

The poem should progress like the manifestation of Christian Revelation: a gradual unfolding from the outermost least-defined symbol toward the "heart of the multifoliate rose": the tainted inversions of paganism, the dark intimations of the Old Testament, the definitive revelation of the New, and then the long groping toward full theological comprehension of the event. An ambitious undertaking, no question. But why not be ambitious? If the poem is a failure, I simply won't publish it. It it's a success, I shall have at least put Christ into the memory of a man I loved dearly.

## Wednesday, 24 February

THERE ARE TIMES of awful introspection when at the core of your inner darkness a window suddenly opens on complete self-awareness. The involuntary reaction is to throw up your hands and admit to being an intolerable mess and then at once burst into a tirade of prayers and aspirations. That reaction is betrayal. You must steel yourself for a good long look at whatever the window reveals. Who can tell—out of the cumulative horrors within me, I may discover a few seeds of love.

## Thursday, 25 February

RAIN. A nice soft rain, warm almost: it could convince me that spring is hiding somewhere down in the valley except that I have a chest cold that rather effectively cuts off my breathing. And that's not very springy at all.

I worked until after two this morning on my Kennedy poem. Threw out everything written so far. It will open, I've decided, with about twenty rhymed tetrameters, nice tight rhyme with an unpleasant undertow of irony. Keep the reader on his guard. Seduce him with music and with meter and then club him over the head with the ironic thump at the end. None of the verses so far are effective but they present me with a nice clean challenge and I feel I can whip them into properly ironic shape.

St. Paul and Fr. Fitzmyer take on the Woodstock community on Saturday; word is that the test will be objective—what color were Paul's socks, who opens the door in Acts 12, that sort of thing. Under the pressure generated around here, and it is considerable, I've turned more and more to books. Besides great mounds of poetry, I've read *Things as They Are, The Wide Net, The King Must Die,* and Saul Bellow's *Herzog. Herzog* is several cuts above the usual Jewish contemporary novel handed out today by practically everybody writing. Still I find its method limits its possibilities terribly. The investigation of the convoluted mind becomes an end in itself in *Herzog;* the reflection on reflection twists back and back upon itself until the book is strangled in its own umbilical cord. One step beyond *Herzog* lies the death of writing. Perhaps Bellow's method hits off the illness of our society as well as Dickens' hit off the congestion and moral suffocation of his London. Perhaps. But I've had enough of it. The characters are hard enough to accept: Herzog's wife is a cheap hypersexed shrike with handsome breasts and interesting legs; Herzog himself wallows alternately in the sweats of lust or philosophy (strange bedfellows?); everybody else in the book is pretty much consumed with self-interest. I'm being a bit hard on the book. I've read it at the wrong time, maybe.


## Sunday, 28 February

SCRIPTURE EXAM yesterday was an objective test with scores of questions, many about Jewish intertestamental literature. Scarcely an adequate measure of how well we had studied St. Paul's Epistles. I was fortunate, having just reviewed the sheets Fr. Fitzmyer had given out on this stuff. So I did well.

As soon as the exam was over, I set about bringing to full flower my migraine. By three in the afternoon I was partially blind (sounds dramatic, doesn't it), then I mopped the second-floor corridor, which I had been assigned to do the day preceding and neglected, then I lay down sick. No dinner. Orange juice at ten, and a piece of toast. By midnight I felt all right again, so I read Eudora Welty's *The Bride of the Innisfallen* until one. What bothers me about the headache— and this was a good one, going away in almost record time—is the notion that I can't even take a simple little test without bringing on a stroke. What a mess I am. How will I ever survive the final dogma exam this year?

Two nice things. Dr. Duhamel of the English department at Boston College has asked me to review books for the *Boston Herald*, one of Boston's two Sunday newspapers. He says he'll send me a pile of books and once a month I can give a running commentary of some five hundred words, and he adds: "I hope you will because I want a fresh voice about these poems, and you can say what you will as I have noticed you usually do." I wonder in what sense he intends "fresh" to be taken. And Sister Mary Enda writes that the Catholic Evidence Guild of Baltimore would like to have me give a lecture on writing poetry. These things are unimportant in themselves, but I really can't afford to turn down anything that might sell a few copies of my damnable *Dandelions*.

I'm off to New York on Tuesday to see Albee's new play, *Tiny Alice*. And to rejoice.

## *Saturday, 6 March*

NEW YORK should be made obligatory three times a year for everybody. Marvelous time. I come back from each little raid on the city renewed inside and out, ready to lick any unwary dragons.

First off I saw a splendid film, *Seance on a Wet Afternoon*, whose stars ought to get Academy Awards but won't. The acting is some of the most exciting I've ever seen on film; Kim Stanley can build a three-dimensional character out of tissue and Richard Attenborough rises to her performance in every scene. Julie Andrews will get the Oscar because Hollywood feels it has to make up for not giving her the Eliza Doolittle role in *My Fair Lady*. That's how Hollywood is. It's an odd kind of justice, but since nothing is ever quite fair in this world, I rejoice that at any rate the magnificient Andrews will profit by it.

That evening, Tuesday, I had dinner at The Lambs with John McCabe, who teaches drama at New York University. Very pleasant and chatty. The Lambs Club won't admit you unless a member signs you in, so there was an embarrassing scene when I arrived early (my watch apparently had a nervous collapse and began running fifteen minutes fast) and stood looking clerical and wan in the antechamber of a private theatrical club. A very pleasant and rather bumbling Jewish man signed me in as his guest, led me to dead center of the main dining room, and abandoned me. I sat there self-consciously teasing a martini until McCabe showed up. Silly.

I dashed from The Lambs to *Luv*, an hilarious two-hour joke about people so caught up in expressing themselves that they haven't the least idea who they are. It's a satire on Albee and the other neo-Absurdists; it devastates a society that has all the labels and none of the values, that has psychoanalyzed itself into meaninglessness. Terrifically funny. Strange that I kept finding myself laughing most where other people weren't laughing at all. The funniest things were not really the lines or even how the lines were delivered but the heroic *rightness* of the humanly inconsequential. (Whatever that means.)

Ash Wednesday my clock rang itself into silence and I slept on and on straight through nine o'clock. I felt remorseful, appropriately so for Ash Wednesday, and then went and found myself a neat little breakfast. In the afternoon I saw a matinée performance of Barbra Streisand in *Funny Girl*, a show that would be only fair except for the presence of this sad and lovable girl. She is so terribly talented and so desperately determined to be great. She gives the impression of having willed stardom. Her nose is monolithic, her accent pure Bronx; but she can act and make you feel deeply, cavort and make you roar, sing and you forget her nose and her accent and everything else except that she so very much is *there*. I fear she's going to have a very very unhappy life. I suppose I'll add her to the list of abandoned theater folk I pray for. She's murder.

Wednesday evening I had dinner with Joe Healey, another Woodstock man in New York on some business or other. We saw *Tiny Alice* together. And what can anyone say about that show?

*Tiny Alice* is interesting. Mostly, I suspect, because of Gielgud's superb acting. As drama it has technical values that few plays today can boast: exciting and sure-fire pyrotechnics, genuine literacy in some areas (and awful pseudoliteracy in others), some morbid humor, a great deal of magnificent acting. And it marks Albee's return from the country grotesques of *Ballad of the Sad Café* to his own proper territory, where people are at ease with the finer wines, don-cha-know, and with that peculiar malice bred of refinement and perversion. How good is the play itself? I'm not sure yet. I'll have to study it first. I suspect, though, that Albee has been too clever for his own good. He dances so many symbolic puppets in and out of physical-metaphysical dimensions that he seduces his audience into playing the symbol game—what stands for what?—and thus vitiates the impact of a unified impression his play might otherwise have had. He lards the thing with Christian symbols, everything from a black Mass to a crucifixion, in the way

Kandinsky will take a circle and bisect it with a triangle. But with this unfortunate difference: Kandinsky violates the eye in innumerable small areas while creating a whole in which discords are meaningfully resolved; Albee violates the imaginative and symbolic sensibility on so many different levels that his only effect is diffusion. Even the mind willing to play hide-and-seek with itself in the symbolic mazes meets only frustration because the symbols are not self-consistent or continuous; they cannot sustain themselves. Albee has traded the image structure of his previous plays for a string of penny fireworks: pop pop pop pop pop.

What he is trying to say (I think) is interesting enough. He gives you a contemporary man, a Catholic lay-brother named Julian, who is intent on living a life conformed to the will of God and shows you how he is progressively seduced by Church, by law, by money, and finally by love—the ultimate deception—to which he no sooner gives himself than he is shot in the guts while his erstwhile seducers look on passive and unconcerned. It seems to me that Albee is affirming what he only limned in *Who's Afraid of Virginia Woolf?*: that man's isolation is complete and unalterable, that to give oneself to love is an act of self-deception that must end in despair. Julian's God is only the projection of his desperate need for something larger than himself to live for, to believe in. One must *affirm* nothing—not negatively, not nihilistically—but positively, as if nothing were a reality. There *is* nothing.

The play would be more powerful if it were less pretentious, less cluttered with the silly symbolism Albee has heaped upon it. Post-factum symbolism, it looks like. If only he had remembered to be funny, to break your heart laughing, he could have written a first-rate play. As it stands, however, *Tiny Alice* is a first-class presentation of third-rate thinking. Albee can do better than that.

Thursday morning I saw the Op Art Exhibit at the Museum of Modern Art—it makes your eyes cross—and came home. To Woodstock. Where the landscape is very gray.

## Tuesday, 9 March

SOMEBODY named Morse Allen has reviewed my *Dandelions* in a New York newspaper called *The Courant*, and he says that though my book left him "cold" he was nonetheless interested in my "intelligent, handsome, lively face." (He's afflicted with not only a cloudy mind but cloudy eyesight as well.) He concludes: "Before John L'Heureux can become a poet, I feel he must be born again." That last bit struck me as a wonderful epigraph for a poem and for the last couple of days I've been letting the thing mull in the keg. And today, *voilà*.

### Compliance

"Before John L'Heureux can become
a poet, I feel he must be born
again." Morse Allen in a book review.

I died last night,
Was born again this morning
Poet.
Six A.M. and there I was
Singing with a cuckoo's voice
An Easter antiphon.

Everyone came running
From the bathroom not to miss
Rebirth.
(We rarely see a miracle
And even faith can profit by
A little oomph.)

A cuckoo sings,
They said, where only yesterday
L'Heureux
Flapped his clumsy wings
In ribald limericks. They left
To shave and marvel.

Song all day. Already
They and I are tired of me
Poet.
Tonight I hope to die once

More—and resurrect again:
This time, real.

## Monday, 15 March

FR. MURRAY'S CLASSES: I feel sometimes that I'm trapped in a word-house burning to the ground around me. Father is beginning to affect my own mode of expression. I wrote the other day: "Few critics have mentioned that *Tiny Alice* is pretentious: the characters logorrhetic, the symbols hypertrophic." That's pure Murray.

## Tuesday, 16 March

A FELLOW JESUIT asked me today to give *my* opinion (he asked it in such a way that it was clear immediately that my opinions would in no manner reflect the opinions of the sponsor) on the current crisis within the creative community. Geez, I didn't even know there *was* one. Except insofar as so much of what is written today is rubbish. *Herzog is* a reflection of a certain crisis, I suppose: the book is formless, the character is in search of himself. *Herzog* is deliberately formless—well, perhaps snail-formed would be more accurate—because Bellow sees man's inability to know himself and his quest to overcome this inability as a process of reflection upon reflection upon reflection. The artist no longer understands traditional forms as a viable mode of interpretation of his experience. It is not a question of Bellow's disliking the discipline of form or of his feeling that form is in itself a falsification of reality; it is a question of literary agnosticism. Classical forms have nothing to do with Bellow's—and hence Herzog's—experience.

Contemporary man, Herzog if you want, knows himself only phenomenally through his experience. And experience of its nature tends to be chaotic. Order imposed upon experience will of *its* nature tend to be subjective. Result: *Herzog*. An oversimplification, of course, but it embodies at least a large part of the modern difficulty. Man is alone in trying to understand himself; the ancient understanding man had of himself as self and as a member related to his community has disappeared.

Perhaps his lostness explains his inability to love himself, since some appreciative knowledge must precede love if it is to have any degree of stability. And Herzog, if anybody, is a loveless man . . . o.k. back to reality.

I must surrender my pen now and go talk French with Jim Linehan. He comes in three nights a week for a little French session, the only result of which thus far has been to indicate to me how hopelessly my own French has lapsed. All these years of English and God-knows-what-else studies have merely ministered to the unseasonal death of my mind.

## Wednesday, 17 March

DINNER WAS FUNNY. Jesuits like to celebrate the feast of St. Patrick, but they decidedly do not care to celebrate it with corned beef and cabbage. And the cabbage was like stone. People were annoyed when they got a gander at the *pièce de résistance;* but they were infuriated when we ran short of dessert—a cake of bilious green dotted with some horrific green cherries. Some wise guy provided green hats for the waiters, but the crew—with names like Baumiller, Bowes, LaMartina, L'Heureux—put its collective foot down and refused. It's just as well; the community might have found green hats the last straw.

## Thursday, 18 March

I STOLE THREE cubes of sugar from a table in the fourth-floor corridor and this afternoon I fed them to a marvelous horse who was grateful. I had no idea horses were such agreeable people. I'm going to bring him an apple tomorrow.

*Continuum,* lushest and most elegant of all quarterlies, bought my six-page poem "I Fall in Love Heartfirst, Once or Twice," which comprises the second section of *Rubrics.*

"Heartfirst" isn't a very impressive piece and their choosing it confirms me in my suspicion that it would be madness ever to underestimate human folly.

Later. Leonard Woolf's autobiography, *Beginning Again,* has some funny things. Describing the debacle that attended the first Post-Impressionist showing in England, he says: "Large numbers of people came to the exhibition, and nine out of ten of them either roared with laughter at the pictures or were enraged by them. The British middle class—and, as far as that goes, the aristocracy and working class—are incorrigibly philistine, and their taste is impeccably bad. Anything new in the arts, particularly if it is good, infuriates them and they condemn it as either immoral or ridiculous or both."

He offers, too, some wonderful accounts of the people who made up the Bloomsbury set, but what impresses me most about the book is the open and completely honest way he discusses his wife's madness. Without his love and constant watchfulness, clearly there would never have been a Virginia Woolf, author.

## Sunday, 21 March

THIS WEEKEND HAS been for me the most profound spiritual experience of my Jesuit life. It would be absolute folly to try to put it in words; naturally I'll try, but not now.

## Thursday, 25 March

YES, STILL UP THERE on that marshmallow cloud. This is a strange experience; I completely distrust the surface manifestations of a love that makes everything easy. Life is not easy and when even the most difficult things—prayer for instance —become a lark, you have to cast a cold eye on whatever is behind it all. And I have cast my cold eye.

The prayer and the great happiness I experience these days flow directly from that essential grace—whatever it was—in which one of the things I realized was Christ's love for me.

The prayer and the happiness are, it is true, part of that emotional overflow, which is the quickest and most disappointing betrayal of any real spiritual rapport with Christ, but beneath the overflow there is something far more real and more important, something so real and so important that it tolerates the superficial manifestations. I think of an example that, though inappropriate for a number of reasons, will illustrate what I mean: the Little Flower's granite spirituality manifesting itself in the most awful sentimentalisms.

This all came about through the casual workings of God: Woodstock held a little institute on American Spirituality last weekend and among the many visitors was Don Maloney, S.J., a friend of mine from California. Don and I talked on several occasions; on Friday night until three in the morning. Things he said about grace and faith and Christ's personal love for him reached me as few things ever have. Not at the time, mind you, but by Sunday I began to realize that something quite extraordinary was going on within me. It has continued to go on within me and I am not going to make myself more foolish than usual by trying to explain what it is. I am in Christ as I have never been, and though my emotional and intellectual and even spiritual house may collapse upon my head, I can't imagine anything that will ever change that fact.

## Friday, 26 March

WE HAVE A NEW Rector, Fr. Maher being apparently too ill to continue in office. The immensity of the job would make anyone ill. They have my sympathy; Fr. Maher going out and Fr. Cardegna coming in. (Self whispers: I wonder if I'll be able to retain my splendid censorship status—disentangling red tape by consulting my two censors directly. I fear not.)

## Monday, 29 March

IN HIS FIRST couple of days Fr. Cardegna has made something of a hit. He gave a wonderful little talk in chapel the other

night, explaining that Fr. Maher is ill and unable to continue
as Rector and that he himself has no immediate plans for us
except the promise that if we don't panic, he won't either. The
next day a note went up to the effect that all lunches hence-
forth will be buffet style, a sensible thing considering there
are almost three hundred of us crammed into that tiny refectory and one third of us would prefer to go without lunch
anyway. So things promise well for the remaining terrible
months of tests and general house-panic.

A strange thing happened to me Saturday night. One of
my closest friends here suddenly told me, so far as I could see
with no provocation, that he found my overly strong personality a threat to his liberty, my visits to his room too frequent,
my way of trying to find the summation of our whole relationship in even our most passing conversation at the least distressing. So try that one on, L'Heureux. I was dumbfounded,
and since my first reaction in the face of any criticism is to
consider the possibility that it may be accurate, I considered
whether or not it is accurate; I was even more dumbfounded
to discover that in large part it is. So I spent yesterday, Laetare
Sunday, cloaked in an uncomely mantle of grief. He is right.
I am a pain in the tail. I could not have guessed it, however,
and so my being such a nuisance is more forgivable than
if I had been one with even an intuitive awareness. I *should*
have known of course; as he pointed out, I am not the only one
with sensitivities and feelings.

So what is the upshot of this? Lay off, that's the upshot.
I love the fellow like a brother. He knows far more about
me, in fact, than my own brother does. And I know him. But
love and knowledge do not give the right to go trampling
through another's privacy. So often loving means leaving alone.
Well, I shall try. He said, and I see the grace in his saying
it, that to love and to be shut off in this way is to experience
in a finite human way precisely what Christ must have experienced all during his life. And this experience can teach me
more about Christ and the life of the spirit than many many
hours of joy or of prayer or of good works. There is nothing
like the shredding of the soul, like the disciplining of love,
for growth in Christ.

I sound, I suppose, awfully unconcerned about this, cavalier almost. Well, dammit, I'm not. A kick in the belly is still a kick in the belly even when you offer it to Christ. And this has been a kick and a half—be a sport, call it two kicks. And it isn't easy to find Christ in a rejection that involves me so intimately, right down to the core of my personality. It isn't easy because all that I see is myself, my eyes put out. But this new situation is really just an extension of the incredible graces of last weekend. Christ loves me. Now he wants me to love him, just a bit more honestly, a bit more emphatically than I did before. I once wrote that I must find Christ in the cross because only there would I be sure it was really Christ I had found. I wrote more truly than I knew. So now I take a deep breath and examine the other side of the shiny coin I was given last weekend. In my way, I am happy.

## Thursday, 1 April

I WAS JUST completing Schillebeeckx's *Mary, Mother of the Redemption* when it occurred to me with an overwhelming clarity how, when Jesus at twelve remained behind in the temple, Mary's world must have come to an end. She had, after all, no clear knowledge that this was meant to be: she must have seen only her negligence (she must have been talking and having a wonderful time when the news reached her that Jesus wasn't among them) and she must have experienced the death of the heart at a profound level. She lived by faith, more completely and more perfectly than we can grasp. The loss of her child must have been the most awful test of that faith. Everything gone. She wouldn't have thought of the Annunciation or of the Flight into Egypt; she would have been numb and broken. With just that hand tight about the heart so that breathing is impossible and everything is meaningless. The inability to go on. Love thwarted through her own fault. Loss and never.

All this is obvious, I suppose. But I've just seen it for the first time—experientially almost—and it takes my breath away.

*Sunday, 4 April*

THE HORSE IS MARVELOUS. Runs right over now for his lump of sugar; well, he walks over. Lets me pet him and scratch behind his ear. Rub his nose. Very nice horse. Brown and white. I suppose the poor beast is going to kick over one of these days with diabetes, what with all the sugar lumps I give him. But it's nice to have someone look forward to your arrival each day, even if it's only a horse.

St. Paul. Let's hear it for St. Paul. Not only am I picking up enough data to get through the exam without major disgrace, but I'm picking up something far more valuable for my spiritual life. I have been deluged with graces in the past month, graces extending even to studies, which have come alive for me in a far more relevant and personal way than ever before. The season of visible grace is drawing to a close no doubt; perhaps it has ended already. No matter. It has been a glorious time of integration . . . a time when I couldn't properly speak of an intellectual life or a social life without being forced simultaneously into a consideration of the spiritual fabric from which they are cut. True, we never can properly speak of an isolated spiritual or intellectual life *anyway*; what I mean here is that I couldn't categorize my life even for the sake of consideration. For the past month I've felt like a whole man and I have been happy. And am. I still am.

Later. Peace shattered. Late this afternoon I received a phone call from Carolyn Kizer, who, stopping in Washington on her return trip from Pakistan where she's been doing cultural exchange work for the government, asked me out to dinner with Allen Tate. Honest. I dashed around the house trying to see people who give out car keys, trying to hitch a ride with people on legitimate business, trying in short to beg, borrow, or steal a ride. No luck. And so no dinner. I called Carolyn and told her I couldn't make it and she very nicely asked me to come to Washington tomorrow for a talk and for Muriel Rukeyser's poetry reading at the Library of Congress. It's quite late now and there seem to be no rides available; I'll get there.

## Tuesday, 6 April

QUEL DAY! After the four-thousand money and transportation mishaps attendant upon any Woodstock trip, I arrived in Washington in time to meet Carolyn in the hotel lobby at five. She's a beautiful woman—what made me think she was around fifty?—in her late thirties, very blonde, very elegant, very very tall. She must stand six feet in her high heels. And she wears these crazy black glasses that are perfectly round, with the bows and the nosepiece dead center: you know, the lenses don't hang down from the bows, they just sort of free float.

So we sat in the cocktail lounge for a great while, talking and reading each other's poetry. I had no idea poets really *read* poetry, let alone talk about it. Carolyn is quick, with a fine, penetrating intellect and a well-honed tongue. She made some wonderful observations about poets, their work, their neuroses.

We met in the lobby after she changed for dinner. Unlike most women she was ready in only a few minutes. So we set out across Connecticut Avenue to the hotel where we were to meet Reed Whittemore; she six feet tall and glorious, with her blonde hair and black glasses and brocade dinner dress, I skinny and self-conscious in my clerical collar—we made quite a couple. Mr. Whittemore arrived late. He's young and very pleasant and I suspect a bit shy, though, as Poetry Consultant for the Library of Congress, he must have plenty of occasions to work off his shyness. Chat was good, exciting for me since I have almost never before had dinner with poets-at-ease. The dinners I've attended at Boston College for Auden and that crowd have always been huge, with everybody reverent and adulating. Poor. The reading by Rukeyser was not exciting; it was soporific at best. Carolyn and I left at intermission. More chat and then home.

I had never met Carolyn and feared we might not get on particularly well, but we liked each other instantly. Quick minds and sharp tongues do not often harmonize. Nevertheless.

And I almost forgot the most significant thing; she asked me if I would like to read on a shared platform with her in the fall at the Guggenheim in New York and—get this—under the auspices of the Academy of American Poets. Apotheosis at age thirty. For some reason, pessimism maybe, I feel the whole plan will fall through, but it's cheering at this grim moment of the school year to think that next fall I'll be mouthing my verses at the Guggenheim.

Now back to the grim reality of Scriptural exegesis.

## Friday, 9 April

EVERBODY LIKED THE Scripture exam this morning. I hated it, felt I did rather poorly. I hit the exegetical questions with less vigor than I might, though I handled the essays with some degree of competence. What I really messed up were the multiple-guess questions at the beginning; and since it was the beginning, I got a little panicky and then the whole time was spent anxiety-ridden. I console myself that I learned a good deal about St. Paul even though my knowledge may well fail to emerge on that test paper. So much for Scripture; now I must begin work on my *Critic* review of Teilhard's *Hymn of the Universe*. Well, I suppose I'm no less qualified to review that than to take an exam on St. Paul: drawing courage from my comparative ignorances.

## Monday, 12 April

FRIDAY AND SATURDAY I immersed myself in Teilhard. Saturday afternoon I saw Julie Andrews in *The Sound of Music* and was only half aware of being at the movies; I was steeping in *Hymn of the Universe*. Sunday at Mass I prayed for inspiration to write the damned review; suddenly the idea came to me to write down what I was sure I wanted to say about the parts of the book I had already given most thought to. I began writing at ten minutes to eight and finished at twelve noon— finished the entire review. I spent Sunday afternoon rewriting and re-rewriting, submitted the finished manuscript to Fr. Dulles, got it back in the evening approved for publication in the form I submitted it. Fantastic. Of course, it's only a book review. But it's six pages long and it's about a book I am hopelessly unqualified to review in the first place. The whole awful experience has had one great merit; I've learned never never again to undertake any book review merely because the author is important and hence it is an honor to be asked to review his book. Why needlessly parade my foolishness?

## Friday, 23 April

EASTER WAS A time full of extraordinary graces for me, so extraordinary that I had the good sense not to try to write them down. Lots of finding myself and Christ in the Passion: that terrible awareness of being forgotten, of not mattering, of being desperate to give love which nobody cares about. The Passion wasn't just lived out once a few thousand years ago; it's going on and on and on right now in people who never heard of Christ except as something you holler when you get your hand caught in the door. If only I could realize how fully the whole life of Christ is being lived out in me and in everybody I meet, surely it would make some difference in my reverence for them; surely I'd be aware that they also are frightened and lonely, in need of someone to show them Christ's love. Anyway I pray for that grace of awareness. Christ rounding out his suffering in the people I meet must become an obsession with me. Then I will find him and them.

But nothing is ever going to be profoundly different. Always the deceptions and little lies to myself. Always the comfort that I'm doing the best I can with my limited resources. And always the suspicion that I am tricking myself into a most fatal complacency. So Easter was a great grace, and almost everything else since then has been an extension of that grace.

My summer plans have been approved by the Provincial. Which means I'll spend a week after ordination seeing plays in New York, three weeks teaching creative writing at Boston College High, one month in my poetry chair at Georgetown, two weeks at villa in New England. Now I ask you. I mean. Surely the summer plans alone—spiritual motivation and private desperation aside—ought to be enough to carry me through these dreadful exam days.

The Kennedy poem moves along at about the pace I had hoped for. It satisfies me . . . which is probably a dangerous sign.

One last word. I am in a horrible black depression. I am tired to death of obeying, of doing what I have to do rather than what I want to do, of sitting at this damned desk with these boring notes. I would like to throw everything off, tear up the notes, pitch out the books, have done with the whole sick business of study. Surely God doesn't take all this nonsense as seriously as we take it. He couldn't and be God. But I don't pitch out the books. I sit here blackly and do what I ought. Three cheers for me? Don't be a damfool.

### Thursday, 29 April

THE MORAL THEOLOGY EXAM of Tuesday was half glory and half rout. They questioned me first of all on jurisdiction for hearing confessions, on which I acquitted myself somewhat more handily than I would have thought. Then they launched into birth prevention and the rhythm method. Any fool can tell you all about rhythm, so I rushed ahead—proving myself not only precipitous but an idiot as well—with elegant comparisons of what happens during the ovulation cycle when one practices rhythm and of what happens when one uses the pill. It seemed eminently sensible to me, incomprehensible to them. They wanted me to talk about the psychological difficulties for the couple who practices rhythm, as I discovered later. I made a mess of the whole business, the L'Heureux touch you know, and so I have no assurance that I passed. A life of terror, that's what it is. Pain and fear and like that.

Some other cheery news. Carolyn Kizer, generally the best critic I've ever had, saw a copy of *Rubrics for a Revolution* while she was visiting Doubleday. She wrote today saying "the autobiographical poems are juvenilia. If they are ever published, it should be long after you are famous. You simply can't afford the luxury of publishing them for many years." O.K. lady, drop that poker. Well, first off, the poems are the ones about coming to the priesthood, the best stuff I've ever written. Granted that I may be mistaken about their merit and that Naomi and Carolyn are right in hating these poems, then what justification can there ever be for publishing them at all? Yet Naomi says if I should drop dead dramatically Doubleday will probably publish the book just as it stands. And Carolyn says I should afflict the public with these poems only when I'm famous. If they're no good, it seems to me they should never be published. Period. This way, it's too much like eating your moral cake and having it tucked by your bedside for a midnight snack. Don't care for it.

*Critic*, to change the subject to happiness, liked my review of Teilhard's book. Quite a bit, in fact; they've decided to run the lengthy version (I sent them two), which delights me. And besides, they sent me fifteen clams, which I'm going to use this weekend to entertain some Jesuits who are coming here from Weston to receive the orders of Subdiaconate and Diaconate. God always seems to provide just when the larder is bare. A lesson to Mother Hubbard.

## Monday, 3 May

THIS IS SUCH a season of grace. Yesterday and the day before we had the Subdiaconate and Diaconate ordination ceremonies, to be followed by Priesthood in June. They were all the more forceful for me by reason of Don Maloney's being one of the men ordained. It is astounding to receive Communion from the hands of a fellow who the day before had no more right to touch the host than I myself. In one day he has become the giver of good gifts. Beautiful.

Don and I had several long talks, and although there were not the extraordinary and overwhelming graces of our previous visit, it was certainly a prayerful time for us both. I am looking forward to the priesthood with more eagerness than ever.

*Monday, 10 May*

SHADOWBROOK BURNED to the ground in March, 1956. Four men burned to death and several others were injured, some quite severely. I was in the fire, warm as toast but safe as you'd expect, and stood outside barefoot in the snow watching the house burn for a good part of the night. I didn't come near getting hurt, really, and I had always been under the impression that the fire didn't affect me much.

Last night at two o'clock the fire alarm went off. I hopped out of bed with an alacrity I haven't exhibited since the Novitiate, popped into the corridor to check for smoke, awakened my neighbors. Some of the men were already streaking down the stairwells, others were pounding on doors or just standing there looking confused. I dressed, took my glasses and my contact lenses, deliberated on whether or not to rescue the manuscripts of my new poems, the Albee book, the journal, and decided that my shame would be greater than my loss and so I left them. We waited outside for almost an hour while the fire crew rampaged through the house trying to locate the fire. It turned out to be a defective fire-alarm box that one of the workmen had joggled loose while painting the stairs; he had repaired it with a rubber band that broke in the middle of the night.

So everybody laughed and went to bed. And I sat for the rest of the night in a mild state of shock, the whole horrible Shadowbrook episode coursing through my mind. It didn't really wear off until noon today. And tonight I have a poetry reading at the Novitiate of the School Sisters of Notre Dame.

Later. The reading was o.k., I guess, though the Sisters seemed a good bit more pleased with it than I was. The poems sounded so dull and lifeless to me. I kept thinking: "How can you be such a bore? They want to scream." The drive home sort of capped the evening. Halfway home I suddenly realized I was passing any number of cut-offs with familiar names. I suspected that when I entered the turnpike I had somehow managed to take the wrong direction and was rapidly on my way back to the Novitiate. So I reversed directions and, yes, finally *did* find myself back at the Novitiate. Then home again, wiser, furious at myself.

## Wednesday, 12 May

I SERVED MASS this morning for a fourth-year Father, Frank Winters, whom I probably won't see again for years and years. He is an extraordinary man, brilliant, esteemed by the most orthodox of an orthodox faculty, yet with a streak of the Christ-Rebel in him that ought to terrify the comfortable conservatives. We never really talked until two weeks ago: my loss and his too, I suppose, given the fact that we are sanctified by everybody in whom and through whom God chooses to make contact with us.

In some small way I have been a grace for Frank, with my quiet nonconformity (I'm not intelligent enough to risk being noisy about it) and my unshakable conviction that not to love is to die. That startled him. He had looked upon our Jesuit lives as a choice between giving ourselves to studies or to people. Why not both? God knows, I've learned more from people than I've ever learned from my studies, especially the arid soulless texts we use in theology. Anyway, he has decided to enter the human race—and he's done so with a vengeance. You *do*, though. You have to spill yourself out completely for men; it's not easy and it soon ceases to be pleasant; Christ never said Christianity should be a fun-thing. And it's precisely by this complete entry into the human race (that's what the Incarnation is) that you most fully realize Christianity, that you most perfectly imitate Christ. And of course you're going to stick out and look silly. Why do you think they were always trying to stone Christ? He stuck out. People who go around loving are always going to be an embarrassment to a world that finds sex more interesting than love.

I just reread the second section of my Kennedy poem. It's over a week old now and I can see it a little more objectively. There is something wrong with it; I don't know what. I cover the lostness of the human soul before the coming of Christ: the centuries of metaphoric exile in the desert. The ideas are o.k. but ideas have never yet made a successful poem. I'll wait a month or so before cutting it. Now for a short devastating passage on the crucifixion. The poem is building nicely.

### *Thursday, 13 May*

OUR DENTIST FILLED two teeth for me today. Fillings about the size, say, of your fist. I feel like I've just been hit in the jaw with an ax. I offered the pain in thanksgiving for all the wonderful graces I've received this year; they must have been even more considerable than I had imagined if the degree of pain was any index to their quantity or quality or whatever you measure a grace by.

The *Atlantic*, wonderful dear good old *Atlantic*, bought two of my poems today: "Compliance" and "The Window." The first is my response to that reviewer who told me I must be born again before I can become a poet and the second is about Ned and time and how ghastly it is to be me. Now that I think of it, they're both in this journal. I'm rich.

### *Sunday, 16 May*

FOLKS JUST LEFT for home. It is wonderful to visit with them; they're alive and vital and interested in practically everything. And we talk about God and religion without any of that constraint most people seem to feel. I'm glad they're *my* parents. Since there are only two of them to go around, I prefer to have them for myself.

### *Tuesday, 18 May*

IT'S ALWAYS so easy to be perfectly honest and frank and open in admitting failings—so long as they're somebody else's. I find it very easy to admit my failings, except when someone points them out. All of which is to say I'm smarting from a recent encounter with the truth about myself.

Theology absorbs every second of my time. It seems impossible that I'll ever be prepared for this exam on 1 June. And the wild thing is that, whenever I get caught up in what I am studying, the objective matter knits up neatly with my subjective dispositions and I find myself praying when I should be pounding the books. That's a real temptation. I believe it. The devil (do we still hold there is a devil?) is that subtle: to drag you away from what you're supposed to be doing on the pretext of doing something intrinsically better. And of course it *is* better to pray than to study, but *not* when you're supposed to be studying. So what I do is make an offering of the prayer I'm not going to engage in. Then the studies lose a lot of flavor, you know, but that's how it is, Charlie.

## Friday, 21 May

IN THE CHRISTIAN dispensation there is no longer any death without a resurrection. The source of hope.

## Saturday, 22 May

LOTS OF THINGS. We have a new Superior General of the Society of Jesus. He is a Basque, former Provincial of the Japanese mission, a medical doctor (can that be right?) at Hiroshima immediately after the bombing, and—if all the reports are true—one of those Renaissance men we don't see much any more. He looks very promising and the future of the Society looks brighter to me than it ever has. Thank God. It's important now that the Holy Spirit work overtime.

Two other things. Thursday I saw the Royal Ballet and the incredible Rudolf Nureyev. He was dancing *Les Bayadères*, the ballet he has reconstructed with many opportunities for his fabled virtuoso leaps and twists and spectacular negations of the law of gravity. He is great, no question, but I felt kind of bad that the couple of thousand in the audience had come to see him jump. He is a consummate artist; I imagine jumps mean no more to him than a dazzling display of verbal pyrotechnics meant to Shakespeare. Yet they come to see him jump. How awful. He is asexual, beautiful, almost the soul without body. A wondrous experience for me.

And yesterday I did a painting for the first time in well over a year. It's a huge abstract done with palette knife.

## Sunday, 23 May

ANOTHER PAINTING TODAY, a big black one, two by three feet, all scratches and bumps and attractive lines. I underpainted the canvas in ochres, vermilions, yellows; then I slapped black enamel over all of that; while the whole mess was still wet I sprinkled pencil sharpener shavings in blobs down the left side and drowned them in more black enamel. Finally with several nails and an old razor blade and a wire spring I scraped away some of the black. *Eccolo.* "Convergence." Everybody hates it. I think it's terrific.

## Sunday, 6 June

TIME. A résumé before I leave Woodstock blessedly behind me for the summer.

My dogma exam was quite successful. The examining board was easy to talk with and, as a group, seemed disposed in my favor. The Dean examined me on Mariology, giving me a chance to talk about Schillebeeckx and Rahner with—it's true—more heat than illumination, but nonetheless with a degree of confidence indicating more than a casual acquaintance with their ideas on Mary. So that was good. Then Fr. Clarke questioned me on Christology and I did all right there too. The five days which have passed since the ordeal have (maybe) made me a bit more objective than I customarily am; it still strikes me that I fared well. Marks in September will probably indicate once more that I've embraced hyperbole as a way of life.

Since the exam I've been in grim depression. Can't sleep, can't read; its driving me frantic. The only solution, of course, is to get away from Woodstock for a while. Being here after exams is like burying a dear friend and then standing around his grave trying to make social chat. Poor show.

Shall I pray? I mean, shall I just write off all plans for New York—forget the writing and reading and play-going I had promised myself—and just try to burrow back into the center of me where the only fire is the Spirit? I can't think of all that now, not even long enough to decide on what I intend New York to *be* in my summer scheme. I can't think at all. Not at all.

Tomorrow I have lunch in Baltimore, then a cookout at the pool, then off in the morning for New York, where, with luck, I'll see Ned Lynch and Frank Winters.

## *Monday, 7 June*

THE BEST LAID plans, etc. One of the brethren, moved by the spirit of the New Frontier, tossed me into the pool as I knelt to pick up his plate. I went under like a bullfrog: a clean quick plop. I emerged with my dignity considerably dampened and my spirits warmed. I have never understood the practical joke mentality. Only the rich can afford the luxury of casual destruction and I am not one of the rich. I sit here now in my shorts contemplating my drowned wristwatch (another trip to the repairman) and rejoicing that I'll be getting out of here tomorrow morning. Deo Gratias.

## *Wednesday, 9 June*

YESTERDAY WAS MARVELOUS. The first man I met on Fordham campus was Frank Winters, with whom I immediately repaired from the terrible heat to the air-conditioned comfort of a neighborhood pub.

Frank is doing research at Union Theological for an article on contemporary ethics. He's brilliant of course and an exciting conversationalist so we went right at it, the two of us, talking about Christianity and Christians and the necessity of the full Christian life if you're to make any sense out of the business of being born and its few consequences. And all this in a marvelous pub full of people who probably don't even know that they're redeemed or that Christ is pursuing them with his impulsive patient love or that the hotfoot they feel isn't only the New York pavement but the Spirit sneaking in by whatever way he can. Since Christ has come and the time has been redeemed, we witness for one another—gross and uncomely in our limitations, blundering and stupid in our affections—but witness all the same that Christ lives and moves in us, that our salvation is ultimately a question of letting God love us as completely as he wants. We have to let him let us live. Christianity is exciting. Even in a pub. Maybe especially in a pub.

Then at dinner I ran into Ned. Complete day. We went to see two James Bond movies. *From Russia with Love* and *Dr. No*, both of which struck me as vaguely amusing and little more. Maybe I'm losing my sense of humor; everbody else is wild about James Bond. I find him merely a caricature of that glacial sophistication I used to see all the time in summer theater. Brittle dilletantism. Tiresome. Anyway Ned and I had a good talk afterward. Ned is wonderfully patient with me even when I inveigh against people who toss people into pools, and the tosser happens to be one of his closest friends. Ned Lynches of this world, we salute you.

I have decided not to decide on what I expect from my New York sojourn. If I get something written, o.k. If not, no loss. Mostly, I want to spend some time contacting the Holy Spirit —if he'll let me.

## Thursday, 10 June

ORDINATIONS TO THE Priesthood this morning were beautiful. Healing. (Have I said I'm all cut up? I am.) I attended Fr. Cardegna's Mass and then the ordination ceremony, and during the ordination Mass, I served Frank's Mass. It was a wonderful morning. I want to be a priest. Never mind about anything else.

## Saturday, 12 June

IN THE COURTYARD beneath my window there is the magic twang of an electric guitar, its horrors magnified many times by a microphone that carries, I should imagine, to the farthest limits of the Bronx. Fordham Prep Class of 1965 is holding a farewell throb of some kind. Nobody seems to be dancing very much; they just stand around vibrating at one another. And I upstairs studying *Tiny Alice*. Which of us do you suppose is squandering his time most profitlessly?

Ned and I went to the Bronx Zoo this afternoon and watched three clever gibbons making fun of the spectators. It was like an Albee play—you couldn't be sure at any given time just whose leg was being pulled. There was also a very docile camel carrying hordes of screaming children on a mercifully brief and joggity ride at fifteen cents a shake. O money-making camel! And some interesting birds, several fantastic flamingos with hideous bills and rickety legs and the most beautiful plumage any bird should be allowed. They all stood about in a dull flamingo manner, periodically raising one incredible leg and stretching it with deliberation straight out to the side like a skilled but scornful ballerina. Something to see. The lions were quite satisfying but we didn't see any bears. I should like to have seen a bear or two, fat in their fuzzy scuffies, padding about in their ancient housecoats. Which reminds me that we saw a rhinoceros whose skin seemed several sizes too large—as if he had bought it from a Jesuit tailor. I guess all rhinos are that way; poor rhinos. Then we had a beer at Howard Johnson's and came home. I did *not* feel I was returning to a more select sophisticated zoo. No. I did not.

Now I can tell the best thing. Ten Jesuit philosophy students are spending a couple of weeks working in Harlem, going from door to door and offering, where they can, the clinical or financial assistance which government agencies make available, but more immediately offering evidence of the Church's concern for her poor. The work is terribly discouraging since there is very little that ten men can effect in two weeks in Harlem.

Besides, a Roman collar does not necessarily elicit spontaneous devotion in a slum—or indeed anywhere. The ten have the further difficulty of being held somewhat suspect by their own contemporaries.

They are a remarkable group of young men—open and genuine and unabashedly Christian. Frank Winters is serving as their chaplain for these two weeks; this morning I attended their Mass. They stand in a semicircle around the altar, sing hymns not out of obligation but as an expression of devotion (one chap leads them on the guitar), place their hosts individually on the altar during an Offertory procession, receive Communion standing, and sing "We Shall Overcome" as a recessional. More remarkable, one of them gives a homily each day—the one I heard being structured in the incomprehensible patterns of Chinese logic but alive with a sincerity and love I've only rarely heard in sermons—and at the mementos for the living and the dead each one says what it is he would like to include in offering Mass. They are devastatingly open young men. Witnessing their liturgy, you have no choice: you must laugh at them or you must admit that this comes close to what Christianity should be—lives lived in Christ forming a continuity of revelation. We witness for him or we simply are not Christians. I begin at last to think the people of God shall inherit the earth.

## Sunday, 13 June

TRINITY SUNDAY. Work all day on Albee has left me tight as a tick. His characters talk and talk and I listen while the living word mourns his isolation . . . about which I wrote a poem today. "The Pilgrimage." Caustic and pained.

## Tuesday, 15 June

I LEAVE IN A few minutes for a luncheon date with Bob Giroux of Farrar, Straus, and Giroux. It's awfully complicated. He was Naomi's godfather at her entrance into the Church and he submitted my first two books for Lamont Awards. When I wrote recently to say I'd pick up the manuscript of *Rubrics*, which I had sent him for comment, he wrote back inviting me to lunch. I'm afraid he's going to administer me a loyalty oath to Naomi, make me promise not to go niggling about from publisher to publisher. Quite embarrassing. Then dinner this evening with Naomi. God help me. How do these things happen?

Later. Giroux was superb. He was very positive the book as it stands is right, very certain in telling me not to mess with the basic structure. He feels *Rubrics* is an advance over *Dandelions*, that I have a rich career ahead of me. He also told me—curious—that authors know more about what they're doing than their editors; that, if they didn't, they wouldn't be worth publishing. I had always heard the opposite. He was displeased that Farrar cannot afford the loss involved in publishing what he assured me would be an unpopular book (ah, realism), something I *do* understand. He was most encouraging. For the first time in a long time I have confidence in *me*. Someday *I'm* gonna be a writer.

Dinner with Naomi was exhausting. We talked businessly for over two heated hours. She didn't want to discuss *Rubrics* and I insisted on discussing it. She feels she never said Doubleday was unwilling to publish *Rubrics*, they just didn't want it in its present form. I tried to explain that the form—the semi-autobiographical structure—is precisely the one thing I will not change. She relented to a degree: she'll go through the book marking for cuts or changes, I'll rewrite and resubmit, and we'll publish in fall, 1966. That is, *if* Doubleday approves. Her main objection seems to have been time; she is reluctant to bring out another book of poems so soon after the first. But the form difficulty will yet prove to be the cause of several squabbles, I feel sure. But I'm not about to give in. It will be published as a whole or not at all. I hope I have the courage to accept the alternative of nonpublication should that dilemma ever raise its ugly horns.

## Friday, 18 June

FRANK AND I went to see *The Glass Menagerie* last night. Such a beautiful play and so eloquently acted. Maureen Stapleton can do anything and I was astonished at Piper Laurie's beauty and ability. The scene in which she gives to the Gentleman Caller the glass unicorn he has just broken is one of the most affecting heartbreaks I've ever seen. The naked terror of it shows how hollow the emotions of *Tiny Alice* really are.

*Menagerie* is perhaps Williams' strongest play. Its strength, ironically, flows directly from its reliance on dream and memory; its fabric is wispy—an hour in a troubled man's mind—and only so delicate a structure could support these semi-illusory characters and draw from them the reality they are. In conventional dramatic structure they would appear attenuated and insubstantial. The pathos of faded beauty and regret and hopeless love are all there. It is a moving, a wonderful play.

## Saturday, 19 June

I'M LEAVING FORDHAM a day early to visit my folks in South Hadley. Grace: it suddenly occurred to me at Mass this morning that I've had a chip on my shoulder ever since coming here. I've taken every opportunity to rip off clever cutting remarks. I've whined and moaned and felt bad for myself. I'm depressed at my pettiness—when will I ever grow in Christ? I *resolve* to be pleasant with the folks tomorrow, at least to spare them my ugliness.

## Monday, 21 June

LIFE DOES TEND to be a series of confusions. After an awful bus trip on which the bus collapsed and another was sent to pick up the stranded passengers (some of whom—guess who— had to stand in the newer smaller bus), I arrived at Boston College High and was informed at the door by the rather

aggressive Dean that my course in creative writing had been
canceled and I would therefore be teaching vocabulary to
eighth graders as part of a larger remedial reading program.
Since he was almost accusatory in his explanations, I lacked
courage even to protest. I smiled. But this morning I trotted
in to the Rector and told him I was returning to Woodstock.
He bargained: I will teach vocabulary for thirty-five minutes
daily all this week; he will send me to Boston College for the
next two weeks. I am delighted that I'll be with my friends,
pained and embarrassed at how things here have turned out.
And the vocabulary business is a fright. I have never felt so
incompetent as this morning facing thirty washed uncompre-
hending faces and trying to explain what "apathy" means.
Fierce. God is praised, I hope, in the sincere efforts of fools.

### Thursday, 24 June

DELIVER ME, O Lord, from ever again teaching vocabulary.
Nightmare experiences do have their value, however, and this
one will at least make cheery tales for villa. But never never
will I repeat the ordeal.

I am capitalizing on my time at B.C. High to have my
eyes examined and my teeth looked to, so that at least I'll
leave this place in good physical repair though psychologically
an ash heap. And I've managed to see David Morrissy for
lunch, will see Jim Linehan tonight for a movie, and be with
Leo Fahey tomorrow. Socially, at least, things are fine. But,
dear God, *vocabulary.*

Later. Two random thoughts to which I ought to return
sometime. (1) Why do people always tell me I'm so "alive,"
especially it seems when I'm about to drop from exhaustion
or self-pity? David mentioned my "aliveness" right in the
middle of one of my diatribes on how much I disappoint
my friends and how sad my disappointing them makes me.
(2) Bonhoeffer in one of his letters says: "I shall be writing
about Christian 'egoism' next time—selfless self-love. I think
we agree about that. Too much altruism is a bore, and makes
too many claims. There is a kind of egoism which can be more

selfless, and makes less claims upon us." Too much altruism isn't my trouble, though perhaps the wrong kind of altruism is. Perhaps I only want people to like me. Perhaps really my exhausting "selflessness" is not that at all, but just a sublime selfishness wearing a spiritual disguise. I hope not. But perhaps?

### Sunday, 27 June

I AM LIVING in a fool's purgatory.

### Tuesday, 29 June

I HAVE TO DROP artificial tears into my left eye four times a day. Exquisite irony. It seems my tear ducts don't care to operate any longer (compensating for former excesses?) and consequently my eye lacks fluid and tends to just give up its normal functions like—say—seeing. Quite poor. The eye doctor warned me I could have a great deal of trouble with this, though what he meant by a great deal of trouble he didn't say. He spoke with that ominous tone doctors use when they want to make sure you're going to put witch hazel on the soles of your feet every half hour. In his defense, though, I should say that the eye has felt better with its ersatz sorrow injected before meals and as my last prayer ritual before bed. It's all so silly.

Boston College is fine. This is my fourth day here, each of the four being given over to visits and parties and reading Karl Rahner. I came with the intention of beginning no work until Wednesday and I've kept gloriously to that plan.

### Saturday, 17 July

I ARRIVED IN Washington on Wednesday amid the chaos that customarily attends my leave-takings and arrivals. That is, I imposed upon strangers, enraged my friends, and generally proved myself short on social acumen. I borrowed a car from a complete stranger to get to the Boston airport; he gave it willingly. But I threw the Minister of Georgetown into wrath by writing to him a week beforehand and asking if he could spare a car for an hour to let one of my Woodstock friends pick up me and my luggage at the Washington airport. His response was to demand who the hell I thought I was that I expected to be met at airports, etc., etc. Once on campus we instituted a search for my suite, which of course had never been readied for me. I ended up in a student's room between the elevator and the showers where no noise escapes me. I get tired. I just get tired.

Later. I've put in a good day's work now, so I feel less shredded. Yesterday I wrote part five of the Kennedy poem; it's rather good, I think, factual and removed. It's taken almost verbatim from the Warren report: I can think of no other way to handle the assassination than in terms of cold unassailable fact. The poem is shaping up nicely.

Here's a tribute to my firmness of purpose. I've decided to restructure *Rubrics for a Revolution*, retaining only the three strictly autobiographical sections on being born, living the religious life, being ordained. I'll use the three as a single section and toss in poems written during the past year as other sections. I've begun to realize, you see, that unless Naomi is willing to die for the book, there will be no book. I am at the mercy (worse, at the enthusiasm) of publishers so long as my writing is not worth money to them. No wonder so many writers who have hit success only after a long wait drive such ruthless bargains. So I restructure *Rubrics*. (I feel like I'm concealing poison darts in my trench coat.)

## Sunday, 18 July

I SUDDENLY FEEL that my spiritual life has gone to hell. I'm praying less, am distracted, seem always to be doing something frivolous. And I haven't read a spiritual book in far too long a time. The one thing that matters is that in less than a year I am going to be a priest: ergo it's high time I started living like one. I don't want to spend the last few months of preparation for the priesthood agonizing over whether I can in conscience go through with it. I've seen too many men do that and it's a tragic thing to watch. And so unnecessary. God doesn't call men to his service to torture them but to fill them so full they overflow with his goodness and drench everybody within splashing distance. But you've got to *let* him fill you, and that means you've got to keep open to him, you've got to be receptive, responsive to the subtlest workings of grace. Which means you've got to pray, chum, and you've got to maintain an interior silence even in the midst of hurricane social activity and all that cavorting you engage in.

## *Tuesday, 20 July*

THINGS ARE HAPPENING quickly. Last night I gave a poetry reading, which was surprisingly well-attended considering that (1) nobody knows me here and (2) the reading was advertised for *June* 19. About forty people came and they were wonderfully responsive, picking up all the little snidies I dropped and getting a good bit of the poetry on first bounce. It was the best reading I've given yet; well-structured and fresh; anyway, they liked it.

Afterward a Jesuit friend of mine gave a small party for me in his digs (he's sort of prefect of the dormitory I'm staying in) and there I met a great lady. She's Joan Caryl, a sculptress. She's lived in Maine for some time and has kept roots there: she's sort of tweedy and rockbound and earthy in a balanced sophisticated way, if that isn't contradictory. She loves people and she loves to sculpt. I'm eager to see her again. Relax, she's a good forty years old.

After the poetry reading and the party last night, I rose promptly this morning for a double feature: Patricia McGerr and Riley Hughes and I taped a panel discussion on "Who Shouldn't Write?" for radio and then the whole thing over again—with a completely different discussion—for television. It was a ghastly experience. They sat me down dead center, and as I listened to the talk whistling back and forth in front of and in back of me and I unable to interject a syllable, I

figured that at last I knew what it's like to have a flat tire
in the Holland Tunnel. Talk talk talk. And nothing said.
It was a grim experience. Doubly so on telly, since everybody
could see me—green—in living color. I don't know when either
tape will be played, and I don't want to know. I prefer to forget the whole sorry business. Who shouldn't write indeed.

## Thursday, 22 July

FRANTIC PACE. Tuesday night I went to a party for a going-
away Jesuit and whom should I meet but Joan. She's great.
We talked about writing and sculpting and being alive in a
sick society and it was wonderful. You so rarely meet someone
with whom you have everything in common. She invited me
to her at-home, which she holds every Thursday from three to
six, just as they did fifty years ago in the bettah circles.

So I went. Right off I admired a beautiful Madonna and
Child in the center of her table. She gave it to me. Just like
that. It's baked clay, looks like bronze, and for all I know is
probably worth a great deal. I prize it highly, spend most of
my prayer time (small rations these days) looking at it.

The at-home went on all around us and of course we made
good chat with everybody but we continued to converse
underwater, if you follow me. She is a great lady. I love her.
Every so often Christ brings a real Christian parading through
your life; usually they knock you out; not this one. She has
filled me with such gratitude and joy that I don't even mind
being me.

## Friday, 23 July

I'VE BEEN WORKING for some time now on the last section of
the Kennedy poem, "Death of Kings." Can't get anywhere
with it. In just a few lines, around twenty, this one section
has to pull together all that's gone before, make some sense out
of the sorry spectacle of hatred and murder and human per-
versity, state positively where redemption lies. That's a large

order. Perhaps I'll put off writing this last section until the retreat at Woodstock. I haven't sufficiently digested all the material I want to include.

Much later. Midnight. I finished "Death of Kings." I took a tranquilizer and went to bed much troubled by the poem, gave up trying to sleep after an hour or so, and suddenly bashed out this last section. Is it good? I think so. I'll tell you in a month.

## Wednesday, 28 July

THE REVISED standard version of *Rubrics for a Revolution* is restructured, typed, and ready to go off to Naomi sometime next month. It's not bad. More things will have to be cut; the tone of the book is not so even as I could wish. However, that's an alp we'll scale when we get to the end of the ski tow: confer Madison Avenue.

## Thursday, 29 July

EVENTUALLY of course it had to happen. I hadn't expected it to happen quite so soon, nor indeed in quite so folksy a manner. Even now, scrunched in embarrassment over my machine, I blush to think on't.

A week or so ago Bill Somebody called me up to ask if I would give a poetry reading to the Sunday Evening Club of the Presbyterians of Washington, which meets every Wednesday. He had seen my Georgetown reading advertised in the paper and thought his Presbyterians would like some of the same. I said "sure," thinking it both a good ecumenical gesture and the likely source of another hundred clams. He assured me he would pick me up in time to get there for the steak dinner before the reading. His mentioning a "steak" dinner should have clued me in, but didn't. "Neat," I said.

So last night, *the* Wednesday, it rained. The business went like this. The car is bulging with wet and commodious Presbyterians. Nobody talks; conversation is apparently to be my

contribution to the evening. I try some witty patter; I begin
to melt at the edges. Gloom. Meanwhile the car starts making
obscene noises, roaring and coughing with little belches inter-
mixed. Scenting disaster, I begin to coin excuses for a rapid
getaway immediately after the reading. Bill decides to break
the silence:

"Where you say you were from, Father?"

"I'm from South Hadley in Massachusetts. It's a little town
in the western end of the state, near Springfield."

"Oh, in Maine."

"No. No, in Massachusetts."

"Right outside Boston?"

"Well, sort of. About a hundred miles west."

"Never been there."

"Oh, you must come some time. We're on the Connecticut
River, you know, and there's beautiful scenery in the fall."
Pause. "It's really lovely."

Girl from the back: "Shucks, we've got plenty scenery right
here."

Other girl in back: "We sure don't need scenery."

I try other conversational tacks. They don't work either.
I grow desperate, marvel at the layout of Washington, admire
the Georgetown houses, inquire about the Sunday Evening
Club. Silence and monosyllables. Things will take a turn for
the better at the party: a Jesuit consolation.

The Presbyterian meeting place is the former Irish consulate.
It was once handsome. It looks abandoned today, with long
grass and great unfurnished rooms; in the rain it is Bleak
House.

The car stops at the end of a long winding drive; everyone
simultaneously assures me, as if I had been stricken blind in
transit, that this indeed is the house. Everyone struggles out.
I notice with alarm one girl carrying a bowl of salad, her
transparent raincoat draped over it as protection from the
elements. And a young man, dear God, is carrying a movie
screen. Inside it smells musty. People are milling about with
strained expressions on their faces. Surely they can't *all* have
stomach disorders. In the center of a large room, four men
are settling huge planks on saw-horses; this is the dining table.

I wonder will we begin swilling great flagons of mead? I look about for battle trophies. Skins of animals? Scalps? Nobody speaks to me. They look unutterably miserable and I feel that way. I put my raincoat in a corner, careful not to disturb the spider who has set up housekeeping there. I try to engage a fellow about my age in chat. Having answered my question, he literally turns his back. I have almost decided to make a break for it, run like hell down that long winding drive and disappear forever, when a bunch of new folk come in behind me. My escape is cut off. We all stand in the entrance to the room with the not-yet-groaning board when a very short and very fat man slaps my shoulder and says:

"Say, Reverend, where you from?"

"Well, I'm studying theology at Woodstock College. That's . . ."

"Never you mind, Reverend." Another mighty clap on the shoulder, the bursitis one. "I guess as how you've gotta do a lot of that studying if you're going to go around eating free with folks."

I grow red, laugh stupidly, embarrassed. I can think of nothing to say. But he's not stalled; not on your life.

"My name's Horace, Reverend. I'm not your religion, of course. I'm not even theirs. I'm kind of a lapsed Baptist. But these folks don't mind me coming to their club long as I pay like everybody else."

"I'm sure they're pleased to have you, Horace."

"Don't matter if they aren't. I pay just like anybody else. Say, Reverend, I got a question for you. Don't you priests miss women?" He leers wetly.

My feet turn to cement and I assume that at any rate the evening can't do anything but improve. I take a deep breath.

"I'm not sure what you mean, Horace. I see lots of women. I sometimes give talks to them. In summer I go to secular schools and there are lots of women in my classes. I don't have as much contact, I suppose, with women as with men but . . ."

I'm beginning to breathe easier; I've put the question in

the area of safe discussion. Horace, however, is not to be put off.

"Oh, come on, Rev, you know what I mean." He joggles me chummily in the ribs with his surprisingly pointed elbow. "I mean *having* um."

Everyone has fallen silent; they listen to Horace's little exhibition, some with interest and some with bewilderment but none with understanding for my godawful plight. I try to explain celibacy. Mercifully somebody summons us to get in line for steaks.

"Looks as how we're fixing to eat." Horace forgets my bleak chastity.

A sweet-voiced lady with a downy black mustache urges me: "You first, Father. Hurry up, hurry up." And she thrusts a paper plate into my now trembling hands. I wonder will I survive the evening without a breakdown.

I did survive it and I am pleased to think that if the Lord applied my sufferings in the areas I offered them, then I liberated a good portion of the population of Purgatory. The remainder of the evening was, if possible, more embarrassing.

The meal was a mélange of desperate conversations that kept me crimson. From one end of the twenty-foot table to the other, the shout: "Hey Alice, don't eat all them rolls; pass some down here." Alice passed the rolls and sure enough everybody on that side of the table took one. Nobody talked, except about food. Stevedores could not have done justice more quickly or more efficiently to the scared little steaks or the delicious rolls that Alice had set her mind and maw upon. And at the end, yes, a gentleman did pass from person to person collecting a dollar from each. Inexplicably he asked none of me.

My reading was the intellectual analogue of the meal. After twenty minutes, Bill suddenly interrupted with the question: "Now, Father, you undoubtedly had something in mind when you wrote these poems. But we've always understood that poetry has to have rhyme and meter, and you don't seem to have any of that. So how do you know you're writing poetry?"

The reading stopped there and for the next forty minutes

I tried to explain, to justify to these people, what poetry since the 1900s has been trying to do. It was hopeless. I am too depressed by the whole affair to repeat some of the hilarities, even those from the woman who informed me in some wrath that she was herself a poet and, personally, had never *heard* of poetry that didn't at least have meter. And on and on.

When I finished, Bill explained that he was grateful and felt they all were and that he regretted (I had told him I must leave right after my talk) that I couldn't stay for the special attraction of the evening: a sixteen-millimeter film of the recent astronaut space walk. I came home and drank five beers right in a row.

### Friday, 30 July

ELEVEN YEARS AGO I entered the Society of Jesus; God somehow has lasted it out with me. What have they been, these eleven years on the mountain? In so many ways chaotic and undisciplined and wasteful, yet beneath the surface there lies a stratum of continuity: my desire to desire what is good. God will forgive me these eleven years.

### Wednesday, 4 August

JOAN CARYL. Joan Caryl. I had dinner at her home on Sunday and then we settled down to a six-hour talk—about Christianity and being a Christian and our pasts. We are alike in so many ways, even to our years spent in theater, to our wild appreciation of the zany and incongruous. She told me of her marriage and conversion to Catholicism and her husband's leaving her for greener pastures. Tragic. Beautiful, too. It is her suffering that makes her so very lovable.

Tuesday was a big day: squabble on radio, good meeting with the president of William Morrow publishers, chopping away of calcium deposits in my bursitis shoulder.

The squabble occurred because I didn't think the lady interviewing me should call me John; I preferred Mister or Father, both of which she found tiresome. And she found *me* tiresome, as she made abundantly clear. We exchanged pointed, if not sharp, words just as the "on the air" sign flashed red. So there we sat with smiles on our faces and venom in our eyes, frozen. Made for a rather interesting forty-five minutes.

Also at the interview was John Willey of William Morrow publishers. We talked about the impossibility of teaching anybody to write, about Albee and the fraudulence of *Tiny Alice*, about Connecticut—where he lives and where I taught school. He was interested in me, took my address, asked me to dinner in New York: I find this all the more astonishing because nobody of his age and position has ever treated me with such respect before. He seemed to think I had something valid to say. I am flattered still, some twenty-four hours later.

That afternoon I hotfooted it into Washington, where, with the aid of a five-inch needle and the roadmap of an X ray, a good doctor invaded the joint in my left shoulder and smashed the calcium deposits to chalk dust. As I bit my lower lip half through, he assured me that I couldn't feel a thing. It was ghastly, but at least I can move the arm now. And I don't feel any longer as if I'm carrying a golf ball in my arm socket.

Tomorrow, the big reading. I'm going to try out my Kennedy poem on the audience. Please God, don't let me make a consummate ass of myself.

## Thursday, 5 August

MY READING tonight went swimmingly. Not quite up to the level of my earlier performance at Georgetown, it was nonetheless better received by a good-sized audience of over a hundred. They seemed most enthusiastic and, what pleased me especially, were evidently quite touched by "Death of Kings." Pin-drop silence for the entire ten or fifteen minutes, and after that, no conversation whatsoever. The poem may be good. Not so good as I had hoped, but good. I'll be able to see better in a month. Meanwhile I have the satisfaction—a minimal one—of knowing it goes over well with an audience.

This is my second day of workshop conferences on how to

write poetry. Naturally I left at Woodstock all the notes I methodically collected during the past year, so now I'm reduced to improvisation. I just let words run along until I stumble over an idea. Then, as I actually did in class today, I stop and say: "Hey, I said something. I just said my first thing." Having called attention to it, I promptly forgot what it was. Some attentive soul had made a note, however, and I was able to repeat three times that an image must be the embodiment of concepts rather than a source from which the poet draws concepts. Ideas are *in* the image. I was able to illustrate this with two poems: Carolyn Kizer's "The Ungrateful Garden," which is the perfect fusion of thought and image; Ralph Waldo Emerson's "The Rhodora," which is such an awful mishmash of poor images, sentimental theology, and opprobrious aesthetics. The group seemed satisfied. I was elated. It's not pleasant to contemplate two hours of having your ignorance systematically unveiled before a crowd of forty people who have paid money to be taught something.

## Friday, 6 August

I OFFERED Mass this morning for Horace and my Presbyterian friends. The reading turns out to have been yet another exercise in God's humor. So I must laugh.

## Saturday, 7 August

TODAY'S SESSION with my poets was the best class I've ever taught. I don't know how much I said about poetry, but I do know what I said about Christianity and I know furthermore that what I said is true. They drank it down like water from the fountain of youth—and some of those gals could use the fountain of youth. I had two perfect reactions. One Jewish girl said to me: "That was a wonderful talk because it was so comprehensive; it encompassed your entire cosmology." (Cosmology, prithee.) And Sr. Thérèse told me briefly: "Father, that's the most beautiful retreat I have ever made." How pleased I am.

I was excited, almost paranoid. I poured out practically all of my spiritual life, certainly my most personal and most long-pondered convictions. Using the last part of my Kennedy poem, I explained how it got to be a poem in the first place. By way of introduction to what the poem contained, I read the original notes and scribbles, punctuating them with my unshakable convictions. That the Incarnation is not only a Christmas event. That compromise is another word for the golden mediocrity of failure. That mourning changes the nature of the insides of you. That to be known by God means to live forever, but that to live in Christ is to learn the art of dying. That to die is not to cease to be but to begin to be in Christ. That experience merely defines the shape of the gap where our love of God ought to be. That truth is an eternal now; philosophy is not the history of truth but the history of man's search for truth and it is riddled through with frustration and disappointment and mistakes. That a miracle is an itch that draws us back to the ordinary daily content of our Christian existence. That death is an action coextensive with a whole lifetime, a sharing in Christ's death, the token of our numinous encounter in eternity. That to live the Christian life is to accept. That purgatory is a state where we learn to accept the help of Christ's Church, to accept the love which in life we rejected. That Christ pursues us from the earliest moments of our existence, drives us into the desert of himself where we encounter the nothingness of ourselves and the totality of him. That without the Incarnation everything is meaningless and with it everything that is is holy. That heaven involves a condition of such total self-surrender that the joy cannot be described as being ours but merely as being. That life is a question of exposing ourselves to the dangers of being loved, that to accept love is much more difficult than to give it, that we cannot receive God until he is willing to give himself, that he cannot give himself until we are willing to accept. That the Blessed Mother's pre-eminence lay precisely in her having received Christ as completely as he desired, to the point of physical motherhood . . .

So I said a lot of things. And I suppose I'll spend the rest of my life saying these same things with varying degrees of success. But today was beautiful. I hadn't planned this kind of talk. When God wants people to hear something, he arranges it. Uses even me. They have little idea of what they've heard; on the other hand they won't forget *every*thing: it was rather an intense session. I am elated that God is willing to use me to tell his people something. I must be careful now to keep the meddling self out of the way, not try to play God or God's will for these people. I'm beat. This one session has made the summer completely worthwhile for me.

## Friday, 13 August

FRIDAY THE THIRTEENTH. *Rubrics for a Revolution* went off to Doubleday this morning. Now I settle down, metaphorically at least, for a long long wait. I do hope Naomi likes it; I cannot, absolutely cannot, make any more significant changes in it.

I leave tomorrow for villa at Lake Sunapee. Exhausted but in fine spirits, I hope only to sleep and carouse and to talk a little. Not another word until I return to Woodstock and the beginning of my ordination year.

# III
# BABYLON: THE
# NEW JERUSALEM

AUGUST 1965–JUNE 1966

## Tuesday, 31 August

HOME AT WOODSTOCK. I'm glad to be here too. The summer was stimulating in many ways but I am eager now to get on with ordination year, to begin retreat this evening. Villa was great—lots of rest and a chance to gather up my soul—and the couple of days I spent with my family were perfect; I have no excuse for not making an exemplary retreat.

## Friday, 3 September

ISN'T IT STRANGE? I was so eager to begin retreat and now here I am bored to death with the whole business, desperate to talk, to escape from the hard realities of prayer into the frivolities of chatter. Despite my boredom and lethargy, however, I remain aware of a substratum of happiness.

## Saturday, 4 September

WHY SHOULD the attempt to love God give me headaches? I guess because I worry about *me* loving God instead of me loving *God*. I can't quite believe God has called me to his service with the intention of seeing how miserable he can make me.

Later. Terrible depression. I am a dilettante at everything I've ever undertaken: painting, criticism, poetry, the spiritual life. And I'll always be this way. Never an expert anything; all superficial gloss, and in the end even the gloss will go.

Reactions are funny. Instead of being humbled by the depression, I'm angry. At everything around me. At Superiors passing judgments on my suitability for ordination, at Superiors passing judgment on my poems before I'm allowed to publish, at Superiors because they are Superiors, I guess. It's the ancient story. Eve blamed the serpent; Adam blamed Eve. So I've nominated myself dilettante of the year and I've made Superiors autocratic tyrants. Exaggeration always. And somewhere, deep beneath the anxiety and foolishness, I exist.

## Monday, 6 September

REREADING THE JOURNAL I suddenly discover what Naomi means by saying that I am not present in it. For instance there is no real indication that I spent an agonizing week in New York last June; the impression is that things ran along pretty smoothly and that I realized at the end of my stay that I had been a sorehead. That, of course, is also true. Things did run smoothly. And I did have a miserable time. Is it ever possible, I wonder, to capture the multiplicity of fact? That things are horrible even while they are wonderful? Virginia Woolf does it in *Mrs. Dalloway*, but we're a little short on Virginia Woolfs these days. *Why* can't I write? Are all these pages just a self-conscious arrangement of selected lies? God, no wonder I get headaches.

## Wednesday, 8 September

THERE IS NO HUNGER like the taste of you: good opening line for a poem. Something is forming about how God first loves us and how we must open ourselves, letting him love us as he wants, if we are ever to be able to return his love. There is no hunger like the taste of you. Splendid line.

Later. How does the Spirit want to speak through me? Mystery. But what does that mean?

## Saturday, 11 September

RETREAT, thank God, is over and we've lapsed into the routine of school. There are a certain number of changes. Cafeteria-style breakfasts are a novelty. You enter this vast refectory and see three long lines of blackrobes waiting for their eggs and gruel, faces grim with first morning, nobody speaking: ah, you think, here we are—the Albert Camus Memorial Bus Terminal. And then there's a new approach to the teaching problem, quite inexplicable at this juncture either as approach or as problem. And finally the over-all sense of urgency about everything. Already I'm worn out at the idea of all the things I must learn before they'll go through with it and ordain me.

Since returning here, I've done nothing but read: O'Hara's *Sermons and Soda Water*, three rather interesting novellas that engaged me while I was with them but inspire in me no great longing to return to the flaky sophistication of O'Hara; Tennessee Williams' newest play, *Slapstick Tragedy*, which is weak in many many respects but engagingly funny at times; Flannery O'Connor's *Everything That Rises Must Converge*, which is a magnificent collection of stories I'll write about tomorrow; and now Sitwell's *Taken Care Of*. Perhaps high-level escape reading is the best way to ease into some form of responsible work. I may even tire of carrying on with novels and hotfoot it back to the marshes of scholastic theology. Dear Lord, deliver us from teachers who aren't desperately eager to tell you *some*thing.

## Sunday, 12 September

I'VE FINISHED reading and keep coming back to Flannery O'Connor's last book of short stories, *Everything That Rises Must Converge*. It's a first-class book exploring the O'Connor territory of grace and sin, corruption and the unfathomable mercy of God. Her grotesques are all here: an inhuman social worker who is "a big tin Jesus"; a self-pitying woman who insists a neighbor's bull be driven out of her pasture, gets her way, and is impaled upon its horns; the incredible Mrs. Turpin.

In the best story, "Revelation," Mrs. Turpin, a woman of cagey intolerance and indomitable good disposition, is attacked in a doctor's waiting room by a girl who hurls a book at her, pitches her to the floor, bites her, and whispers: "Go back to hell where you came from, you old wart hog." The revelation is only partial. Later, while hosing down the hogs, Mrs. Turpin cries out against God: "What do you send me a message like that for? . . . It's no trash around here, black or white, that I haven't given to. And break my back to the bone every day working. And do for the church." She continues on and on raging against God until in response to her "Who do you think you are?" there comes the final revelation: she sees marching through the sky armies of white trash washed clean for the first time, bands of Negroes in white robes, freaks and lunatics shouting and clapping, and in the rear people like herself who always had had a little of everything and the wit to make use of it. "They were marching behind the others with great dignity, accountable as they had always been for good order and common sense and respectable behavior. They alone were on key. Yet she could see by their shocked and altered faces that even their virtues were being burned away."

Terrific story, it packs a punch like few others ever. And it's profound, a searching analysis of the complacent-saved, a revelation of the inadequacy of being a self-conscious Christian. I'd really like to do a theological investigation of all her books. I think it would be profitable for me both as a critic and as a person. She's as theological as Rahner and a hell of a lot more interesting. She liked to quote Cyril of Jerusalem's passage: "The dragon sits by the side of the road watching those who pass. Beware lest he devour you. We go to the Father of Souls, but it is necessary to pass the dragon." Once she commented on this passage: "No matter what form the dragon may take, it is of this mysterious passage past him, or into his jaws, that stories of any depth will always be concerned to tell." That's just about a summary of her work. All her stories deal with this passage by or into the dragon.

Hazel Motes, the hero of her first novel, Wise Blood, is an inverted St. Paul who preaches the Church Without Christ:

"I'm going to preach that there was no fall because there was nothing to fall from, and no redemption because there was no fall, and no judgment because there wasn't the first two. Nothing matters but that Jesus was a liar." His grandfather had promised him "Jesus would never let him forget he was redeemed" and it is this which constitutes Hazel's strange integrity: that he cannot escape his own redemption.

Her first book of short stories is all about the grace problem too, about people in flight from or in search of grace. In the title story, "A Good Man Is Hard to Find," there is a murderer called the Misfit who says: "If He did what He said, then it's nothing for you to do but throw away everything and follow Him, and if He didn't, then it's nothing for you to do but enjoy the few minutes you got left the best way you can—by killing somebody or burning down his house or doing some other meanness to him." The ineluctable logic of the fundamentalist takes your breath away.

Similarly her second and last novel, *The Violent Bear It Away*, investigates grace and the freedom of the will. As in *Wise Blood*, she develops the theme of the inverted apostle, the reluctant prophet doomed to execute God's will in violence to his own, pursued by a grace he cannot understand and cannot wholly evade.

Four books; that's all she has. But I think you could document from these four books a pretty sound theology of grace and redemption. She probes the nature of the Christian life, the mystery of grace in a graceless time, the status of Christ in a world which sees distortion as natural and spiritual purpose as personal whim. And she is savagely funny. She shows you the wounds and makes you laugh and makes you wonder what's the matter with you that you can laugh at wounds. She is dead at thirty-nine; only she, I suppose, would have seen in her early death the perfection of God's irony.

### Monday, 13 September

A FRIEND is someone who leaves you with all your freedom intact but who, by what he thinks of you, obliges you to be fully what you are.

### Tuesday, 14 September

I'VE BEEN TRYING lately, probably because of my reading in Flannery O'Connor, to think through some ideas about heaven. If it's just the contemplation of infinite perfection, in the same sense we generally think about contemplation, it's going to get awfully dull. And yet this is the idea most Catholics have of heaven, I'm sure: we sit around *looking at* God. I, for one, would get a headache.

How about taking another tack? How about beginning with this life as the Christian life of grace, working toward death as the flowering of grace in our lives, terminating in a "heaven" that is the constant ecstatic living-in-love with someone? How about that? With some*one*. With a person. With God, who is a person. Maybe this approach would be more fruitful, or at least more palatable, a way to talk about heaven. I'll think tomorrow.

### Thursday, 16 September

BECAUSE IT STRUCK me as crazy, I didn't record that Californian's request of a year ago that I write an opera libretto to which he would compose music. I don't know who he is, save that he's a Jesuit who has read my verse and knows some people I know and is apparently quite an accomplished musician. Well, he did ask me and I told him I'd think about it and suddenly I've thought about it. I don't know if I'll have time to execute the thing, but it would be fun to try.

"The Waiting Room" is the tentative title. The whole thing came to me yesterday during meditation, probably because I was thinking about heaven and distracted by Flannery O'Connor's story "Revelation." In a fairly naturalistic waiting room, several patients wait to see the doctor. They are types of wounded humanity—not symbolic representations, but the real thing—and they reveal themselves to each other by a sort of Pirandello gravitation from superficial conversation to the resonances beneath that conversation and finally to the subconscious and primitive urges that skulk beyond anything they suspect about themselves.

I can swipe all the techniques of Absurd theater and turn them to advantage: the banal and meaningless chatter, the cliché as a substitute for communication, the totally inclosed psyche, the desperate need to escape self, the ritual action without commitment and without validity, etc., etc.

A nurse, for instance, wanders in and out of the room rejecting some patients and giving medicine to others but rarely— probably never—admitting anyone to the doctor's office. To an especially importunate patient she gives an outsized monkey wrench.

NURSE: The doctor says take this according to directions.
PATIENT: But what do I do with it? What do I do?
NURSE: Take it according to directions.
PATIENT: [*Examining it*] But there aren't any directions.
NURSE: That is one of the difficulties we face.

Some patients she will drive out of the waiting room altogether, kicking and punching them. Mostly, she will ignore them.

A Negro who wants to be turned white will be smiled over and coddled and then told to wait in an adjoining room. A man with a bandaged and bleeding head will be made to leave because he is getting blood on the carpet. A nun who observes all this will be outraged by it and will denounce the absent nurse and sing a hymn to charity. Later, refused admittance to the doctor's office, she will beg and then insist and finally with great violence try to force her way in. The patients themselves will wrestle her to the floor, the nurse will give her an injection: as they carry her off limp, her companion turns her back and sings some mawkish hymn to the Sacred Heart.

When the nurse is out of the room, the patients reveal themselves deeply and painfully; when she returns, they become silent and alien patients in a waiting room.

Eventually someone—probably clean, poorly dressed, crippled—is told the doctor will see him now, if he will kindly step into the next room and be blinded. He emerges with his eyes swathed in bandages; the nurse leads him to the door of the doctor's office, now visible behind a transparent scrim; he either stumbles and feels his way to a guillotine where he collapses with his neck upon the block or else he is forced to crawl through a long tunnel and then, wriggling through a small dark aperture infinitely distant, disappears forever. The patients all shake hands and congratulate one another silently while the orchestra plays a prolonged and triumphant Alleluia.

What is it supposed to mean? Don't be silly. It's corn.

### Sunday, 19 September

"THERE IS NO HUNGER like the taste of you" is now the last line of a rather good poem called "Landscape." It has some other nice things too: "we wandered in the gardens of our flesh" and "the weighted vines go down upon their knees" and "the light wingbeat of love behind the storm." I've been working on the poem for about a week. Done with it at last, I seem to have given myself over to total inertia. I need a good kick in the behind.

Later. Do you know what I was thinking of tonight in chapel? When we used to go tobogganing by moonlight—Mother, Dad, Jerry, me. The snow was new and slick and the moon full and, because I was only seven or so, the hill seemed very very steep. We'd go down and down and down and the snow would stick to our eyebrows, seep into our boots, and fluff down our necks. And then we'd go home and make popcorn. With butter and salt. Was anybody ever so happy?

## Monday, 20 September

HERE'S A GOOD THING. *The New York Times* reviewed my *Dandelions* yesterday, and pleasantly too. The newspaper strike began sometime during last week, but not before the Book Review section had already been produced. Thank God.

The reviewer, DeWitt Bell, says some good things: "The language sings for him . . . to his often excellent metaphoric language, he adds wit, playfulness . . ." things like that. He has a few reservations: the poems that do not leap from the conventional framework remain merely conventional; Jesuitism "constricts him to a tradition and limits his range of subject matter." And he's right: many of the poems in *Dandelions* are merely conventional; I am limited in range and subject matter—but because I am *me*, not because I am a Jesuit. Anyhow I feel great to be favorably reviewed in an important place.

Later. How about this? I've had my prayer schedule approved by my spiritual father so that the freedom I've been giving myself in the matter of time is now given with the blessings of Superiors: no prescribed time for prayer, no "duties" I must accomplish. Tentatively I've chosen noon to twelve-thirty and nine-thirty to ten as rendezvous points with the Lord, but I'm free to choose other times, to shorten or lengthen prayer periods whenever I wish. This is neat. It makes prayer possible, even likely. (And I think back to the time a few years ago when I was threatened with expulsion from the Society of Jesus for not getting up at five-thirty, "the time prescribed for prayer." Fantastic.)

## Friday, 24 September

INERTIA AGAIN. I work one day and then rest for six—sort of the creation story in reverse. Surely there must be some pill you can take to throw yourself suddenly into high gear.

My new poem, "A Sufficiency of Women," celebrates the five women in my life. Good? I think maybe. The opening lines are nice.

Women—when they cease to be soft mice—
are brilliant feathered birds or animals
or tropic rains. They happen: total,
without warning. I have known five.

It's good to be writing again, though I suppose it would be better to be studying for the Confessions exam of next Wednesday. Canon law is not exactly my forte.

## Saturday, 25 September

JESUS CHRIST was a *man* as well. A real one—not God dressed up in flesh for a thirty-three-year charade—but a real man. He had gas pains and he wept real tears over Lazarus and he loved Mary Magdalen, a poor type. Furthermore he encouraged her to love him, even though the neighbors must have been horrified and though he surely must have sensed the risk he took of breaking her heart. And what do I risk?

## Wednesday, 29 September

CONFESSIONS EXAM was quite successful; I'm approved, even commended. I enjoyed the exam, since it was the first time I can ever recall having everything under control, even voice and composure. Thank God *that's* over with.

To celebrate my new status as approved confessor, I wrote a fan letter to Muriel Spark. I was brimming over with good cheer and it seemed only right to share it.

Dear Miss Spark:

You are the best novelist writing today. Period. Each of your books is better than the preceding and *The Mandelbaum Gate* looks to be the best of all.

This is my first and, I think, only fan letter. I am thirty and too old for frenzied enthusiasms over people I've never met. But you are great and therefore an exception.

I pray for you now and again and shall. God's blessing on your work.

Sincerely,

Now, some hours later, I feel a little bit silly. Still, it's true, people don't tell other people often enough how good they are. I'm glad I wrote.

Later. With the Incarnation, all things become holy. Christ, assuming flesh, assumes into his divinity the destinies of all things finite and limited; they become integrated into the divine plan of things. We do. We men. Our flesh will be in heaven. But we fulfill this integration into the divine by responding, as Christ did, to the Father's call to pass through our own special crucifixions and deaths and burials. And then, and only then, do we rise triumphant with Christ. Death, therefore, is the most frightening ratification of our lives; it is the seal on all that we have done and on all that we have neglected to do. No wonder we fear death. I fear it.

## Thursday, 30 September

Do YOU SUPPOSE my mind is giving out this early in the year? Here is a little verse I wrote today under the title of "Intimations of Immorality":

> Humpty-Dumpty sat on a wall
> Humpty-Dumpty had a great fall.
> All the King's horses
> And all the King's men . . .
> Were secretly pleased.

I could do a whole series of cynical nursery rhymes, call it "A Child's Garden of Perverse." I'm sure the idea isn't new.

> Old Mother Hubbard
> Slickered and rubbered
> Took her dog out in the rain
> And shot him.

I'd better stop. Right now.

*Saturday, 2 October*

Is IT ONLY when our friends are absent, I wonder, that we feel we most want to talk with them. I keep feeling I want to talk openly and honestly with somebody—maybe David or Frank—but I half suspect that if they were here in the house, I would just fall silent and wait for them to draw me out. Is that my way of missing people perhaps?

I rejoice in the people I love, rejoice even more that my love for them terminates in mystery. I can't explain why I love them; imagine them trying to explain why they love me. But Christ loves me. And them. And his love for us goes far to explain why anybody can love anybody else, why in fact we are driven to love one another. Of course his love for us itself remains a mystery, *the* mystery I suppose. So we come back to it again and forever: mystery and fact.

Later. Truman Capote's *In Cold Blood*, an account of the brutal, calculated murder of a family of four in a small Kansas town, is being serialized in *The New Yorker*. Capote some years back had the idea that a novelist working with only a newspaperman's reportorial manner and matter might be able to bring something quite new and individual to writing. With this plan in mind, he chose from *The New York Times* a small account of the Kansas murders, followed them up, spent several years living and researching in the town in which they were committed, and now has produced this truly breathtaking account. Composed in fluid and highly civilized English, it is without the novel's embellishments of any kind—even the dialogue is said to be exact transcription. As the action unfolds and the murderers move in for the kill, Capote cuts back and forth between the family and the men who are about to murder them; the effect is Greek tragedy, an almost ritual action barbarous and irrational. The horror and the grandeur of life collide head on. The impossible seems inevitable. It is a splendid piece of writing.

## Sunday, 3 October

WE ARE ALL so separate, so lost. Trees in a storm. "This too is fiction." "The heart wants what it wants, or it does not care." Lines from Emily Dickinson keep pattering on my brain. Another South Hadley recluse. She left Mount Holyoke College because she could not stand the stuff that passed for piety there.

Not long ago we were given permission to have radios and since then you haven't been able to hear yourself think. I feel like a salesman in a music shop.

We have underestimated the importance of feeling in the Society of Jesus. It *does* matter that once in a while you feel loved and respected and successful. Survival can become a full-time occupation.

Lots of work accomplished today. I polished off two more chapters of Cox's *The Secular City* and three chapters of C. S. Lewis' book on the psalms, spent an hour on class work for tomorrow, wrote a review of Tony Connor's *Lodgers* for the Boston *Herald*, and rewrote eight lines of "A Sufficiency of Women," which is now rather good. Since I'm beginning to succumb to whatever that disease is that's running through the house, I rejoice in having done a good day's work. Now I can collapse in peace.

"He is a man whose meager pleasures sprout from his malice and who finds himself, because of his malice, incapable of enjoying them." Line for a story? Or do I remember this from somewhere?

## Monday, 4 October

IKHNATON AND MONOTHEISM. Reading the Old Testament to trace the development of the Israelite conception of the One God, I am overwhelmed with God's infinite (literally) patience with these recalcitrant and hopelessly unqualified people. Wouldn't he have been much smarter and wouldn't it have been so much easier to have chosen the Egyptians for his Covenant? In the fourteenth century B.C., here was this highly developed civilization with all manner of intellectual and artistic refinements, with a Pharaoh—Ikhnaton—who believed so single-mindedly in the unicity of God that he commandeered the wealth and the power of a very wealthy and powerful priest-class for the service of the one and only God. He even erected a new capital city to this God. His religion never caught on. (Moses was not to appear on the scene for some centuries.) Wouldn't it have been practical on the part of God to have stepped into history at just this moment, seeing how Ikhnaton had everything set up for business? But he didn't. He works in his own ways. And that is one of the most marvelous aspects of his choices. When I see how ill-suited and hopelessly backsliding the Israelites were (how they skipped out of their side of the bargain as soon as everything was coming up milk and honey), and when I think of how gauche the apostles must have been (smelling of fish and talking with back-country accents), I take courage and begin to see his wisdom and humor in choosing me. Of course. It all begins to make sense.

## Tuesday, 5 October

Do OTHERS consider as often as I seem to the possibility of losing their minds? I don't think they do. Or if they do, they conceal their thoughts better than I. And why am I ashamed to let anybody know I consider the possibility and fear it? Because they would think that maybe I *am* going crazy or, worse, am crazy already? Possibly. Or is it because I myself might think it? See how the long grass bends in the wind; the mind is supple and will survive.

## Thursday, 7 October

I AM MIDWAY through an awful cold and everything looks gray. Even people. Purgatory must involve that: an absence of color. Despite the cold, however, I managed to complete the dog poem.

Last Sunday I discovered in the magazine section of one of the papers an advertisement for a salve which will restore your dog to its primal health from whatever itch, scratch, or mange might presently afflict it. The advertisement carried a testimonial from Mrs. John Burmester of Hammonton, New Jersey, proclaiming to the world that her Daisy was healthy thanks to the beneficent ministrations of Sulfodene: "I suffered as she suffered almost two years with large, running, itching sores. I had almost given up trying things when I came across Sulfodene. Now her back is all healed, her hair is coming in thick. The Lord should bless you for such a fine product." The extraordinary thing is that the advertisement carries the photograph not of Daisy as you would expect but of Mrs. B. The implication is, I gather, that their identity in suffering was such that a photo of one was for practical purposes a photo of the other. Hence the dog poem, which follows.

### TESTIMONIAL: The Dog of Mrs. Hammonton

"nearly had to be put away, poor Daisy";
her fungus itch had all but made her crazy,
had made the beast a running sore with ears.

"I never could have put away our Daisy.
I suffered as she suffered, two whole years
of frenzied scratching at the frantic itch."

But Daisy's back is healed, the little bitch
boasts the fluffiest behind for blocks.
"The Lord should bless you for Sulfodox."

The Lord has blessed me for Sulfodox.
At better pet shops everywhere am I blessed.
That dog will never die. Be it confessed,

however, Mrs. Hammonton will die.
She—notwithstanding Sulfodox—will lie
beneath the daisies sealed in a wooden box

with pearls and worms twining in her breast.

## Friday, 8 October

A BEAUTIFUL LETTER from Frank Winters. I am overwhelmed. The devotion of my friends will amaze me forever. Especially at this moment it amazes me, since only a short while ago I noted on a memo pad the following bit of edification.

"And sometimes you feel there you *are*, forced back on your own resources—out in the desert, your canteen dry, not another soul for miles—and you wonder how on earth you can survive it and why you undertook it in the first place and who cares. Writing it down helps. Or talking about it. But eventually writing and talking give way, their respective bottoms drop out, and you're *there*: alone, on the edge of that great darkness, and you stare out into nothing, nothing, nothing at all. Don't say this doesn't happen. I *know* it does."

I don't know if I'm just in an awful slump or if I've reached another of those moments in my life when I take a long hard look at me and what I'm doing and what I'm supposed to be doing. Some men look and turn to stone. I myself tend to die. I've died several times in the past years. But only on the greater feasts.

## Saturday, 9 October

I AM OFF to tea now. Yes, tea. Jake Empereur, an excellent priest who lives next door, makes tea each night and he and Matt Quinn and I assemble and talk theology or scandal—whichever is more relevant to the moment. Sometimes Charlie Gonzalez joins us and we go right at it, exhibiting in pursuit of theology an earnestness that classes have not yet killed. (Ah, but give them time.) As a matter of fact, I learn more theology from Jake during these evening sessions than I do from class during the day. And this despite the fact that I am not very fond of tea.

Later. We talked about death. I can't imagine dying—really dying—ever. I know I will, you understand; I just can't really conceive of it happening.

## Sunday, 10 October

I'M NOT BITTER, only deeply scarred, and that accounts for the fact that I look at things differently from most men. It is as if I had in some mysterious way passed through the Second World War in Europe, seen prison camps, worked in the underground. As if existentialism—which never really reached the United States—were my kindergarten. Why do I think this? I guess because Carolyn Kizer wrote yesterday about my poetry: "At your best you have a kind of intellectual and moral opulence, a kind of shiver with which you contemplate what other, lesser men, would find austere." Contemplate the austere. Or is it a question of seeing the austere behind the opulence? Scar tissue.

## Monday, 11 October

RAHNER SAYS that from the world's point of view, and examined in isolation, history "closes with a shrill disharmony never to be resolved." And right away I think of my poems and my life: attempts to bring some order to the chaos of things.

Rather pretentiously I thought that my poor poems and my dignified-dissolute life may indeed seem to terminate unsuccessfully, but at least they have been attempts to approximate the order and perfection of God and so approach success. Seen from another perspective, God's for instance, their very incompleteness might be their value. We tend always to think of things from a rather distinct and possibly quite limited point of view. And aren't we feeling cosmic this morning.

Later. Muriel Spark actually wrote me a letter. In her own handwriting yet. And best of all, she concludes: "Do let me know if you are in New York and can spare the time to come along for a drink. I should enjoy that very much." I am delighted out of my wits. And I *will* meet her sometime.

*Tuesday,* 12 *October*

I WROTE MY obituary this afternoon. Jim Jurich and I were joking about the high seriousness of tone in the Jesuit obituaries of *Woodstock Letters,* and since Jim is in charge of finding men who knew the deceased and are willing to write about him in fond and pious phrases, he asked me if I would write my own . . . and tell the truth. *Voilà.*

It is to be hoped that Fr. L'Heureux loved much, since it is certain that there is much to be forgiven. Father died the way he lived: causing inconvenience for everybody.

His friends were numerous and faithful; they say he was uncompromisingly honest; in fact, he was not. His enemies, less numerous but easily as strong in their feelings about him, say he was a poetic fraud, a liar, a thief; they exaggerate. He was outspoken and clever, which accounts in some part for the feelings of his friends. He was a writer and clever, which accounts for the feelings of his enemies.

He was limited and never forgave himself that. Intellectually, spiritually, even artistically, he was an average man or less. He prided himself on a keen critical sense, though he had little, and that little was further attenuated by peculiarities of taste so narrowing as to make him blind to the merits of almost any literature not professedly Christian and identifiably witty. Though he thought of himself as a priest who loved God's children with God's own love, he loved all too humanly only those whom he found attractive. As an artist, he knew himself. What willpower and incessant application could accomplish, they accomplished for Fr. L'Heureux. It is greatly to his credit that, fortified with small talent and immense desire, he managed in his lifetime to publish so many books. They are in some degree a craftsman's books. He published too early and too late, but almost everything he published manifests the precision and attention and impeccable care he was never able to bring to the more plebeian business of living.

He is mourned by few, a fact that would not bother him since he considered mourning a futile effort and would have preferred a kind and public word from his mourners, followed by amusing anecdotes and bibulous conviviality. He tried never to hurt anyone, always to make people happy. His efforts were scarcely ever visible in his actions. Dead, he rests.

Fairly objective, I'd say.

## Wednesday, 13 October

THREE NOTES. During meditation this evening I asked myself *why* I pray and was astonished to hear: because I love and because I live with death.

With Adam's fall, all material things become subject to a legal irony: the law of vanity (the pride we take in what we are and how we look) and the law of corruption (our inability to preserve what we are and how we look). And so many of us spend our lives trying to beat the law.

Joan Caryl has offered to design my holy card for ordination: I'll provide the text and she'll take care of everything else. I've decided on this:

> Lord,
> Make me your bread.
> Then break me up
> And pass me around.

That's good, I think. Better than a poem.

Later. At tea this evening Jake asked me to help him prepare the Dutch Canon of the Mass for use in English. He has a translation of the Dutch but it's a bit rough, so I'm going to help him smooth it out. I'm not quite sure how I feel about monkeying with the Mass this way. Jake assures me, however, that this Canon, drawn up incidentally by a young Dutch poet, has been submitted to Rome for approval as an officially recognized Dutch Mass and that furthermore it is already in use in certain Holland areas which are experimenting liturgically. Well, I suppose if everyone is doing it in Europe, we'll begin doing it within the next ten years. Still, revising the Mass strikes me as a rather revolutionary notion.

## Friday, 15 October

UNSEASONABLY WARM with all the leaves wilting from expectation rather than dying brilliantly in the fall holocaust. Such strange summer weather. I suppose we'll freeze to death all winter.

*Critic* has asked me to review John Updike's new novel, *Of the Farm*. I'm flattered they consider me worthy; but I should have preferred Muriel Spark's *The Mandelbaum Gate*.

I've read *Of the Farm* once and my first impressions are far from favorable. Updike is dreadfully overrated and I'm going to say so in my review. That sticky style of his meanders like watery molasses all through the book; every so often a little lake forms and you drown in it. Listen:

My wife is wide, wide-hipped and long waisted, and, surveyed from above, gives an impression of terrain, of a wealth whose ownership imposes upon my own body a sweet strain of extension; entered, she yields a variety of landscapes, seeming now a snowy rolling perspective of bursting cotton bolls seen through the Negro arabesques of a fancywork wrought-iron balcony; now a taut vista of mesas dreaming in the midst of sere and painterly ochre; now a gray French castle complexly fitted to a steep green hill whose terraces . . .

And on and on. This is his "fine writing," an amalgam of hypertrophic language and stunted sensibility which, attempting to be profound, succeeds only in being funny. This linguistic hysteria occurs again and again; any real writer knows where to stop.

## Sunday, 17 October

I'M GOING TO WRITE my review this afternoon and want to get off a few thoughts by way of preparation. *Of the Farm* is Updike's best book so far; it's his simplest too. He is back again with the characters he knows best: the precocious adolescent, the *zoftig* redheaded mistress-wife, the dying querulous mother rooted to her land, the trapped father-teacher full of compassion and confusion and sex. It is *The Centaur* revisited, but this time honestly, without all those mythological horse droppings.

Updike tells an interesting story, I guess. The problem is that his characters are not strong enough to bear the burden of the theme he lays upon them: the moral responsibility of a free choice. They're not morally conscious folk and so you can't expect them to act with either the guilt or the greatness of characters from *Anna Karenina*. Yet Updike places them in a Karenina landscape of value and consequence. At one point the hero's mother locates the difference between men and women as a sexual one, explaining: "I'm a very coarse customer. I believe only in what I can see or touch." O.K., I say, if that's how your characters are, but then you can't expect them to get very upset about intangibles. Indeed, you can't expect much of anything from them.

The hero's moral dimensions are too circumscribed. How can I explain it? If a small child chooses to eat fistfuls of green grapes and then comports himself well during the sickness that follows his action, then we're grateful. We're grateful but we don't deceive ourselves that we've witnessed a Greek tragedy writ small. And I'm afraid Joey, the blah hero of *Of the Farm*, is closer to the boy with grapes than to Greek tragedy.

I find Updike's style distressing. The book is shot through with minute descriptions of light striking walls and floorboards, faces observed through screens, the curves of flesh beneath clothing and without it . . . the result is a naturalism that describes rather than illuminates. Updike tries to do with language what Andrew Wyeth does with paint: to represent a selective reality with such accuracy of detail that the real is forced to yield a depth of meaning not evident on its surface. Where Wyeth invariably succeeds, Updike presents only more surface.

And he badly needs control. A ponderous blue pencil and a less pretentious approach to his theme might have made *Of the Farm* a fine short story. So . . . on to the review.

## Wednesday, 20 October

UPDIKE'S VERBAL excess has been haunting me ever since I read that damned book. Hysteria with a fountain pen. I dashed this off this morning in a half hour.

*"Of the Firm"*
by Dike Upjohn

We veered off the speedway onto a glassy tar road, then off the tar on to a double mint ribbon of car ruts. We went down a gully and there, from the ditch where Hinkeldorf's exhausted wife lay on her back gazing at the flies that flickered at her running eyes like minute buzzards on the corpse of a calf, my mistress-wife first saw the firm. Protectively, she leaned toward me and I felt her shoulder bone quiver against my shoulder bone as her son's head heavily plowed into mine. He was seven and, topheavy from reading Plato, his head was always plowing into everything.

"That's our firm," I said. "Mother put up the smaller buildings by herself."

The walls of the big main building rose stark and white, catching the sunlight like the white ash heaps lining the streets of the mind from New York to Alldun, the Pennsylvania town near which Mother's firm asserted itself, astringent and displaced. Behind the main building we could see Mother, a mattock swinging from her meaty fist, shooing the sows up the shuddering ramp and through the squealing back door. From the front door there wound a procession of local rustics, all dressed alike and all with interchangeably fat wives, carrying on their shoulders brown sacks of silk purses. Mother had discovered how to do it, had emasculated my worrying galloping Father with her passion for the firm, for making those corrosive silk purses.

I felt my mistress-wife's nails dig into the white puckering flesh of my thigh as if she were testing a turkey for firmness. "Not now," I said, "think of Mother."

I thought of Mother. I thought of how it would be, my weekend at the firm: Mother sweet and folksy to outward appearances, wrapped in her purple sweater like an ambulatory Passion narrative, picking at the small scab that always festered an eighth of an inch to the right of her lower lip.

I thought of how the light would strike the walls in the bedroom, cleansing and softening my city vision and reminding me that I was home at the firm, reminding me how the consecration of time had blessed my father's razor which corroded on the washstand and which I loved for its aquamarine mold. Nothing, not quiescence of lust, not the chthonic thwack thwack of flesh upon flesh, not the pulsing tumescence in the throat and the sweet strain along the cranial arch, appeases like sunlight on the bedroom walls.

I thought of my mistress-wife. How beautiful and stupid she is and how she satisfies me in bed. My wife is like a firm. She is broad, expansive in herself with innumerable small outbuildings, and, surveyed from a distance, gives an impression of a factory, of a wealth whose ownership imposes upon my tax report a deepening source of anxiety; entered, she yields a variety of offices, seeming now an infinite expanse of corridors winding and circulating to some sinister purpose or to some place where a minotaur god keeps court with a bull mask of beaten gold and with rubies for eyes; now she is a tight anteroom containing in itself all the miseries and inexperience of Plato's *Republic*; now she is a French boudoir with tiny chairs of tapestry and carved teak, with a groaning bed of satin; now she is the main converter where ponderous and infuriated machines grind the sows' ears and, by a process too marvelous and too metaphysical to explain, are converted into a silk so fine that it is like sunlight on the wall or in the bowl of my wife's navel; and then she is a receding passageway of fuchsia and puce where wall-to-wall carpet flows soundlessly between shadowy walls of pictures that are never observed. Over all, like the factory roof, elevated and witnessing, presses her awareness, a nonpossessive giving that protects me from the claustrophobic inclosures of life with Mother.

I came out of my reverie. There was Mother coming toward us, limping a little to possess me with her weakness, her purple sweater like a floating banner, her mattock hanging earthily in one limp hand. I turned the car around and raced to the speedway, leaving the firm and Mother behind. "What the hell," I said, "that's enough experience for one novel."

## Thursday, 21 October

I'VE JUST REREAD my little Updike parody. It's so awful that it's good. I'm going to send it to *Critic* as a lark. Maybe they'll want to print it instead of the review.

Later. I took Joan Caryl to lunch today. She has an At-Home every Thursday from three to six and, since we delayed at the Little Vienna, the guests arrived before we did. But we had a marvelous time; I never laugh so much as when I'm with Joan; she radiates a truly impressive Christian joy.

Much later; three in the morning. I lie awake remarking to God that I am very pleased he wants me to be a priest. It is

Pentecost right here in my cluttered little room and I keep a vigil of astonishment. Love is battering at the windowpane. Come in. Come in.

### Friday, 22 October

How TIRED you get when you're awake at three. You feel like you've held your breath too long under water.

Poor news. Macmillan finally wrote about my *Rubrics for a Revolution* (early version), which I left at their office in New York sometime in June. Their very cryptic note has as its main burden this sentiment: "You can well imagine that we are wondering why your second book of poems will not be handled by the house which so recently did your first book." I replied at once and with some heat: "No, I cannot well imagine that you are wondering, etc.," explained that the enclosed postage was for the immediate return of my manuscript, and concluded: "I find you incredible." That should take care of me forever with Macmillan. I wrote the note in annoyance and mailed it for the hell of it; I wanted the experience of telling a company the size of Macmillan to go jump. Glad I did, too.

Later. Maybe we all want the dignity of dying our own death, the privacy of our own suffering. But again, and awfully, the need to console people who are miserable is borne home to me. Two of my friends are leaving the Society: one at the urging of a psychiatrist and one because he has been wretched for several years. The latter of course is relieved to have made his decision, but the other one is a wreck. He doesn't want to leave; he does want to be a priest. God, what an awful situation to be in. And I, helpless to do or say anything to console him. I try to imagine how I'd feel if I were told now that I ought to leave. I certainly wouldn't want to listen to some idiot whining out condolences. So I try to respect his anguish, to understand. And I am all aches.

## Tuesday, 26 October

I AM THIRTY-ONE today. I feel seventy. Another step toward senility. If only the damned *Atlantic* would write saying they'll print my Kennedy poem, I could grow old happy. Frank Winters sent me a box of assorted cheeses. And a beautiful letter in which he mentioned that occasion when I forked a piece of cheese from my own plate on to his and, when he protested, I remarked: "No, take it, they'll think we're Christians." So here I sit, melted.

## Wednesday, 27 October

JAKE'S EXPERIMENTAL Mass is a thing of wonder. I finally attended it this morning and I must say I'm converted to belief in the true Jake. The liturgy of the word is longer than in an ordinary Mass because after the two Scripture readings anyone who wants to can make a comment. Some say a little prayer but most just remark on what strikes them most vividly about the epistle or gospel. There are some astonishing things said; the liturgy becomes a beautiful prayer session, honest and without pretense. The eucharistic liturgy is shorter than we're accustomed to because the Dutch canon (which Jake uses very effectively, I think) is without the many accretions that encumber the Roman canon. For the first time ever I saw what the outlines of the Mass really are: it is a meal, a sacred one. I rejoice that the liturgical commission in Rome has this Dutch canon at hand. Imagine making the Mass once again meaningful to people. Exciting.

## Tuesday, 2 November

I RECALL WHEN I used to resent God. It seemed to me that no matter what I did to please him, he was not satisfied. I felt he was making me bitter and resentful. What a truly sick concept of God I must have had and how fortunate I am to have shaken it. Where do we get ideas like this, I wonder. That God is somehow against us, waiting for us to step out of line and then gun us down. The infinite IBM noting all our errors, not giving a hoot about our noble efforts. The Big Eye watching us. We want to do things our way, work out our salvation according to our own plan. I wonder if that isn't the essence of Adam's failure: his refusal to let God love him the way God wanted.

Later. Reading about Camus this evening, I thought that the notion of suffering here on earth in order to enjoy an eternity of bliss makes no sense to me. We do not *buy* happiness any more than we buy love. And when that happiness *is* love and for eternity, then where does the suffering fit in? Is it a chance for us to love magnificently? Christly? I think so.

## Wednesday, 3 November

A BEAUTIFUL MORNING. Sharp fall weather with just enough bite in the air to keep you from spring leap-frogging and not too much bite to remind you that winter is almost here.

I've been thinking about Communion, mostly I think because of the real impressiveness of Jake's Mass. The Eucharist is a sacrament of union and a sacrament of faith; a perfect sacrifice. Jake tells me that all the sacraments serve to elicit a commitment to Christ by affirming the solidarity of the Mystical Body. I must confess I don't see exactly how that works. But in Communion we make an act of faith that this bread is indeed Christ and we receive that bread of oneness whose purpose is to bind us together, to make us cognizant of our unity in Christ and responsive to the demands that unity imposes on us. But the sarcrament of the Eucharist is more than this, isn't it? Isn't it Christ being with us personally. loving us by actually getting inside us, possessing us in a way all love attempts and only his love can accomplish? I must do a little study on what the Eucharist means.

Later. It's ironic, I suppose, that at the very moment I am coming to an awareness of the living reality of God in and around me, the "death of God" phenomenon is gaining peak popularity in this country. *The New Yorker* is running three long and really excellent articles on the death of God movement and *Time*, our leading theological journal, has just run a little feature on the four American death-of-Godders. Gabriel Vahanian, who teaches at Syracuse, is the one who interests me most. He's a littérateur and a cultural historian. His two books, *The Death of God* and *Wait Without Idols*, are impressive and appalling at once. Impressive because they do anticipate the advent of this "unconcerned God" movement in America. Appalling because they are more spirited than judicious, beginning with a premise and studying only those aspects of a complex reality which will verify the premise. Shoddy investigations of literature can prove anything. Careless analysis of cultural phenomena can do the same. But Vahanian was there first; he did have the initial insight.

I think what I'll do is this: take Vahanian's thesis that God has been disappearing in literature for the past fifty years and apply it to American literature of the past ten or so. Investigate novelists and playwrights—Bellow and Updike certainly, Albee and Williams, maybe others—to discover whether or not God (any old kind of God) any longer has significance to the American literary imagination. This would make a good seminar paper for Avery and would be publishable as well.

## Thursday, 4 November

AVERY HAS approved my seminar plan. Looks like a breeze. Perhaps *Critic* would be interested in publishing it. They found my little parody "Of the Firm" immensely amusing and will print it in the issue following my review of *Of the Farm*. And would you believe, they sent me thirty-five dollars for the dam-thing. I am astounded. And grateful. But I think somebody at *Critic* has a screw loose.

Later. Five minutes ago *Atlantic* returned "The Death of Kings" with a note saying that the parts they understand are admirable but the new final section still confuses them hopelessly. Well, resurrection never was an *in* thing in New England. I am grieved. But I refuse to publish the poem anywhere except in the *Atlantic;* I'll rewrite the whole thing and submit it next summer. I'm not crushed, it's just that I have this ache, see . . .

The same mail delivery brought a letter from David, all excitement about my writing talent. God, if only I had any. My stupid book reviews and my seminar papers and everything I try to do crumbles and dismays me and I want to run and hide.

## *Friday, 5 November*

TONIGHT I WAS WALKING outside, praying, thinking of being alone. I imagined myself standing on a low hill of asphalt (I was standing on one as a matter of fact—a curious commentary on the imagination) with the whole world with all reality sloping away from me. I felt nothing; just hollow and alone. And I thought that I have nothing but God, nothing, because love seemed incomprehensible and because nothing else matters but love. So I thought how I *do* have God and how I'll be ordained in June. And then I thought of the death of God theologians and I wondered if I really do believe in God. Immediately of course all the defenses rushed in, the fears and insecurities, but I pushed them back and looked as honestly as I could at the problem. Conscience kept getting in the way but I think I succeeded in looking beyond that to the possibility that maybe there is no God, that maybe I've projected him out of my deepest need. At least I faced that possibility. I decided that God does exist and moreover loves me and I spent some time then praying for an increase of faith and love. It was a grace-filled experience for me, I think. Perhaps it is unwise to flirt with temptations against faith; I do think it *is* really; I also think at some time in your life you have to challenge yourself on what matters most to you. The year of my ordination is making me a bit hyperconscious, I think, of my state before God.

### Friday, 12 November

WORK IS GOING splendidly: mind sharp, tongue fluent. Vahanian is a hard man to explain to people. He's given to making statements about "the radical immanentism of our cultural religiosity" when really what he means is that today we experience a cultural incapacity for God. I feel much of the time as if I'm translating from a language with which I have only dictionary familiarity.

### Sunday, 14 November

I SPENT MOST of yesterday in bed, fever-ridden and vomiting. Quite a performance. I seem to have the flu or something. It may be a reaction to Vahanian.

Jake said to me tonight when I mentioned that his red plush shirt struck me as a bit much: "You must face the fact that not everybody goes through life the way you do, deliberately trying to look *drab*." I laughed so much at his righteous indignation that I couldn't assess the truth value of his thoroughly enraged injunction.

### Sunday, 21 November

I'M JUST PULLING out of my disease though I've managed to work steadily through the whole thing. Almost done with the damned paper. The hardest part was getting Mr. Vahanian to agree with himself (sometimes I had the impression he was deliberately proposing a thesis in one chapter and refuting it in the next); the analysis of Bellow and Updike and Albee and Williams fell rather readily into place. If I do get this thing published, it will be my first prose in print . . . my first *real* prose, I mean. And then they'll all know I have no mind, that I've been operating all these years on a quick tongue and a bad eye.

## Monday, 22 November

JOHN KENNEDY is dead two years. I offered Mass today for him—in gratitude that he was our President for a thousand days, in confidence of peace for his soul.

## Monday, 29 November

MY SEMINAR TALK was on Friday and it was o.k. except that I was so nervous I thought I might choke. Avery seemed satisfied with it. Explaining something in Avery's presence always strikes me as though I'm trying to explain divinity in the presence of God. I boggle.

I gave the same talk to the community on Sunday night. Most dissatisfying. I lost my own point at one juncture, got all red, made people nervous. Reactions were mixed: the Dean told somebody it "was truly brilliant" whereas one of my contemporaries remarked that he had not come "to hear somebody talk off the top of his head. His attitude was flippant and the whole hour was devoid of content." So take that, L'Heureux.

What do I have to show for my month's work? A talk I can give to Newman Clubs, I suppose, and a paper I can probably publish. Doesn't seem proportionate to a month's investment.

## Thursday, 2 December

DEPRESSION. I am appalled at my lack of love, my *dislike* for so many of my fellow Jesuits. My ugliness is certainly a comment on the absence of charity in my life. I must pray for grace to stop hating, to start living a responsibly Christian life.

Later. Here's a splendid quotation from Sr. Charles Borromeo, CSC, in the December 1 *National Catholic Reporter*: "The sign of the Spirit is not agreement, but rather the love that is strong enough to support diversity. Where Christ's love is concretely effective in persons who live together, all are accepted, all are trusted, all are listened to, all are taken seriously as unique members of Christ." Way to go, Sr. Charles!

Which makes me think of Matthew. Matt Quinn. There we are each night at Jake's having tea and talking about celibacy or something and I know Matt is leaving the Society and he knows it and Jake doesn't. It's awful. I think Matt is wise in not talking about this with anybody. On the other hand I feel bad that Jake and Charlie Gonzalez don't know something I know and that there's a whole area of my thoughts that I can't in any way reveal to them. And worst of all, of course, is that I am no adequate consolation for Matt. I don't know what to say to him because I don't know why people leave the Society. For that matter I don't know why they enter. And I'm afraid to influence his decision. And I'm afraid he'll feel I'm not concerned. And I'm afraid he doesn't realize he's one of my closest friends in the world. So I dislike some Jesuits and can do nothing to solace the ones I love. (That's called life, Mr. L'Heureux.)

## Wednesday, 8 December

I'M TRYING to catch up on all the theology I have not done for the past month. It's desperate. I'll flunk everything in the January exams.

Meanwhile in an attempt to de-Romanize the Preface of the Mass—to get rid of the incredible abstractions of the Preface of the Trinity for instance—I have written a little hymn of praise and thanksgiving that conforms in every necessary way to what a Preface must be and, in addition, is comprehensible and readable and (Jake says) theologically sound. See if you like it.

PRIEST: Lift up your hearts.
PEOPLE: We have lifted them up to the Lord.
PRIEST: Let us give thanks to the Lord, our God.
PEOPLE: It is right and good.
PRIEST:
We give you praise and thanks, Almighty Father,
that you are God,
creator and father of all men.
You know us and so we live.
You love us and so we are your people.

Blessed are you, Father, that you have given us
this day and this hour.
Blessed are you, Father, in all the things you have made:
in plants and animals and men; in all the wonders of
your hands.
Blessed are you, Father, for the food we eat;
for bread and for wine; for laughter in your presence.
Blessed are you, Father, that you have given us
eyes to see your goodness in the things you have made,
ears to hear your word,
hands that we may touch and bless and understand.
We thank you, Father, that having made all things
you keep them and love them.
And so, with all your creation, we praise you through
our Lord, Jesus Christ, saying:
holy, holy, holy
Lord God of all things
heaven and earth are filled with your glory.
We bless your name.
Holy is He who reveals your presence among us.
We bless your name.

## Friday, 10 December

I AM COMING to face the fact that there will be no theology
learned in my room this year. I'm always involved in semi-
theology, something which unfortunately is of little interest to
examiners.

Between one and two hundred girls came to my poetry
reading last night at Notre Dame of Maryland. (I must learn
to estimate the size of my audiences more cannily.) They were
very sweet and "nice" and I don't think they knew what the
hell I was talking about most of the time. A beatific nun
asked me afterward, simply, sincerely: "Do you always read
everything with a sneer, Father?" *That* certainly knocked me
off my pins. How do we explain it? I must have felt they
weren't reacting and so took a rather defensive tone. That sort
of thing always comes through. I must keep that in mind the
next time I read to an all-female audience: they like pretty
things, nice things, and I mustn't let their reaction—no matter

what it is—betray me into being something I'm not. I wish I could go back tomorrow and do the reading fresh.

## Sunday, 12 December

THE FOLKS just left for home and I feel dreadful. Friday evening we were sitting at the motel talking about something inconsequential—oh yes, how kids take for an ideal whatever is proposed to them as an ideal—when I remarked that I, for one, had grown up in my brother's shadow and had spent the larger number of my adolescent years trying to live his life. Mother protested this with some heat and I, rising to the task of presenting evidence, began reciting incident after incident in which I seemed to play the role of second son. I convinced Mother and Dad that this emulation of Jerry had been a reality for me, a painful one, and they were of course deeply hurt. When, *when* will I ever learn? I was anxious only that the truth of the matter might appear, not that they should feel they somehow failed to give me the love I badly needed during adolescence. And yet the one thing I really convinced them of is the fact that they had tried to love me as best they could and went about it in the wrong way. Dumb. Dumb. Dumb. How could I have been so dumb. Parents are parents; what they have done is sacred; I wonder can I ever unconvince them now.

## Monday, 13 December

I JUST DID unspeakably poorly in my rites exam. Which is funny because, with my panic about doing things wrong in public, I've taken great care to know rites well. Fr. Fitzmyer rattled me right down to my shoes, kept at me with the same questions over and over; finally I told him I had gone blank and couldn't think. (I suspect he thinks I went blank years ago.) He asked me where I anoint someone who is dying; it was less a question than an accusation. I replied, uncertain and anxiety-ridden, that one anointed the five senses. He asked me what the five senses were. I told him, quite truthfully at that moment, I don't know. For some reason best known to God and possibly known to the examiners, they passed me. God, the things that happen to me!

## Thursday, 16 December

AN END OF GRIEF. I have been moping around since my folks left; I have been hateful and hard to get along with; I have been unchristian.

So today I went to Washington and had lunch with Joan. Then we went and bought an art book for Mother and Dad. And when I got home there was an incredible letter from somebody called Mr. J. Blazkiewicz at the Harvard Coop telling me in the most elaborate form that a book I had ordered would be sent to me soon and that meanwhile they wished me Merry Christmas and best wishes for the new year. So in the spirit of whimsy I wrote right back, thanking Mr. B. for his information and his good wishes and telling him I am now ashamed of having said to people that if I can't get into Yale I'll go to Harvard. I'm sure the Harvard Coop can cope with that: they'll conclude I'm merely mad.

## Sunday, 19 December

EACH SUNDAY one of our newly ordained priests says Mass for the patients at a nearby mental hospital. Charlie Gonzalez and a couple of other scholastics go with the priest and help with the singing, with keeping the patients in order, with maintaining some level of conduct short of the bizarre. There is one woman who, each Sunday before Mass begins, thunders into the room and greets Charlie with a great handshake, greets the others in the room with some glad word for the day, and then retires to the back row comfortably aware that everyone knows of her presence. Well, this morning she came in with special determination. Marching up to Charlie, she clicked her heels and shouted: "Heil, Hitler!" Charlie returned her "Heil, Hitler!" (not to respond is to reject and so he always responds), whereupon she greeted everyone there similarly and repeatedly until they responded. Then she asked Charlie if she might give him a gift. He told her she was very thoughtful, that it was very nice of her to think of giving him a gift. At once she whipped open this huge satchel she carries with her and from among an unbelievable stock of improbable items she withdrew two, presented them to Charlie, and gave him a resounding kiss on the cheek to accompany them. He looked in disbelief and embarrassment at her gifts: an ancient torn brassiere and a prayer book. Merry Christmas, Charlie.

### Monday, 20 December

FOR THE LAST three days I have done nothing but write Christmas cards. Two hundred twenty of them. Never again. I shall cut all Jesuits from my list next year, writing brief notes to those I'm closest to. This annual madness has to stop somewhere. Still, I suspect that next year I'll just go ahead and spend three days addressing cards. Madness.

After dinner this evening I took my many-colored canvas of last spring and glued to it a collage representing an immensely fat nude lady bending over a pitifully small stool. She is wearing only a hat, an enormous hat with a feather. I then painted her with blobs of oil ranging in color from salmon to purple. The result is hilarious. Everyone who sees it immediately goes into wild laughter, apologizes, and then laughs some more. It *is* funny. I'm delighted with it. Title: "Venus on the Fourth of July." The many colors of the background look like nothing so much as fireworks. Wonderful painting. Do you suppose I've missed my real vocation?

And another pleasant thing. After a long long period of silence I've begun writing poetry again. Time spent with Gabriel Vahanian and in "getting up the matter" that you've missed is not particularly productive of the best poetry. But now all at once I have three new poems. They're strange poems, different from all my others in a way I can't quite define. In any case it's nice to be entering on a new period, even if you don't know what that period is. Here's my favorite, "Thrasher."

### Thrasher

We are betrayed by what is true.
He leaped out from behind his face,
he always did, and said things
we don't say. Poor Thrasher.
Poor dim lodger. We grow to hate
the innocent we injure most;
the famished heart devours.

Winter dawned and settled in his eyes.
He stopped his leaping. When
all the guests went home at Christmas,
no one thought of Thrasher who sat
and hugged his toes. We were relieved
when at the end he took the hint
and passed on quietly. Rest in peace,
Thrasher, you poor leaping toe-hugging
innocent slob.

## Thursday, 23 December

LOOKING BACK in the journal, I discover that unaccountably I neglected to record the good news that Macmillan, immediately after I hit them with that persnickety fresh letter, wrote me apologetically and said they would like to submit my book for a contract if I was willing. Of course I was willing, especially since the continued silence from Doubleday grew more and more to resemble the sound of one hand clapping. And today, in memory of Scrooge, it happened. Macmillan wrote saying they are returning my manuscript. "It has come to my attention recently that Doubleday still has the option on your book, and that you have been negotiating with them for a contract. Under these circumstances we, of course, do not wish to keep your manuscript any longer." Whomp. So that takes care of that—and, I wouldn't be surprised, my writing career, short-lived and inglorious as it was. Now Doubleday will write and say they don't like my double-dealing (as a matter of fact, I am *not* under option to Doubleday any longer, at least not as I understand the term option, and negotiations for a contract have consisted principally in my waiting during the last year for them to tell me what they think) and so will I kindly peddle my papers elsewhere. And then no major company in New York will come within printing distance of me. Happy Christmas, Mr. L'Heureux. Oh yes, and New Year.

## Sunday, 26 December

YESTERDAY was the nicest Christmas I can remember in the Society. Prayerful and joyous and kind. Thank you.

## Tuesday, 28 December

IN MY OWN WAY, I've begun to pray again. It might be just the good feelings induced by a cozy Christmas (my first, I think, in the past eleven years), or it might be that the Spirit is once again claiming some small corner of my soul: whatever it is, I rejoice to be praying again. There's not so much formal prayer as I should like, but I do have good talks with God now and then. We'll settle for that.

Naomi wrote this morning. Doubleday has nixed *Rubrics for a Revolution*. Somehow I'm not in the least surprised and somehow I'm not very disappointed. I feel free, whatever that means. Naomi explains that *Dandelions* has not sold well, though fourteen hundred copies were bought in the first six months, which, for a book of poems, is rather exceptional. So I don't quite understand. She concludes her letter: "You always tell me that you are strong, philosophic and not easily wounded, but I never have quite believed it. All I can say is, give us another chance if you can and when you can and personally I don't think the sale of *Dandelions* is *at all* bad." This is a chance to prove to myself at least that I don't go to pieces over a rejection. Pieces, maybe, but I do stay intact and rational (pretty much) and like that. So I wrote Naomi a nice soothing letter in which I told her everything was fine about the book and not to worry.

I then went on to tell her some of the good luck I've been having lately with poems, the flourishing condition of my heatlh, the arrival of our superduper new baker. So that should cheer her. She *is* good and she did publish me at a time nobody would. And—furthermore—I'm not being a martyr; the truth is, I'm not all shocked up over this. I'm a phoenix; keep your eye on those ashes, baby. Here I come.

## Wednesday, 29 December

LATE LAST NIGHT a good friend of mine explained why he's been acting a bit strained: he's leaving the Society in a day or two. All day I've been dragging around trying to be cheery, but all I can think of is the waste and the loss and how love's chief labor seems to be pain. Him, the other one, and Matt still deciding (what is a foregone conclusion). I've prayed more frequently of late and that's something to be grateful for. Everything keeps reducing to essentials: God's wisdom, our folly, etc. It's enough to drive one metaphysical.

## Friday, 31 December

NEW YEAR's EVE. And the place is really hopping. Five are watching television, four are playing bridge, everybody else is madly typing up term papers due on the third of January.

So many wonderful things have happened in 1965. My parents feel they have somehow grievously failed me when I was growing up, one of my friends has found me too much to cope with (and I him), another is about to leave the Society, Macmillan has written me off their lists forever, Doubleday has rejected the book which I thought they had all but bought, Carolyn Kizer writes telling me that all my poems of the last year fail because they substitute violence for inspiration.

On the other hand, I still have those princes of the earth, my friends. David and Frank and Ned, who are off priesting somewhere, Jake the True Theologian ("Let us rise and kill the conservatives!"), Charlie and Matt and Ed Glynn, James and Justin and Ken and on and on and on. What would I do without them? And I *am* going to be ordained in a little over five months. And my parents still love me despite my stupidity. And somehow, miraculously, I'm happy. To hell with grief. L'Heureux shall overcome.

## Saturday, 1 January

I BROUGHT in the New Year well, talking until almost two o'clock this morning with Ed Glynn. Ed is one of those saintly men who is brilliant and athletic and nevertheless accepted by everyone but whom no one, you suspect, really knows well. I know him well, am richer for knowing him. He says astonishing things with an utter ingenuousness that knocks me out. I hope that, since I seem to be cracking up emotionally and psychologically with the advent of ordination, I won't be a bother to him. I'm turning into rather a mess.

## Sunday, 2 January

ALL AFTERNOON I've groped toward a poem beginning "A darning egg is good of course but scarcely what I had in mind." Nothing has come of my scratchings. But if I never do another poem, I'm going to do this one—if for no better reason than to get that damned darning egg out of my mind, where it's been lobbling about over the past month.

What is it I'm trying to say about loving someone? That when someone loves you what they really love is what you aspire to be; they love you for your desires? They love the self you want to become? And by loving you they help to make you that self. Yes, that's it. You do become good, you do become what you desire. If love compels, it does so by liberating. You are suddenly freed to become what you had always hoped you might be but never really dreamed you would be. Is it the disappearance of the last illusion or the proof that even illusions have value?

*Tuesday, 4 January*

BARRY LEFT the Society of Jesus today. And it's raining. I've been in somewhat of a grump all afternoon, sorry to see him go, sorry that such an excellent man will not become a fellow priest. Just when life has become so livable around here, what with an excellent rector and an interested faculty and everybody trying to live like Christians, suddenly all my friends are pulling out. Good men. A shame.

Tonight I learned that my rites exam was indeed the disaster I thought at the time. Fr. Fitzmyer flunked me (to be fair to him, I *did* deserve to flunk), the other examiner passed me, the Faculty Secretary—who has the power to do so—resolved the toss-up by passing me. Dutifully I trotted in to thank the other examiner for a show of charity I've not met in other similar situations (though thank God there's *never* been a situation quite like my rites exam) and he asked me how things were going in general. I told him I was getting a bit nervous, perhaps because of my approaching ordination and all; damned if he didn't launch into a spiel about how I ought to look into the sources of my nervousness in case it might be I have some reservations about becoming a priest. O God, how do these things happen? I told him I had been through a number of vocation crises over the past years and had decided quite coldly and rationally and with the guidance of my spiritual father that I wanted to be a priest and, since Superiors seem willing to carry on with me as I am, intend to become one. He was nice, of course; anxious only that I not rush into something I haven't thought about. Well, maybe I shouldn't be ordained, but unless an angel comes and tells me so—straight out and in English—I intend to be priested. God is humorous and will prevail.

Later. That is what we are, of course: a summary of all we have been, of all that has happened to us, of our love and our hate and our suffering. More than that, yes. But that certainly —the walking compendium. So there will be some profit in reading my journal during tertianship; discovering who I've been, I might also come to understand who I am, who I might become. I'll write nothing except a retreat and an occasional poem. No major projects. And no journal.

### Wednesday, 5 January

WELL, YES, as a matter of fact, I have finished the darning egg poem. Who could have guessed way back then that it would be about Ed Glynn, or me, or whoever it's really about? Rather good poem, I think.

### The Gift

A darning egg is good
    Of course
      Though not exactly what you had in mind.
        He meant
        To give you
      Something better. Growing up,
          He learned soon to ask for bread
          And take the offered scorpion.
  Dusk settles;
  It is all the same.

What from the first
    You loved
    Was his outrageousness, you thought.
      After, you
      Were pleased
      With his pitiful austere desires.
        He had grown up in desire, always.
        He woke at night, your name
  Upon his lips.
  You slept, smiling.

A darning egg is good
    For socks.
    Lodgers make repairs that slip
      The mind.
      They must.
      And you and he are lodgers—never
        More than that—waiting to move on
        In fear and insufficient wisdom

Groping to
A kind of truth,

A home, a you to love
        For good
With talk and laughter and desire.
        He meant
        To give you
        More than this. Much more. But
                Take it anyway; you will remember
                Him, his one last foolishness.
A darning egg
Is good, and serves.

### Saturday, 8 January

FOR THE PAST five days I have been supremely happy. Grace.
It's ironic that I am studying for a midyear exam in grace and
predestination with no idea what either of them means at the
very time when I am smothered in grace and perfectly aware
that whatever predestination means it's completely tied up
with God's loving presence to you. He is present to you, in
you. And we rant about the great theories proposed by the
great minds of those far-away great centuries and I don't know
what the hell anybody's talking about. But I do know that
grace goes stalking about among all kinds of crazy and unattractive people making them less crazy and quite attractive.
Me, for instance.

What's happened is quite clear in one respect. I have en-
countered Christ in one of my fellow religious. Like meeting
Ned or Frank or David or that ethereal lady sculptor, Joan.
But different. Because each one of them is himself, just as Ed
Glynn is himself. All good. Open. Pouring out Christ in all
directions. I am privileged to know him. The whole epiphany
makes me pray more, makes me so much easier to get along
with, makes me go out to people I normally avoid. God is
really something: You are; You knock me out (when You
want to); with one jump I could clear this house.

Later. Look what I did. After months in the desert I have

hit miles of oasis, and here is the most joyful glorious happify-
ing poem I've ever written.

### The Unlikely Prophet

Struck by the lash
of your eye
and your soft laugh
I leaped over the house

twice, maybe three times,
like somebody in Chagall.
A happy comet all
bright blues and reds

and streaming more joy
than philosophy. An end
to grief: fireworks at ten
this evening and at midnight

we will drink beer
and be riotous with God
who likes a good time
too. I will say

implausible things. You
will understand, ignite
your eyes and laugh.
Our words will make

the black sky sunrise
with a host of roman
candles. Clear out. Run
for your lives. The house

will catch on fire. They
will dance upon the roof,
the whole damned crowd
of them, seeing that

it does make sense.
Chagall will weep—
fulfilled—as Jesus sings
triumphant in the flames.

## Monday, 10 January

OH GOD, I'm not going to survive till June. Yesterday I took off first thing in the morning to Georgetown, where I spent a large part of the day with Frank Winters, who is serving as assistant Chaplain at the Georgetown University Hospital.

On the way to the hospital I met a former student, we talked, I leaped up and down. (I leap up and down . . . at age thirty-one.) A dignified gray-haired man looked at me with apprehension as I stood there in the street waving my arms and carrying on; I looked back; he looked; I looked. Voilà. John McGuinn, my college roommate, whom I haven't seen in twelve years. He lives two minutes off Georgetown campus. I'm going to look him up next time I'm downtown. It was good to see John even if he did catch me performing at my poorest.

The day with Frank was superb. We talked about prayer and helping people and preaching and what Christianity is all about. He's the first person who made me feel, *understand*, it wasn't such a bad thing to be me. Do you know what I mean? I hate being me, hate to inflict myself on others, and yet he made me feel it was all right, that he liked having me inflict myself on him. Ed makes me feel the same way. Don't misunderstand; I'm not saying these men flatter me to the point that I forget I'm a crashing bore; I'm saying they value me for the Christ in me, the Christ who uses even me to tell his poor children he loves them. It was a Christ day.

I can't remember half the startling things Frank said. He mentioned that the raising of Jairus' daughter from the dead demonstrates the power of love and forewarns scoffers that at the last judgment we shall be asked, each one of us, Whom have you raised from the dead? Whom have you loved back to life?

He mentioned also the parallel scenes of Mary Magdalen washing Christ's feet and drying them with her hair and Christ at the Last Supper washing the feet of the disciples. Taken in conjunction with the fact that the first recorded appearance of the resurrected Christ is to Magdalen, these parallel scenes describe symbolically the center of the Christian message:

service out of love. The consequence (I avoid "reward" because this kind of service doesn't understand the concept of reward) of Christian service is the vision of the glorified Christ, who shines into you, out of you.

One last thing. Immediately after the Resurrection we find Christ summoning his crowd to breakfast at the lakeside, a breakfast he himself has prepared for them. That's it again and again: to love by giving and serving.

I'm overwhelmed. There is the further problem of *living* this life, a more difficult but even more exciting prospect than thinking about it. I can leap over buildings.

## Wednesday, 12 January

IT's ALL VERY WELL to be wide open about people you love and what their love means and what Christ has to do with all this. It's quite another thing to publish your lucubrations on these matters. Isn't it an awful lot like undressing in public? Admittedly, you may undress to show the teeth marks where you were bitten by the tiger; nonetheless you're still naked. Further, why show your tiger-scars? I like to think people should know that priests are people and have emotions and experience personal crises. But should people know? Is it possible to let them know without terrible misunderstandings, without their being scandalized? Maybe this whole month should be dropped right out of the journal.

## Thursday, 13 January

DOGMA EXAM lasts for two and a half hours tomorrow and here I've spent the whole day reading Peter Fransen's *Divine Grace and Man*. If I had plowed through the thing a couple of months ago, I'd now know more about grace than anybody in the whole world . . . give or take a few thousand theologians. But this is not the time for building a background; it's the time for putting the decorations on your battlements, polishing shields, checking armor. Tomorrow, total war. God help me.

Grace is the life of God within us. It is a life of love, a gift from God to us which allows us to return his love, to live in his love, to live *in* him. Grace is the prelude to a life of glory, an assumption into intimacy with God. I'm so caught up with this that it doesn't matter much that I'll do poorly in to-morrow's exam. I should pray for the grace to pass and have done with "getting up the matter."

## Sunday, 16 January

DOGMA EXAM on Friday came off rather well and Scripture yesterday wasn't nearly so bad as I had feared. It seems un-reasonable that the older I get the more I go to pieces in the presence of exams.

I gave a poetry reading last night at St. Steven's Church in Washington. It was very well attended, the best reading I've given yet. The audience was literate and wonderfully responsive, I read more humanly than I have in the past (usually I am brittle, glacial), and best of all my friends were there: Frank Winters and Charlie Gonzalez and Ed Glynn. Afterward we had a party at Joan's, where we met all sorts of mad and de-lightful people and where I felt that if things were any better I'd have to flap my arms and fly away. Marvelous.

And tonight at haustus I asked Fr. Dulles why he didn't finish his beer and he responded that since reading the auto-biography of the Little Flower he has tried to imitate her by always leaving a little beer in the bottle. Fabled man.

Tomorrow I leave for New York.

## Thursday, 20 January

NEW YORK is still up there. I've just returned from three smash-ing days in the wicked city; the main purpose of my visit was to take the revised standard version of *Rubrics for a Revolu-tion* to Macmillan. It all came about this way. A week or so ago, mid-afternoon, I flung myself upon the sack in a deep gloom: the writing career finished before it ever got started, both Doubleday and Macmillan thinking I'm a little crooked. Mentally I sorted out dates of rejections, etc., and came to the astonishing conclusion that at the time Macmillan contacted Doubleday they both must have been serious about my book: otherwise Macmillan wouldn't have bothered investigating my sales, otherwise Doubleday wouldn't have bothered saying I was negotiating a contract with them. So if Mac was once interested, it probably still would be. Swallowing my pride, a deep swallow, I got on the phone and called Miss Bartelme at Macmillan. Being a lady, she chewed me out in a ladylike manner, but it was a good firm chew nonetheless. She had talked to Naomi and was under the impression I was playing one company off against the other for the best contract available. She agreed, with no great enthusiasm, to look again at *Rubrics*. So I took the manuscript to New York, left it at the desk, and now begin once again the endless vigil. But at least now there's a possibility of getting the damned thing published.

While in the city (there's only one city), I attended the ballet with David Morrissy, who is working as chaplain in some New York hospital. And I went with various other friends to *The Royal Hunt of the Sun,* which is the most gorgeous show in the world and a pretty good one too, to *Hello, Dolly!* which is fun, to *The Persecution and Assassination of Marat as Performed by the Inmates of the Asylum of Charenton Under the Direction of the Marquis de Sade,* which is admirably described in its title. *Marat-Sade* is the most startling theater piece I've ever seen. At least twenty types of madness are unforgettably delineated by the patients while they are acting out the murder of Marat as an early venture in dramatic therapy. More chilling than the sight of a primitive insane asylum is the author's suggestion that the whole world is a madhouse and that all our revolutions are projections of our radical instability. Growth is impossible. Sanity is perversion. Needless to say, the play is disquieting. And here I am back at Woodstock.

### Sunday, 23 January

PERHAPS GOD CONDEMNS us to the heaven we had imagined; perhaps precisely that is our purgatory.

### Tuesday, 25 January

WALKING IN THE SNOW today, our first snow and somewhat unsatisfactory by its crustiness, I tried to formulate what seems to be lacking in the classroom presentation of the Beatific Vision. (What's really lacking, I suppose, is any philosophic orientation on my part.) One can't think about the mystery of the Beatific Vision until one has spent years in the antecedent mystery of God's personal love for each of us. If I could realize what it means or how it could be that God loves me, then I might be able to talk about the mystery of the vision of God.

Perhaps we should begin from an analogy with human love. At the moment in which two of us are closest, in which we love to the point where our individualities almost cease and we melt into each other and nearly become one another, at that moment I realize that you love me unfathomably and that, though I would gladly, I cannot *become* you. I am aware of your love, aware of the desire to become you, aware that you— though completely mine—are unalterably other. This is the moment of ecstasy: presence before the mystery of love. Presence and mystery and love.

From this pale and momentary human shadow we can speculate upon the divine reality which lasts forever. It's a way of beginning.

### Thursday, 27 January

WE HAD an English luncheon today: they emptied the refrigerator of all leftovers, covered them with a crust, cooked, and served. Very mysterious.

Walking today, Justin told me this story which he insists is true. Two nuns studying for degrees at Columbia University were living last summer in a very small apartment down around Sixteenth Street. One of them fed a stray dog which promptly moved in with the Sisters and in three days died. What do you do with a dead dog in a hot summer in a tiny New York apartment? They phoned some dog-disposal agency which informed them that, since it was Friday afternoon and everybody was about to go home, the nuns had the option of keeping their dog in the refrigerator until Monday or of bringing it to the disposal place at once. They chose the latter.

Unwilling to be seen carrying a rather large and very dead dog down the street in her arms, one of the nuns dug up an ancient battered suitcase into which, by force of much pushing and folding, they managed to fit the dog. They decided the subway was the cheapest, quickest means of getting doggie uptown. While they were lugging the suitcase to the subway, a nice young man in his mid-twenties saw them, took pity on them, and offered to carry the bag for them. He was astonished at its weight; the nuns offered no clue to its contents. He engaged them in chat and not only took them to the subway but provided them with tokens as well. He was charming and helpful. They were charmed and grateful. The train came, they all got on, they chatted some more. The train stopped, admitted people, and just as the doors were about to close, the young man leaped up, grabbed the suitcase, and disappeared with the stolen dead dog in the useless suitcase. He was last seen trying to run *up* a *down* escalator with this prodigious weight dangling from his hand. People on the train were surprised to see nuns laugh so hard in public.

The story is funny, I suppose. But the part that strikes me most funny is the part we know nothing about: the young man five years later glancing suspiciously at every nun with a suitcase, confident in his knowledge that she is only part of an enormous dead-animal-smuggling ring. In what could the poor young man ever believe again?

### Monday, 7 February

LOTS OF THINGS have been happening and I've been giving myself the pleasure of letting them happen and then reflecting upon them like normal people instead of rushing to the machine to record them badly and haphazardly for a posterity that doesn't wish to hear about them anyway.

I've been praying and thinking, learning how to love a little less selfishly, beginning to see that, since I'm so much more awful than I had suspected, the only sane reaction is not to think about it . . . or to think about it less.

I wrote to Ken Hughes, S.J., tonight. Strange how with some friends we grow older and—although it's not supposed to work this way—grow together. Sometimes we meet people when we are not ready for them; we don't understand that all love involves death and that only the selfless love survives. But that sort of frustrated encounter becomes part of our past and hence part of our present grace. Kenneth is part of my present grace. He is good.

Love is learned. Faith is chosen. The dark *must* be light enough. Sometimes paradox makes your head spin, doesn't it?

And here I am hanging on a twig waiting for spring to blossom me, an unlikely butterfly wrapped in brown uncomfortable leaves. I'll survive, of course, because I am indestructible. Nearly.

### Tuesday, 8 February

I'VE JUST FINISHED reviewing that enormous (1274 pages) anthology, *American Poetry*, for the Boston *Herald*. I enjoyed reviewing the book since it gave me an opportunity to fulfill an obligation and at the same time take my licks at some American poets. Poe, for instance, has done inestimable harm to the estate of American poetry with his jingles. And Whitman at his best was never more than an overdeveloped ego attached to a bellows. The review says: "No poet in history has carried on so hysterically at such length about so little—himself." And

I pointed out what is becoming increasingly evident to a number of people: that poetry of the last sixty years demonstrates
beyond the powers of criticism that, with the singular exception of Emily Dickinson, there *is* no American poetry until
1900.

The review makes rather pleasant reading. I sometimes
wonder if perhaps my vocation as a writer is not to be a
poet or dramatist but merely to spend the rest of my life
passing comment on what real writers are writing. What a
dreary possibility.

## Wednesday, 9 February

THE MOST PECULIAR thing happened this afternoon. Fr. Mc-
Naspy, S.J., invited me to Fairfield University for the weekend
to discuss with a number of Jesuit artists what the agenda
should be for a summer conference on the status of the arts
in the Society of Jesus. I had to see Fr. Dulles to ask if I might
be excused from our Friday seminar. He was willing. But I
delayed for a moment to talk about the seminar and he began
to tell me about Altizer, whom he saw last night on television.
To my astonishment he began to act out Altizer's performance.
Avery acting. Imagine. Leaping out of his chair, he waved his
arms like misbegotten semaphores and shouted at full voice:
"Of course I don't believe in God. No sensible man today
could possibly believe in God. That's what Christ has done:
liberated us from servitude to every alien creed." He raved on
wilder and wilder until the door flew open and the priest who
is Avery's neighbor rushed in to see if I needed help. They're
old buddies and evidently flail away at one another like this
not infrequently; my embarrassment quotient, however, isn't
up to sustaining anything quite so brisk. I damn near died.

I told Father later that I would write an account of his disgraceful conduct and entitle the story "Avery's Recantation."
He scarcely thought I was serious.

Later. I wrote a verse tonight called "The Foundling." It's
about me as poet. As poet, I'm a foundling. Left on the door-
step of a generation that is interested, at its best, in the work

of proven greats—Auden and Eliot and Lowell—and at its worst in those cryptic things that appear in *Poetry*, word jugglings by poets who have elected each other to an in-group both sterile and exclusive. Am I feeling bad for myself? I hope not. I've got too much to rejoice about to waste good spirits on self-pity.

## Thursday, 10 February

WEATHER IS CLEAR and cold today. And silent. This afternoon I was looking out my window at an endless stretch of winter and it was so unearthly quiet that my mind conjured up a lady with blue hair and a long white gown running, hysterical, through the snow. Nothing strange about L'Heureux.

## Friday, 18 February

I HAVE BEEN noisily ill with flu since I last wrote. Fortunately the peculiar virus didn't take up total occupation in my withered corpus until after I returned from Fairfield; once it did, it was thorough: unremitting vomiting, diarrhea, a roaring fever, and even delirium for one vivid night. Poor show. I know I'm well again because I feel mean.

On the trip up to Fairfield I stopped in New York to have lunch with an ex-Jesuit. He wasn't available and neither was anybody else (I called four other friends), so without any hope either of her being in the country or her being willing to have lunch with me, I rang up Muriel Spark. She said she would be delighted to lunch with me.

She is the most charming, unaffected woman. Somewhere between thirty and fifty (who can tell, besides other women?), she is very tiny and very pretty with a vivacity and quiet wit that immediately put me at ease. She never once gave the impression of trying to please me, trying to make me think what a good or interesting or intelligent person she is, trying in any way to make an impression. That comes, perhaps, from being aware who you are. She knows, and is at home with, who she is. Thinking back to the lunch—which lasted between two and three hours—I am amazed at how much we talked and how at one we were. We hadn't, after all, ever met before.

She said so many delightful things. I asked her what she planned to do now and she replied that she would write another book: "A small book. I'll begin next Tuesday. At eleven." (Like an idiot, I was so delighted with the notion of beginning a book on a given day at a given hour, that I forgot to ask the title.) She told me also that she sometimes gets ugly letters from mothers complaining that Spark books are corrupting their teen-age daughters. "I usually write back saying 'I showed your letter to His Grace who reads all my books before publication and he was most shocked at your reaction . . .' so that at least they have the satisfaction of knowing their complaints were reviewed by an unidentified prelate."

The most wonderful thing she told me, though, was how she came to write her first novel. She had published a number of stories in some rather good English periodicals but was hampered from doing any major writing by reason of having to work all day to support life and soul. One day a literary friend of hers was lunching with Graham Greene, who happened to mention some rather good stories he had seen recently by somebody named Muriel Spark. Friend said he knew her, that she was good, that she needed a patron to support her if she was ever to find time to turn out that first novel. More chat, new subjects, end of lunch. The next day Greene phoned the friend to say he would like to be the patron. Then —imagine—for the next year and a half he sent a weekly check to Muriel via the friend; no meetings; no communication of any kind. At the end of the year and a half she had published her first novel, which was selling busily, and was well into her second, so she wrote Greene and thanked him for his help and explained that she didn't need it any longer. That was the end of their acquaintance. Then some years later they met at a party, and though they have never met since, they now correspond regularly. That sort of thing doesn't happen even in movies. Besides illuminating the glory and the necessity of charity, it indicates that Greene has one sharp eye for young talent.

Let me see now. Fairfield. The meetings on Friday and Saturday were satisfying beyond anything I could have imagined. Fifteen Jesuit artists gathered and not one nut in the bunch. Think of that. We all got on well together. There was no griping or story-telling about how "I as artist have been persecuted." Discussions were smooth, eminently civilized.

We talked about a number of things, everything really, but mostly about how we might most effectively operate as artists within the Society of Jesus, how best establish ecumenical links with practicing artists outside the Society, how we might benefit each other as artists just by knowing one another. We talked, rather excitedly too, about the possibility of having a house in New York where we might live together under our own Superior and work in our field with other artists—musicians, painters, dramatists, etc. This house would be both a place to work and a place to go when you can't work; cross-influence of the arts, shared enthusiasms, community of interests—so much is possible in a house like this. There are, moreover, precedents for such a center. We concluded that, if we meet as a group several times each year, our Superiors will grow so accustomed to the notion of Jesuit artists that there will be no panic later when we broach the idea of a residence in New York. This sounds very ambitious. It's one thing, an easy one, to get together and get excited over a future that's rosy; it's quite another thing to exercise the necessary patience and tact and selflessness to establish the grounds for such a future. Still . . . is there really any good reason why we today cannot accomplish what was done so effectively by the Jesuits of the sixteenth century?

Meanwhile, back to reality and the pile of work I missed while planning tomorrow.

### Saturday, 19 February

Rev. Father Provincial of New England wrote me today granting me all the wild permissions I requested some time ago. They are, in order of astonishment:

1. to postpone tertianship for three years

2. to spend those three years at Yale (or Harvard or Princeton or wherever they'll take me) getting my Ph.D. in English
3. to apply to Yale this September for the following year
4. to go to Yale for a week at Easter in order to check out the English department and see if Yale is the wisest choice
5. to spend a week at Fairfield this summer for the Jesuit artists' rendezvous.

Though I gave Father well-thought-out reasons for all these requests, I never for a moment expected an affirmative answer to all of them. I laugh. I dance. I jump up and down in place.

### Sunday, 20 February

SOMETHING HAS GOT to be done about the liturgy. Usually I attend Jake's Mass (and usually that is an experimental one of great simplicity and beauty), but weekends, when Jake is out on call in parishes, I have to go to the main chapel. The contrast is astounding. At Jake's Mass, we not only attend, we participate, we are involved; the Sacrifice, while remaining Christ's offered in the person of the priest, is ours also because we are caught up in it. But at the community Mass in the main chapel, we watch. We sit out there and watch. At the right time we go up and receive communion and then we sing a hymn and make our thanksgiving. But it's all so perfunctory, all so objective and cold. I don't want to turn the Mass into an emotional jag but, my God, I would like to feel involved in it. Something has got to be done. I would begin by putting everything in English. Then take out of the Canon the many accretions of the centuries, especially those dark ones when salvation was so often "achieved" by heaping up good works and by the multiplication of prayers. Then smooth the language so that it can be well *said* as well as read. Then simplify so that the words are plain and basic and readily comprehensible to anybody. Then smooth again. Then pray.

## Thursday, 24 February

VOWS ASK MUCH MORE of a man than may appear. The vow of chastity, for instance, asks not only that a man abstain from sexual activity which is perfectly legitimate for other men (married men, perhaps even bachelors) but also that in his deepest self he surrender to Christ all hope of ever possessing or being possessed. That most natural desire of every man to give himself to another, to one other whom he can hold through a long and terrible dark night, must be quietly put down again and again and again. Thus one risks with a vow of chastity the danger of never becoming a man, a real one.

The whole core of the person depends for its flowering upon being able to give and be given to in love. And though for a religious, giving and being given to always remain possible within certain confined areas, one must keep in mind that those areas are indeed confined—circumscribed by prudence and necessity. Loving God is not the same as loving another human person; with God the physical remains unsatisfied. Constantly to force back physical demonstrations of affection is to risk killing emotion and response, to risk the glacial heart and the hard unfeeling stare. Only Christ; no other. And sometimes the emptiness within the circle of my arms is almost more than I can bear.

## Friday, 25 February

READING THE ENTRY above I can't help thinking I've slighted the other side of the picture: that this sacrifice of giving the self and being given to by other selves is the entrance to knowledge of a hundred other ways to love, a hundred other ways to grow in personal response and responsibility. Married couples my own age are frequently more mature than I in many respects; they have (almost all of them) accomplished more than I in terms of building a life, but I *do* think I know as much about living and loving as any of them, that I love more people more complexly than they, that I am more mature in responsibility to others. This is not to say my way of life is better. It is to say (softly and to myself) that to worry about the human risk chastity involves is to overlook the human riches it offers. And I *am* rich. Like Francis, I am the King's son.

Later. *Atlantic* bought "The Gift." To celebrate I just mailed *Critic* my death of God paper . . . entitled "On The Eighth Day, God Died." He is glorified in all his implausible creatures.

## Saturday, 26 February

WHAT AM I doing at my desk this quarter of three in the afternoon? Staring at my books and thinking I ought to be doing something. I've been sitting here for forty-five minutes. For forty-five minutes I have *felt* nothing. It's a good image of death: sitting at your desk, suspended, thinking you should be doing something.

Matt Quinn told me this evening that he has definitely decided to leave the Jesuits. Thank God that at last he has made the decision. He is so good and so honest that he agonized all these months over a decision that more and more came to be a foregone conclusion to me. Matt will make an excellent husband and father, an excellent Christian. He is good. To think that a little over a year ago he asked me if I had ever thought of leaving the Society and I replied I had, at least twice a week, and he replied that he had never thought of it at all, and I—incredulous—suggested it perhaps was about time he did.

This makes how many of my friends who have left one or two years before ordination? Too many. And I, the least likely and the least suitable, stay right here as if my being ordained were not an outrage. I am the poorest religious I know, knocking hell out of the virtues and doing a pretty rough job on the vows as well. I console myself that God knew what a lemon he was getting when he chose me; he's stuck with me now.

I cannot afford the luxury of despair.

## Sunday, 27 February

I AM SAYING the rosary every day during Lent—asking the Lady to help me be a good priest, thanking her for getting me through these twelve years of preparation.

Books. I never mention any more what books I've been reading. Brecht, T. Williams, Bellow, Iris Murdoch, Elizabeth Bowen, Shirley Jackson: who cares. And buckets of poetry. And of course theology. Some Rahner for the course on grace, a lot of Protestant theologians for the Dulles seminar, a little here for medieval history, very little there for Old Testament. The month of May, as always in the Society of Jesus, will be a nightmare. But May is a long way off and the days are very bleak.

## Tuesday, 1 March

THIS IS THE WAITING month. Everything is waiting for a little stir, a little warmth, a little excitation of the blood and then rain and then we'll all burst into bloom. Trees and butterflies and stodgy Jesuits. But that's later. We're just waiting now. And drinking tea.

I practice Mass right after breakfast each morning, that is to say I practice from the Our Father to the end. Fr. Gallen, who teaches us rites, has assigned me to demonstrate this section of the Mass in class on Friday. What surprises me most is how slowly the ritual gestures of the Mass become my own; I would have thought that after all these years so much of the Mass would have become second nature. Not so.

*Critic*, God bless it, bought my death of God piece and paid me two hundred dollars for it. Isn't that immoral? I sent it to them last Friday, received their check this morning. How can this be? Did they even bother to read it? Well, I'm more than pleased. A delight like this makes life, even in the waiting month, seem so much less desperate.

Later. Our library finally purchased a copy of Muriel Spark's *The Mandelbaum Gate*. Reading the first chapter, which I had already read this past summer when it appeared in *The New Yorker,* I am amazed all over again that anybody can write with such wit and economy and that peculiar elegance that looks like fluency. Her writing is even more astonishing, of course, when I consider that she never rewrites anything. Look at the power of this little section:

"It does seem a bit unfair," said Freddy mildly. "It seems a bit extreme, when a couple of grown-up people—"

"Do you know," said this passionate spinster in a cold and terrifying voice, "a passage in the Book of the Apocalypse that applies to your point of view?"

And she proceeds to destroy him with the passage about being neither hot nor cold I shall vomit you out of my mouth. Powerful stuff. I'd give anything, almost, to write like that.

## Wednesday, 2 March

I HAVE FILLED the larder with good things for a going-away party for Matt. The days when the departing religious slipped out under cover of dark are gone forever. He is our friend and we're going to try to show him that. Tea tonight will be one of the highest teas ever.

## Thursday, 3 March

MATT LEFT the Society today. I drove him to the train station with a couple of others from last night's party. We were all jolly and bright-spirited and felt sick to death when he finally left.

There is one awfully good memory though. The party last night, which was an unmitigated success and rather a scandal to those on the corridor who were trying to get some sleep, reached a pitch of hilarity at which Jake quite outdid his most outrageous self, Joe Healey talked louder than usual (something hard to imagine), I laughed my vulgarest loudest laugh, Charlie listened to absolutely nobody . . . and then we all suddenly stopped and toasted Matt with our booze-filled teacups. He shook his head once and then a couple times and said glassily: "No one will believe me. No one will ever, ever believe me." Which sent us quite over the brink of hilarity because he's right. They won't. It was all most unbelievable.

So this morning we drove him to the train. And now he is gone. I feel hideous.

## Friday, 4 March

KEN DeLUCA's first tea session was Matt's going away. He came again last night and tonight. That's nice. But it's kind of awful in a way—as if we were filling up membership in the Academie Francaise. Ken is a delight: he says he is representing first-year theology in the Tea Seminar.

## Saturday, 5 March

A BEAUTIFUL MORNING. I've been out walking, thinking about the vows. If they are to mean anything in my life as a priest, it's high time I began looking at them closely and long. Poverty. If I don't legally possess anything, if I have permission for all the things I use—for my books, for the money I spend, for the shows I attend and the trips I take—then I am officially "poor." But what about the gap between my official poverty and the hopeless, famished faces of Appalachia? The slack jaws and the glistening vacant eyes say a lot more about the nature of poverty than my impeccable black suit and first-rate theater tickets. On the other hand I need books if I am going to be any kind of scholar and my profession as an educator obliges me to be a scholar. I need a good typewriter. I need good tickets for shows if I am going to give the show a fair hearing before I write about it. And Superiors have told me to do whatever is necessary to become the best writer I can. So where does that leave me? Poor in a sense. But then I come back to those terrifying faces of the really hungry-poor and how can I possibly say that my physically comfortable life is a life of poverty? Granted that I have an interior disposition whereby these things I use don't belong to me, whereby I am willing to surrender all of them at any given moment, nonetheless I *have* them. I use things. I don't go hungry. Shouldn't poverty be more than this to me? (Or maybe, just maybe, I shouldn't have a vow of poverty.) Think it over, Charlie, think it over.

Later. Reading the second chapter of *The Mandelbaum Gate*, I'm suddenly struck with something Muriel Spark said when we had lunch: she conceives of every book she writes as a poem, a novel structured like a poem. Something in the allusiveness of the writing and the atemporality of event-sequence made me think of poetry. Image and theme play back and forth in a thousand ways. Scriptural references carry both their own weight and an extra significance by their context within the novel; even place—the constant shift between Palestine and Jordan—assumes another dimension. The second chapter, "Barbara Vaughan's Identity," is a small masterpiece: a penetrating midrash on Genesis' "I am who I am."

## Sunday, 6 March

VERY PRODUCTIVE DAY after a season of creative drought. Nothing seems to get the creative enzymes moving quite so briskly as the sale of a manuscript . . . my first prose . . . it delights me like my first long pants. So today I wrote a little essay called "Among Crumbling Tombstones," a few comments on the survival of moral realism in contemporary American literature. Specifically it looks at J. F. Powers, J. D. Salinger, and Flannery O'Connor and finds them little clearings in a death of God wilderness. The only trouble with prose is that, once you've typed the final draft and submitted it to the censors, you discover that you've chosen the least interesting of perhaps twenty ways of saying what you've said. Dispiriting. Poor.

## Thursday, 10 March

SHADOWBROOK's tenth anniversary. I doubt if I would have remained in the Society of Jesus if Shadowbrook had not burned to the ground. I was so dreadfully unhappy. I don't suppose it's possible to hate a pile of stones; I came close though.

This morning while reading a little article by Rahner on nature and grace, I suddenly experienced the most powerful doubt about God's existence. Not his love for me or his redemptive act, but his existence. It passed in a while. How extraordinary when you think I'll be ordained in three months. I guess I'll stop having temptations against faith and hope and chastity about three days after death.

The sun has taken over quite completely and I have Matt Quinn's plant on my windowsill. It's a strange plant with fat tendrils and waxy leaves; I don't know what kind it is, but it was Matt's and it is green and growing and I like having it. I water it with a funny little copper watering can Matt gave me along with the plant.

Boats (toy ones) and gumdrops and umbrellas and red and yellow jawbreakers and everything nice in the whole world. Do you suppose I'm cracking?

## Friday, 11 March

I JUST FINISHED The Mandelbaum Gate. It is a poem, a long long poem in two parts asking "who am I?" As late as page 337 Barbara Vaughan thinks: "Knots were not necessarily created to be untied. Questions were things that sufficed in their still beauty, answering themselves. What am I doing here on a pilgrimage, after so much involvement? Because I am what I am." The ultimate answer the novel—and life—gives to the question "who am I?" is this: I am the image of God and hence a mystery. Beautiful doctrine. Beautiful book. Barbara explains to her Arab guide: "Well, either religious faith penetrates everything in life or it doesn't. There are some experiences that seem to make nonsense of all separations of sacred from profane—they seem childish. Either the

whole of life is unified under God or everything falls apart."
That's it, lady. Hold on to that. Has there ever, I wonder, been
such a Catholic novel? I hate to say that since it's usually the
ultimate slur. But really there is more solid theology in this
novel than I've heard in most of the Woodstock lectures this
year.

Take, for example, this little snippet of sermon delivered
by a visiting priest at the Altar of the Nailing of the Cross.
He says: "We know the creed of our faith and what we believe.
Outside of that it is better to know what is doubtful than to
place faith in uncertainties. Doubt is the prerogative of the
believer; the unbeliever cannot know doubt. And in what is
doubtful we should doubt well. But in whatever touches the
human spirit, it is better to believe everything than nothing.
Have faith." To which I say: "Wow."


## Saturday, 12 March

GOOD THING. Macmillan wrote today saying my book has been
submitted for a contract and they like it very much; they
hope to add me to their lists. I refuse to pray for this, but I
hope. O God, do I hope.

Later. I'm adjusted to the idea that Macmillan will return
my manuscript. That sort of preadjustment makes disappointment much easier to bear. And my past experiences have proved
that it's wise to plan on disappointment.

Finally I have received the Bishop's permission to con-
celebrate with six other priests at my first Mass. It will be the
first concelebration in the Springfield diocese, so I am quite
lucky to have the permission. It will be an event, the Catholic
Church of the twentieth century turned loose in South Hadley, Massachusetts.


## Monday, 14 March

AS MY TWELVE YEARS of waiting and preparing are at last
coming to an end, I'm somewhat preoccupied with the mystery
of vocation. And about time. Thinking about the priesthood

so much myself, I look around and wonder if everybody else is doing the same thing. I'm not wondering if I want to be a priest; I do. I'm wondering if I ought to be one in view of the history of my failures. However, I'm getting ahead of myself.

Let me conjure up the extreme case. Suppose I'm being ordained as an act of rejection. Perhaps I was not loved enough in my childhood, perhaps I was jealous of my brother who was always so competent in everything, and so I have turned from my family and the world as a gesture: sort of this—you have rejected me, now I reject you, formally, ritually, and I bind myself to this action of mine by perpetual vows. Even this hypothesis, the most appalling I can conceive (good theme for a novel?), is possible grounds for vocation. God *uses* our neuroses, our clouded vision, to call us to himself. His love after all is more powerful than our convoluted motivations.

Now to exonerate my family: they did love me, my brother's success didn't intimidate me. Still, in looking into your vocation you must test all the possibilities, you must question even the most unlikely and disheartening hypotheses. And so, unwilling to be a priest for the wrong reason, I question all my reasons and check the possibility of reasons I'd not suspected.

And I am content that my reasons are adequate. They depend so much on mystery and on God's love for me. Mystery, because I never really wanted to be a priest and because I miss loving and being loved by a wife and family. God's love for me, because of the difficulty of this life and my past failures in living it. There is nothing more traumatic for a religious bound by perpetual vows of poverty, chastity, and obedience than to face honestly the fact that—weakly and because he is a man—he has fallen so far from his ideals and indeed from the ten commandments that he has committed mortal sin. It is emphatically not the same as a college boy committing a mortal sin, or a married man; this is a man who every day makes a meditation and two examens and who is consciously and very slowly preparing for the life of a priest. How it could happen is inconceivable—the imperceptible erosion of principle, the gradual compromise, the sudden collapse into mortal sin —but men do it. I know. I've done it. And then I've been healed in the sacraments, propped up and reassured until I've grown used once more to enjoying the certainty that God loves me. Only his amazing love could whiten such a wound. And so even though I have managed in the last twelve years to kick everything around, to bungle and to fail, nonetheless I am certain that for his own good (and probably humorous) reasons God wants me to be a priest, that he wants to love me as his minister of word and food. As a priest I must recall this—and give and give and give.

## Tuesday, 15 March

I've CHOSEN. A nice free choice. One of those free-will acts we always used to hear about in philosophy lectures. I've chosen to study theology in the way I think best. That is to say, I go to very very few classes, I read books only about those problems that interest me, I ask questions of Jake and other for-real theologians. As a result I've been able to pursue with interest and enthusiasm (and without headaches) such questions as what we really mean by original sin, what grace has to do with living the Christian life, what heaven is and what hell is, and how you reconcile these with an all-loving God. And though I've found no adequate answers, still I have something to say on all these questions which seem very fundamental ones to me. Unfortunately neither my manner of pursuing wisdom nor the fragments of it I've collected are likely to be of interest to my examiners in June. The real glory of the situation is this: that the new curriculum, which has its defects and which is still much in flux, provides for precisely such odd ducks as myself. It's the curriculum that allows us to step outside the well-tempered plan and investigate what really interests us. If I must suffer disaster in June, you see, I would rather suffer it under the law than outside it. In any case, theology as spiritual curiosity is most gratifying.

Later. The Ides, you know. When I wrote the above hymn to Woodstock, it was morning and everything looked possible. But now it's evening and I'm aghast at my repeated failures. How obnoxious I've been. Walking after dinner with one of my brothers, I kept telling myself to shut up, to draw him out more, to care about what he was saying. But no, I kept coming back to my crazy damned views on the artist in the Society of Jesus—it's true he asked, but he scarcely expected an hour-long disquisition. And yesterday, walking with another fellow, I was equally definitive in all my statements. Worse though than the ex-cathedra quality of my pronouncements is the tone of annoyance that accompanies them, as if it were a constant mystery to me how so many could be so badly misinformed, as if it were a personal affront that there are viewpoints other than my own. And at tea I was alternately picky and sullen. Obnoxious. Tiresome. Even Ed Glynn, when I mentioned this nasty dogmatism to him, admitted it was so; he likes me in spite of it, but I cannot expect the rest of the world to prescind from my ugliness in the hopes they may get to like me. O God, when you pick a lemon, you pick a real one.

### Wednesday, 16 March

BOBBY KENNEDY. That's all you hear these days. Well, this is true: he is dynamite and a painful-joyful reminder of his brother and I am crazy about him. But it's distressing to hear the old American heresy working itself out in the Kennedy clan: "We have no God but Jack Kennedy and Bobby is his prophet." Jack was a good man and he ought to be praised for that, not for a whole bunch of specious and irrelevant perfections he never had. And Bobby should be praised because he's Bobby and not for continuing an American Camelot that never existed anyway. We Americans have this terrible need for a national hero, more intense a need, I think, than the normal human need for myth. And I fear that all the greatness of Jack Kennedy will get lost in the shuffle if we start canonizing him for the wrong reasons. And then we'll all be the poorer.

## Monday, 21 March

THE SECOND CONFERENCE for Jesuit artists, this one at Shrub Oak in New York, was quite successful. Emphasis was on performance rather than protracted discussion, so we had an opportunity to see in action some of the rather formidable artistic talent we have in the Society. There was a painting exhibit, a piano and violin concert, a poetry reading, a guitar and folk-psalm performance. What impressed me most was not the presence of two superb pianists, three painters, two poets, a violinist, etc., etc., but the quality of performance, which was invariably first-rate. Jesuits are all right.

The high point of the conference for me, however, was meeting Tom Lynaugh again. He's a most extraordinary young man whom I met two years ago when he spent a weekend here at Woodstock; despite his being in a psychology degree program, he is remarkably sane; he believes on the Lord Jesus. It is exciting, always so, to discover someone who shares your enthusiasm for something as personal as a relationship with the living God. So we talked for several hours about the Gospel of St. John, about the difficulties and dangers and marvelous delights of living. Excellent man. God knows when I shall see him again.

## Tuesday, 22 March

JAKE IS EMBRACING the improbable as a way of life. In preparation for his year in Europe (he'll make tertianship in France), he has bought four ties, gray flannel trousers, and a blue blazer with silver buttons, "because clerical dress is not commonly worn on the Continent and because it may be necessary to visit some places where clerical dress will be more an embarrassment than an aid to devotion." Only Jake could say it with a straight face. I've felt for some time that he was becoming a Protestant, but it appears I've been altogether wrong; he's becoming a libertine. Marvelous man.

## Thursday, 24 March

I WENT to a reception for two English poets the other night. They were nice people to talk with, and so was a lovely couple from the State Department, but the rest struck me as a bunch of phonies. I kept asking myself what in hell I was doing there. Late in the evening a lady, beautiful but faded, told me with a pained expression: "This is my first time in Washington. It's so *unusual*. You know, it's almost like a factory town. Yes, a factory town. Quite frightening, really." I replied with exaggerated sympathy: "How awful it must be for you." I smiled but that didn't help. She was from New York and did not like being whomped by some clod-hopping priest-type from a factory town. Phonies have souls too. I must remember that.

## Tuesday, 29 March

*Critic* has forwarded to me the most marvelous letter with this comment: "Keep the letter. You might want to use it as a blurb for your next book." Here's the letter:

Dear Sirs:

For the sake of society in general, and the Society of Jesus, in particular, I honestly believe that John L'Heureux, S.J., ought to be incarcerated at once and forever in the nearest mental hospital. My conclusion has been reached after reading his article, "Of The Firm."

[signed] Mrs. Joseph A. Lunn<br>Olmstead Falls, Ohio

I think she said that very nicely.

Later. Do you know what I think is nice about God? That having given me this rotten physical constitution that always breaks down completely after a few days' work, he nonetheless gives me these few days' worth of incredible energy that allows me to produce and produce and produce. I'm a dynamo these days; nothing can wear me out. I'm preparing my talk for the Catholic Evidence Guild of Baltimore on Friday, working industriously at theology; reading everything; writing some things. Saturday: collapse.

Great line in Sylvia Townsend Warner's story "The Candles": "This was one of those alarming new children, born into a nuclear age and scornful of everything not potentially destructive."

## Wednesday, 30 March

MACMILLAN SENT ME a contract for *Rubrics for a Revolution* in this morning's mail. I signed it and sent it out in this noon's mail. We're not going to monkey around with this one. Now I'll be on tenterhooks (or whatever those hooks are called) until it comes back from Macmillan countersigned. God certainly accomplishes his will in funny ways.

I had lunch with Frank Winters in Baltimore, as always an exciting Christian experience. My friends are such a tremendous grace in my life; I don't suppose I could make it without them.

## Friday, 1 April

AND GUESS WHO today's April fool is? I spoke to about a hundred ladies of the Catholic Evidence Guild of Baltimore at the Cathedral; subject—the Death of God in today's literature.

It was all very nice except that the car I was assigned to had to be used for another errand before it dropped me off, the driver got lost, and I arrived exactly one half hour late. My hundred ladies were all seated quietly like good children; astonishingly, they seemed more relieved to see me than annoyed that I had kept them waiting. I spoke well, considering that I was frantic, disappointed, determined to accept this as one of the necessary discomforts of poverty and obedience. (But it's not: it's stupidity and inconsiderateness to manage things so that people who have paid to hear you are kept waiting.) I answered questions for only ten minutes at the end of my talk, and though there were many hands still waving, I explained I had to dash off immediately because my driver was waiting out front or would be any minute now. I left. During the course of the next half hour the ladies drifted out of the hall; at least fifteen of them marveled at my still being there and offered to drive me back to Woodstock. I smiled and said no. But by damn I began to think of this whole escapade less in terms of poverty and obedience than in terms of downright unvarnished mismanagement. April fool's day indeed.

Later. Calmer too. Ordination retreat begins tonight. I don't think I have ever needed eight days away from civilization with more urgency.

## *Ordination Retreat, 2 April–10 April*

I'LL JUST FORGET dates during this retreat; I'll record (sometimes) what is going on in my soul, in my mind. Some things will be Fr. John Courtney Murray's, some my own, some adapted from my reading. All will be my own within a month, sinking right down into my subconscious and popping up later without identifying features.

### *First Day*

"In this the love of God was made manifest among us, that God sent his only Son into the world, so that we might live through him. In this is love, not that we loved God but that he loved us and sent his son to be the expiation of our sins." (I John 4:9–10)

"Therefore be imitators of God, as beloved children. And walk in love, as Christ loved us and gave himself up for us, a fragrant offering and sacrifice to God." (Eph. 5:1–2)

Later. Some thoughts on presence: The face of God as a symbol of his presence. God's presence is manifested in his old and new covenants, his presence is that steadfast love with which he pursued Israel down the centuries, it is the grace of his Holy Spirit which unites us. I think of the startling book of Hosea, in which God's steadfast love for his unfaithful people Israel is acted out, symbolized, by the prophet Hosea who takes as his wife a prostitute who then has children by other men, runs away from him, and *still* he takes her back. Renewal in our lives and in the life of the Church must always be a search for the presence of God.

Later. A thought on law: Law is never a creative force. Like poetic form, it gives a symmetry, an order, to what only love can create. It is the boundary line of love. Once separated from the font of its inspiration, law becomes merely a burden.

Later. "I make all things new." Retreat, like the Christian life and the Church itself, is motion toward the coming of Christ. The Word forever comes.

### Second Day

Knowledge of the Father. As transparency is a symbol of God's presence, so opacity is a symbol of his turning away. "Your iniquities have made a separation between you and your God, and your sins have hid his face from you." (Isaiah 59:2) Sin is the source of our alienation from God. Hell is the confirmatory state. Yet hell, like all other created things, is another manifestation of God's steadfast love of men. He is a jealous lover; if he is to have my love, it must be my free gift. If I go to hell, it is because I have freely chosen. He merely ratifies my choice. Psalm 103: "He knows our frame, remembers we are dust."

### Third Day

Apostolic consciousness. We have been known, loved, chosen in a special way. God does not love everyone equally. His knowledge is Old Testament knowledge: it implies love and free choice. We are chosen. We are chosen and sent. "Ah, ah, ah, Lord, I am a child and cannot speak." (Jer. 1:6) So too for Christ, his mission *was* his Sonship. His name is always the sent. And he calls his Father, He who sent me. Christ is priest by reason of his incarnation in the flesh; this is how he is sent; this is how he ministers; this is how he mediates—as God enfleshed.

### Fourth, Fifth, Sixth Days

The desert is a dry, dry place.

*Seventh Day*

Good Friday. Father Arrupe, General of the Society of Jesus, visited Woodstock on Wednesday, said Mass here, spoke to us for about an hour. He is a most remarkable man. Fifty-nine years old, he nonetheless has more energy than most men of thirty. He is indefatigable; his enthusiasm for the work of the Society spills over into all his talk and actions. He is exciting.

Later. God's name is Father: he who sends. Jesus' name is Messiah: he who is sent. Always there is this cyclic movement to the "way" of Jesus. "I came from the Father and have come into the world; again, I am leaving the world and going to the Father." (John 16:28) He does always the Father's will . . . and when he goes back to the Father, the Father sends the Spirit in Christ's name. "These things I have spoken to you, while I am still with you. But the Counselor, the Holy Spirit, whom the Father will send in my name, he will teach you all things, and bring to your remembrance all that I have said to you." (John 14:25–26) Here we have John's intricate Trinitarian doctrine, or inchoate doctrine at least. The Spirit is Christ's continued presence among us; and he who knows Christ knows the Father. Beautiful.

Later. Christ was such an incredible radical, always doing unnecessary things out of love. Think of all that wine at Cana; enough to supply the tiny village for days and days. And then the lady's jar of perfume spilled on Christ's feet; a brilliantly excessive gesture. And again Christ on the cross saying to the thief: "This day you shall be with me in paradise"; a fabulous reward for admonishing his partner in crime. And the crucifixion, the ultimate gesture. My favorite, though, is the breakfast cookout on the lakefront (John 21:9–14) with the risen Christ pottering around the fire, cooking fish and making toast. I'm not being flip; that's precisely what he was doing. What a great apologia for Christian excess.

Later. Love is the only thing that makes any sense.

*Eighth Day*

Holy Saturday night. Only a short while now until the Easter Vigil rolls back the stone and hope arises and peace for which I'm totally unprepared; Scripture and dogma tests coming over the hill; Mass exam lying in ambush. I'm going to crawl under the shrubbery (on the first pleasant day) and die.

## Thursday, 28 April

I HAD LUNCH with Joan today and picked up a thousand copies of my ordination card, which is superb. Dull but strong blue background with a white hand holding a broken chunk of orange bread. At the bottom of the card, in white, there is printed: "Lord, make me your bread. Then break me up and pass me around." It's a unique card and a beautiful one. We celebrated by attending Mass together at Georgetown. Wonderful thing.

In the evening I met my college roommate, John McGuinn, and his wife and two babies. Gregory, the older, is about two and goes about kissing flowers because he thinks they're nice. Kids are incredible . . . knock you right out with their breathtaking innocence. I had never met John's wife, who is a lovely, and I hadn't seen John in the past twelve years, so we had a great deal to talk about and a good time doing it. Charming couples are good to be with. Let it be written.

## Saturday, 30 April

LAST NIGHT at the wee, indeed the most wee, hours of the morning I wrote in one swoop this nice little poem.

### The Startled Flower

The baby kisses flowers.
I saw him.
What untaught harmony
he must shape

to chaos he will learn—
later—with the force

becomes our name. Birth, life, death, buria.
phenomena. The Resurrection falls quite
of the merely human, the empirically verifiai
to the Resurrection of Christ that the init
variably appealed in the kerygma. They proc
over the presence of Christ among them; the n
and what it has worked within them; his presei.
to them but in them; his presence as a guarant
freedom. In Christ, we realize our flesh. In his Re
we find our faith and our hope. In his continued
in us, our love.

### Sunday, 17 *

THINKING ABOUT ordination as I do all the time, I find c
one thing disturbs me and I don't know how to formulate
so that it doesn't sound like the old "I'm not worthy" ple.
(Of course you're not worthy; it would be impertinent of you
to wonder if you were.) I have no doubts that I want to be a
priest, no uncertainty as to why. But it pains and embarrasses
me more than I can say that what I will bring to that altar
for ordination is this nauseating sack of guts: selfish, small,
lecherous; a mind like a whorehouse; a tongue like a longshore-
man's; a soft mousy body that seeks always its own comforts,
a will deluded by hyperactive desires. Poor wreck that I am.
Can I give over to God's service only so little, and *that* so
badly damaged, so in and out of sin and desire? I shall have to
let my grotesqueness testify to his mercy. God help me.

Later. Today's liturgy texts are about the peace of the risen
Christ. For the first time in a long while, I don't feel anything
except a ghastly abandoned ache in the pit of my stomach.

### Wednesday, 27 April

*Quel* month. It's been raining for days—*inside* the house. I
sit down to study and within five minutes I'm off at summer
school or at ordination or anywhere but here with a book in
front of me. There is a test Saturday on Reformation history

of time and tolerance.
He will hate flowers. But now

green anemones
are falling through the air,
Gregory; sea flowers
startled from their stems

by your soft kiss.
I touch your brow
that more than graceful flower
before it crumbles into dust.

And then I slept comfortably late this morning, too late in fact to drop my laundry down the chute by pickup time. So I'll be a scourge to the community until next Saturday.

Later. Joan wrote me this morning a somewhat lengthy description of a project we plan for next year. It sounds a bit ambitious for me. Joan plans a series of sculptures called "Good People," twenty pieces depicting twenty men and women whom we both like, ranging from Adam and Jonah to St. Paul, to Gandhi, to Pope John, and Dag Hammarskjöld. I will write poems for each of them, brief ones, which will be mounted either on bronze plaques or carved in stone bases of the statues. It sounds good. We might even photograph the statues and run the poems—or longer versions of the poems— on facing pages of a small but elegant book. I don't mind agreeing to a project like this; there is no waste of time and material involved for me. But it could be a terrible waste of time and material and money for Joan. I do hope her enthusiasm won't lead her into something she'll regret later. However, here's to it.

## Sunday, 1 May

SUNDAY MORNING and I've just completed the Macmillan publicity questionnaire on *Rubrics*. It's not a bad description of the book, so I append it here.

*Rubrics for a Revolution* is a collection of poems about things that happen to people, about loving and hating and fullness.

Love and hate are the dialectic of living; the commitment is the same, the intensity is the same, only the initial stance differs. It takes a certain depth of personality and a certain openness of spirit to transform hate into love. Most often we lack that depth and openness, cannot rise to it, and so remain in the isolated stance of self-concern. That is the death of the heart: when it closes about itself and atrophies. Sometimes however we do open to the spirit and, taking the risk of losing ourselves altogether, we find suddenly that we have lost nothing and have gained everything. We find joy and that fullness of joy we seem to have heard promised somewhere.

*Rubrics for a Revolution* is a series of observations on this dialectical movement. Its five parts chart a progress from "vengeance is mine" through the darknesses of learning to love and to give and to think only of the other, concluding with "That Mortal Knot," which recapitulates and distills the processes of love. For love is never totally achieved; it is always in process.

These poems then are a record of some of the things I have seen happen around me, have experienced happening within me.

## Monday, 2 May

JUSTIN SAID A GOOD THING the other day. "Just as food is part of the concept of hunger, so is God part of the concept of man." I don't know how well that would stand up as proof of the existence of God, but it certainly makes sense to me—especially when I think of Rahner's explanation of man's situation as being both open to and ordered toward the infinite.

Do you know what? We have had rain for eleven out of the past twelve days. Perhaps Joan and I ought to make Noah one of those "Good People." I keep sending out this pigeon in hopes he'll bring back an olive branch.

And at noontime I'm off to South Hadley to make some ordination arrangements and on to New York to Macmillan.

## Thursday, 5 May

VISIT HOME was quite good. We were able to make final plans about the altar Dad is building for my first Mass and about who should be invited to what, so I feel confident that every-thing in South Hadley (or South Hardly, as David always says) is as it should be. Now if only my invitations would come.

While home, I spent an evening with my brother Jerry and his wife and six kids. At quarter of ten Jerry said it was time for the children to be off to bed: "Better get the books." And to my astonishment little books emerged and the whole family said Compline, or rather a family prayer session of about ten minutes adapted from Compline. Since the oldest child is ten years old and the one reading the Mother's part (Claire was in the kitchen mixing drinks) is only seven, I was bowled over, impressed as I rarely have been by the genuine piety and naturalness of the affair. Imagine growing up in a family where group prayer is taken so completely for granted. There seems to me something wonderfully healthy about Compline and cocktails sitting down elbow to elbow. So I'll treasure that particular memory for some time.

In New York I saw Betty Bartelme, my new editor. She seems kind and Catholic with a capital C (I always feel like a third-rate religious when I'm with first-rate Christians) and a good business woman. We got off to a good start, I think. Best of all, we spoke about this journal and she seemed to be interested in it. I'll find out how interested in June.

And I managed to see two shows, *The Lion in Winter* and *Philadelphia, Here I Come*. They were wonderful. *The Lion in Winter* offers a torrent of the most glittering dialogue I've heard in years. It is really a three-act verbal duel between an aging Henry II of England and an even more aging Eleanor of Aquitaine. For ten years he has kept her prisoner in the castle of Chinon, letting her out according to this marvelous farce each Christmas and Easter to spend the holidays with himself and their children. And each holiday they machinate, the two of them: he to get the Aquitaine and his son John on the throne, she to get her freedom and her son Richard on the throne. The language crackles. The performances by Rosemary Harris and Robert Preston are magnificent.

Eleanor describes her first meeting with Henry (I quote from hope and from memory): "He came down from the north with a mind like Aristotle's and a form like mortal sin. We shattered the Ten Commandments at first sight." She recalls also: ". . . when I went on the Crusades. I dressed all my women as Amazons and I myself rode halfway across Europe with my breast bare to the waist. Henry nearly had a stroke and I damned near died of windburn—but the troops were dazzled." And on and on and on. It is one of the most delightful plays I've seen in years.

*Philadelphia, Here I Come* is brilliantly acted and has a last act that is genius. The construction of the play interested me as much as anything else. The main character has an inner and an outer self, each played by a different actor; it's not the sort of thing O'Neill tried with limited success; it's something quite new and inventive. I like it.

And so here I am back in reality, at Woodstock, where paradoxically it is so much more difficult to find God.

## Saturday, 7 May

I WAS ORDAINED Sub-Deacon this morning. All day I have been ugly and irritable and extremely short of patience. The Sub-Diaconate is the strangest office: one is charged with caring for linens for the Sacrifice of the Mass, supplying the water, carrying the paten about. One is obliged under mortal sin to say the Breviary. One is, in short, a glorified altar boy who is pledged to chastity and the daily Office. Still, that's no reason for the ugliness of my mood.

The Breviary is the most complicated thing I've ever seen. You flip back and forth constantly, scores of little prayers rattle through your teeth while you turn pages, your eyes and fingers develop a life all their own. My head is splitting from this "prayer of the Church." Perhaps it's all been a terrible mistake. Perhaps I should be a typewriter repairman or something less intellectually taxing. Still, think of the number of unclever priests who seem to manage the Breviary adequately. Some day you too, Bill Truehart, will know your matins from your lauds.

Tomorrow I become Deacon. And right here, right here now in print, I want to request a little emotional consolation like anybody else: I want to feel like laughing and singing and rejoicing. I want to feel *glad*, dammit. I'm tired of wanting to swat everybody. You're stuck with me now, so bring on the happiness. A little?

Later. I've spent the evening making long-distance phone calls in an effort to locate my ordination invitations, which seem to have disappeared forever in the murky recesses of the United States Parcel Service. (The chief office of this Sub-Deacon is to keep from going mad.) Nobody has any idea where they are. And I keep thinking that, if they do turn up soon, there will be lots of time to send them out . . . but what, pray, if there is a misprint? Can anyone on earth be counted on to spell L'Heureux correctly? Perhaps I'll just run away.

## Sunday, 8 May

APART FROM a few lucid moments when I was able to pray, my experience of this morning's Diaconate ordination was one of boredom and exhaustion. Isn't that dreadful. I thought the ceremony would never end, that the Bishop's Baltimore accent would just buzz on and on into eternity, that I might never be able to preach and to give gifts but would remain on my knees waiting for the world to end. My few moments of prayer came at the conclusion; I remembered the Provincial and the needs of the New England Province. Fr. Cardegna, my friends, and of course my family. So I was able at any rate to bring together everybody I wanted to include in the ceremony. Though it was disappointing as an experience, nonetheless I am a validly ordained Deacon and can give certain blessings, perform certain sacraments, distribute Holy Communion. And you don't have to feel good or be an emotional whoopee-bag to do that. Besides, I can rejoice tomorrow.

## Monday, 9 May

BUT THERE IS NO rejoicing today either. My ordination invitations have still not appeared and my situation, which till now was unfortunate, is rapidly becoming disastrous. If they don't turn up by Thursday, I'll have some printer do a rush job on a whole new set. The price will be fierce, but at least then I will be able to invite people to my first Mass and reception. As things stand now, I may be the only Jesuit to have *no* first Mass at all.

## Tuesday, 10 May

THE INVITATIONS came last night around dinnertime. Opening them, I discovered they were in large square chunks, unfolded. Ed Glynn, saint of God, helped me fold and fold and fold and then pack them off to Mother who, poor lady, will address them. We finished at midnight. I slept late this morning, lay abed wondering about God's patience. My nerves are strung out like used catgut. I hear myself laughing hollowly and I look around for the little men with white coats. These past weeks of waiting have been the most anxiety-ridden of my life. And worst of all, I'm a royal pain in the neck to all the Brethren. I *must* get some rest and make plans for re-entering the human race.

## Friday, 13 May

FRIDAY THE THIRTEENTH, but everything is going well. I've been following my "May Program" with some success: I rise every morning, retire every evening; in between times I breathe in and out. That's the "May Program." It guarantees survival. Any study or prayer in addition to the prescribed burdens of rising, retiring, breathing, is chalked up as profit. It's a good program.

Carolyn Kizer somehow wangled me an invitation to a

Washington reception for Archibald MacLeish being given by
Dean Rusk no less. It's preceded by a dinner party at the home
of some Under Secretary. White tie and tails. I thought when
she invited me that it might be fun to go; I've decided since
then that I don't have two days to throw away on that sort of
thing. I shall stay home like a good priest-to-be and practice
the Mass. Still, it's pleasant to be invited.

## Monday, 16 May

SCRIPTURE EXAM on Saturday was entertaining. There were
one hundred multiple-guess questions; you know, the kind of
test you had in first year high school where they ask you to
identify the lady lawyer in *The Merchant of Venice* and provide you with a list: "Pauline, Jessica, Nerissa, Portia, Shylock."
That may be very good (though I doubt it) for freshmen in
high school dealing with the characters in a play, but it's another thing altogether for men thirty-some years old dealing
with a major part of the Old Testament. Did you know for
instance that Og was the king of Bashan? Or that the place
where both Joram and Jezebel were slain by Jehu was Jezreel?
Or that the Pharaoh who campaigned in Palestine and com-
memorated his victories on a stele was Merneptah? I knew
these all right. But damned if I knew who instigated the over-
throw of Queen Athalia or what the difference is between a salvation announcement and a salvation assurance. Most disastrous of all was the section in which we were asked to identify
texts. All sixth-century prophets sound the same to me. What
I am building up to is this: I passed but with small commenda-
tion. Nonetheless, be it known in high places and in low, I
passed. One more course finished . . . a terrible attitude . . .
blame twelve years of jumping hoops.

Later. I just returned from my Mass exam. It went rather
well, with only two negligible omissions. Both uglies went unnoticed by the examiner, who spent an embarrassing half hour
heaping praise on me for the way I read the Latin and my
manner at the altar and (God help us) the sense of sincere
dedication I conveyed. I was so nervous I didn't realize where

I was half the time. Another exam over. My name is John L'Heureux and I am thirty-one years old and I am in the twenty-sixth grade and when I grow up I hope to retire.

### Thursday, 19 May

FR. SANDERS TAUGHT dogma here at Woodstock for many years —many years ago. Fr. Gallen teaches Canon Law here now and is celebrated for his orthodoxy. Yesterday, as Fr. Gallen waited with some patience for the elevator (which had been stalled in the cellar by one of the workmen), Fr. Sanders approached him excitedly and demanded to know why the young priests going out on sick calls neglect to light the candles on the altar before removing the Eucharist. Fr. Gallen shrugged and waited less patiently for the elevator. Fr. Sanders is deaf as a board and, not knowing whether he had been answered or not, kept up his inquiries, concluding with a fine harangue and the words: "They *should* light the candles, shouldn't they? I am *right*, am I not?" Fr. Gallen shouted back: "Yes, you're right." Fr. Sanders stared at the floor for a moment and resigned himself to both his wisdom and his impotence to remedy the situation. Then he summed up: "I can't do anything about it and you can't do anything about it, but I know I'm right and you know I'm right, so I'm happy." He shuffled off in rage and dudgeon. Fr. Gallen, surprised at last, turned to Justin Kelly, who was also waiting for the elevator, and said in his inimitable Marx Brothers' style: "Heh, just knowing you're right isn't happiness. Happiness is having the emotions under control." This is, I presume, a definition in accord with the best Canonical thought.

I say Compline each night with Ed Glynn, Matins each morning with anybody who will say it with me. The Office has become a pleasure and Compline has become the best part of the day.

## Sunday, 22 May

I HAVE HAD TO switch gears. I now race along in the "Modified May Program," which is essentially the same as the "May Program"—rising, breathing, retiring—but has the added burden of at least two hours of study each day. More study is recommended, but only if mental and physical health permit. Survival is what counts . . . at least until ordination.

Each morning Denis Woods and I say Matins. We've been doing this for a week now and have decided to make it a fairly permanent arrangement. He is good to pray with: fast with responses while maintaining a sort of ritual attitude to the prayer of the Church (which requires speed and profits by ritual).

Later. In this afternoon's mail the Boston *Herald* sent me a rush review due at the latest by the first of June. Worse than the deadline is the substance of the book: poems by a young American girl who committed suicide at the age of thirty-one. My age. That should cheer me during these hours of crisis.

## Wednesday, 25 May

DOGMA EXAM this morning was long but good: two and a half hours writing about original sin and the supernatural life and what grace does to one's inner life. I did well, I think. Written exams always give me a chance to talk more at length about something I know and can answer well, so long as I'm allowed to approach the question from my own point of view; oral exams always bring me up short because I try to answer the question exactly as asked, not having the art of twisting the question around in such a way that I can assure the examiners I *do* know the subject though perhaps not in the categories in which the question was framed. Anyhow I did well, considerably better than I expect to do on the oral exam which covers the same matter. That little picnic will be five days hence. An hour oral. I get dizzy thinking of it.

*Thursday, 26 May*

I FINISHED the *Herald* review and sent it off in the noon mail. It is a fascinating book and, beginning it Monday afternoon, I was unable to put it down until I had read it through. I went through it again yesterday as a break from my studies and wrote the review this morning.

Sylvia Plath, who wrote the book—it's called *Ariel*, by the way—was an American girl married to the English poet Ted Hughes. In 1960 she published her first book of poems, *The Colossus*. In the same year, she gave birth to a daughter and two years later to a son. Shortly afterward, she committed suicide. I don't know how she died, but the poems lead me to suspect she drowned herself.

*Ariel* is a dazzler in many ways, not least of them the way in which the book was written. Many of the poems were composed during the last months of her life, when she would rise at four in the morning and write and rewrite until it was time to tend to the baby. Sometimes she would turn out two and three a day, not careless poems either, but skull-worn and skillfully crafted. The fiber of her discipline is steel.

Reading *Ariel*, you marvel not so much that she committed suicide but that she didn't do it sooner. The book is a vividly imagined map of the descent to despair. Listen:

> I am inhabited by a cry.
> Nightly it flaps out
> Looking, with its hooks, for something to love.
>
> I am terrified by this dark thing
> That sleeps in me;
> All day I feel its soft, feathery turnings, its malignity.

And listen to this:

> They threaten
> To let me through to a heaven
> Starless and fatherless, a dark water.

And this:

> For a minute the sky pours into the hole like plasma.
> There is no hope, it is given up.

The poems are, almost without exception, about death and despair. They would be cloying, repulsive even, except for the brilliancy of her imagination. It vaults every obstacle of structure or design. There is little love in her book; only loss and terror. There is no joy. No humor. There is wit and irony, but they turn back upon themselves. Reading *Ariel*, I kept thinking of the fabled scorpion who in the presence of danger injects his fatal poison into his own white belly. Only the illuminated freedom of Sylvia Plath's imagination, the splendid discipline of her verse, make reading *Ariel* possible.

Her suicide is a tragedy, I suppose. Seeing life as she did—with the eyes of someone already dead—her suicide, without miraculous intervention, would seem inevitable. And she has left us a great thing. I mentioned in the review that no living person wrote these poems. They are a voice from the unhappy dead.

## Monday, 30 May

MEMORIAL DAY, DECORATION DAY. Well, I'll certainly remember it and I've certainly been decorated. The hour oral in dogma this morning is perhaps the unpleasantest hour I've spent since I was paralyzed at the age of nine. I was examined on original sin, monogenism, necessity of grace, and the eternity of hell. Normally I have something to say on all of these issues; I had very little to say this morning and nothing at all intelligent to commend to the attention of my examiners. I looked stupid and I was. It was an awful hour. It has the one incontrovertible merit of being done. Done. *Deo gratias.*

I might point out before collapsing that my survival is another triumph—and a stunning one—for the "Modified May Program." Now on to better things.

## Saturday, 4 June

ED GLYNN brought me a darning egg from home. It's the one, the same identical kind, etched on my retina from childhood when I used to visit Grandma Clarke and marvel at the contents of her work basket. A darning egg is good. Of course.

I have moved my room to the quiet zone of the corridor upstairs, buckled away under lock all my "secret" papers that I don't want folk blundering into, packed off all my summer goods for New England. *Nunc dimittis, Domine.* Waiting to leave Woodstock is like being suspended a few inches off the floor; you can scrape ground by flailing about but the torment is fierce and incommensurate with the small satisfaction it affords.

Evening. You won't believe this, but it's true. (It sounds like a gloss on the two nuns and the dead dog.) This afternoon I drove to the train station to pick up a Father and on the way home he asked to stop at one of those huge shopping complexes. While he was gone and I was waiting, an enormously pregnant lady scuffed through the parking area to her car, which was fairly near mine. She looked tired and unwell and about to deliver, so I kept looking at her. She got in the car and suddenly slumped over the wheel. Terror-stricken that I would have to deliver a baby in the parking lot, I sprinted to her car and was astonished to find her doubled in two in laughter. I asked her if she was all right and when she finally (it took a while) stopped laughing, she said: "I know what you're thinking, Father, but I'm not really crazy. It's just that I'm on my way to the doctor and he asked me to bring a specimen with me. I couldn't find any little bottle so I used two whiskey miniatures my husband had and when I went into the store I left them on the front seat of the car and now they're gone. And all I can think of is the poor man who stole them." And then she dissolved in laughter again. And so did I.

## Tuesday, 7 June

Bob White and I left Woodstock yesterday in a little rented Valiant. He drove for an hour, I drove for two hours, then he drove the rest of the way—my two hours at the wheel having proved for him something like the living terrors of the Indianapolis speedway. Since Bob is from New England too, we talked a good bit about the friends we have in common at Woodstock, the reasons why we went there in the first place, and generally agreed we had done the right thing. Woodstock is good; though hopelessly large and therefore somewhat impersonal, it guarantees you privacy, the opportunity to grow according to your norms of personal integrity, the choice of being as good or as bad a religious as you want. And the men you meet are first rate. I was most touched for instance that all my friends were out at the car to see us off: Ed Glynn, Jake (in a fantastic garment of blue shot through with silver), Ken DeLuca, Leo O'Donovan, Jimmy Jurich, Charles, and a number of others. Marvelous folk. Marvelous.

Bob and I stopped in South Hadley for dinner. We arrived about five and had a long session of drinks while I opened ordination gifts that had come to the house for me. I hadn't thought of getting gifts. It's a good experience.

I saw the altar Dad has finished for my first Mass, a beautiful white oak table-altar . . . our parish had no altar facing the people and so when I received permission for concelebration Dad suggested he supply the altar and the pastor can either keep it or replace it afterward. He's already decided to keep it. It's nice to say your first Mass on an altar your father built.

Dad and Mother were in rare form, terribly enthusiastic and convivial, so Bob and I stayed until midnight. We talked up a tornado. Driving to Weston I was so sleepy I dozed off while trying to talk to Bob about the wire that was burning in the radio or thereabouts; I slept all the way to Boston; the wire burned all the way to Boston and on through the night and for all I know is still burning somewhere in an Avis dungeon for cars that refuse to try harder.

I was up at six this morning trying to put together a few thoughts for my sermon on Sunday. There is so much to include: my being a priest, the priesthood of the laity, the notion of vocation, the call to the banquet which is refused, the beautiful reading from I John 4. How do I get it all in? I should also say something about concelebration so that the people who have never seen one will understand that all those priests are up there for something more than to help me read the prayers of the Canon. Considering all these things, and reconsidering them, I did what any sane man would do. I gave up.

## Thursday, 9 June

I WROTE MY SERMON yesterday in an hour flat. Since then I've pecked away at the edges here and there, making changes, strengthening the unity. But I think it's ready for delivery now. Thank God, that's done with.

We're caught up, somehow, in an endless round of performance. Rehearsal every evening for the ordination ceremony, rehearsal in private for Mass, and then once more for a concelebrated Mass. Then there is the Breviary to say, people to greet, a homily to prepare for the day after my first Mass. And the general nervousness. And no time to pray. I guess this is the perfect way for me to be ordained, in a welter of confusion, wanting mightily to do the right thing and have the right thoughts and say the right prayers and love the right way and instead doing everything the way I always have. Perhaps that *is* the right way for me.

## Friday, 10 June

TOMORROW AT THIS TIME I shall be a priest. And, except that I will be able to give Christ to others in a visible and sometimes dramatic form, I shall be exactly the same: worried and selfish and loving and wanting only to love properly. So this morning I meditate on God's mercy and humor in choosing me. He *has* chosen me and therefore I rejoice. This is what he makes of the mystery of whatever I am: his instrument, his servant, his other Christ. I am the only Christ some men will ever know. He will have to make me the Christ he wants; the one bit of wisdom I possess is that all my willing has never won me a trace of virtue. God, come; set your tent within me and build a fire. And let them warm their hands at it.

## Saturday, 11 June

I AM A PRIEST forever now. I can bless and give food and restore life to those who have not loved.

## Sunday, 12 June

AT THREE this afternoon I shall say my first Mass in South Hadley, facing the people across an altar my father built, wearing vestments that are a gift from my mother, preaching a sermon taught me by Christ Jesus in the twin mystery of love and suffering. There will be no time to record anything. But I want to share the sermon I will deliver. Here:

We are all priests and so, like Christ, we must talk of food and of love. We are born hungry. We are born with a hunger for food and a hunger for love. We want to be fed and we want to be loved and not all pleasant words, not any cold charity, will ever satisfy us: only food and love will do it.

In the first reading, St. John tells us that those who do not love abide in death. In the second reading, St. Luke tells us that, though we are poor and lame and blind, we are invited to a banquet in which Christ himself is given to us forever. In the combination of these two readings is the summary of the Christian life. John and Luke are telling us that we are all priests.

We are born members of a family. We are baptized into the human family of the Church—a chosen people invited to a life of worship, of love and union with each other in Christ Jesus. We are confirmed, and are invited to bring forth actively the gifts we have received in Baptism; we are invited to give of ourselves to others, to love as Christ did to the point of laying down our lives for our brothers. But as full, mature members of Christ's Church we are more than just ourselves. We are priests.

The priest is a witness and a mediator and—in a way—a sacrament.

Christ, the high priest, witnesses to the love the Father *is* and bears for us. "It is by this that we know what the love of God is: that he laid down his life for us." And we are told to go and do likewise. We must bear witness that we love and are loved, witness to the truth of the Gospel: that unless a man love he abides in death, that to hate is to murder, that to love is to bring back to life.

And we are mediators. As Christ shows us the Father—shows us the Father's mercy and steadfast unshakable love—so do we mirror the patience and love of Christ. "Little children, love one another." "As I have loved you, so do you love one another." "Unlesss a man love, he abides in death." We mediate by revealing in our lives Christ's love of our brother. How can we love God whom we have not seen when we cannot love our brother who stands before us always? He asks for bread. And the bread we give must be our selves.

And, in a way, we are a sacrament. When Christ walked the earth, to encounter him was the sacrament of encounter with God. Christ remains with us today in his Church, his Mystical Body. To encounter a member of that Body must be to encounter Christ. We are the only Christ some men will ever know. We are his image. We must take care that the image is a loving one.

So we are all priests, with the duties and privileges of priests. We witness to the truth of God's love, we mediate that love for our brothers, we bear Christ about in us. As priests we are Christ's bread: we must let ourselves be broken up and be passed around.

An ordained priest is privileged to do more than this. He preaches the word of God. He gives special gifts. He forgives sins to summon those who are dead in hatred to life in love. He has from God the command to preach his saving word. He has from God the power to change bread and wine into the body and blood of Jesus Christ. We are all priests; my priesthood differs from yours in this—that I am your servant. That I give words and life and that food which is your soul's life and—if you will let me—my love.

In the banquet we are about to celebrate, Christ comes to us in bread and wine. He so loved us as to lay down his life for us; he remains with us in the sacrament of his body. We *eat* Christ Jesus; only God could have thought of so obvious a way of saying "I love you." Food and love, the hungers of our lives, find their explanation and their satisfaction in this sacrament. He loves us back to life. He gives us food and vision.

As we approach the altar this afternoon, let us thank God for his food and for his love. Let us ask him to make us increasingly conscious of our priesthood. Let us ask ourselves how well we are living our priesthood. Let us ask ourselves the one question that ultimately will matter: have I ever laid down my life for *any*body? That is, have I ever given myself so completely, so selflessly, to anyone that when he was dead as a person I loved him back into existence? "He who does not love abides in death." "Little children, love one another."

## Thursday, 30 June

IT'S DONE. All of it. Shortly after ordination I went into an extended period of euphoria, which carried me through some trying times at Weston, through the agonies of worrying whether or not I would be able to speak at my first Mass, through the reception which turned into a love feast. It carried me through the horrors of the following day when, after four hours' sleep, Mom and Dad and I drove seventy-five miles to my aunt's convent where I said Mass for the nuns. I was so exhausted that, after saying the Introit, I looked around the strange altar, bowed to the crucifix, skipped the Kyrie and the Gloria, and went right on to the Epistle, Gospel, homily. Furthermore I never realized I had left anything out until Dad asked me on the way home if I had done that on purpose. On Wednesday I left for New York; I realized it was the only way the folks would ever be able to unwind; I realized also that unless I got away I might just collapse, slide to the floor suddenly with blood running out my ears.

New York was a wise move. It brought everything full circle. I saw friends and shows and the superb film version of *Who's Afraid of Virginia Woolf?* It seems right to end this journal with a note on V. Woolf, having spent so much time chasing Albee's play in circles for the past three years. The film is good, the acting excellent. I can't imagine anyone giving a better performance as Martha than Elizabeth Taylor: she instills a womanliness and a lovingness in the role that it never had on Broadway; consequently she gives the film a greater probability, gives the marriage a possibility of hope at the film's end. It is a very Christian and a very moral work of art. Albee has gotten better than he's given.

New York was important at this time for a couple of other reasons. I saw Macmillan and they are rather enthusiastic about my writing: are bringing out *Rubrics for a Revolution* in the spring of 1967 and this journal in the fall. They think I'm a writer. Ironic that my constant fear about not being able to write as a priest seems to be resolved in the moment of my becoming a priest.

Which brings me to the other reason. I heard confessions at Xavier parish on Sixteenth Street between Fifth and Sixth Avenues. I said Mass there each day. I counseled some married couples. In ten days I did some good work, gained valuable parish experience. So I am a priest in more than name now. I administer the sacraments. I preach God's saving word. Christ's is the most joy-filled work I know.

So I end. Randomly and distracted as usual. I like to think of me as living *almost* happily ever after. Or in a 1930 Hollywood fadeout: I climb a hill into a sunset, prayer book under my arm, a small crucifix in my hand. And I am hopping. Hopping. Because I do crazy things like that.

Or better, I should not think of me at all, but of that Christ who has nudged me down the years, cajoled me, urged me, slapped me into shape, wept over me, laughed over me, and who lives in me . . . and though the mountains should collapse and the temperature of New England become predictable, he will not cease to love me. Let us contemplate the infinite and inexplicable humor of God.

# Epilogue

# GOD'S LAUGHTER

1 APRIL 1967

PICNIC IN BABYLON is well on toward publication. And here I sit, April foolish, writing an epilogue so that I may have the last word.

Woodstock deserves a last word said about it; it's unique. It is a place and a house and, I suppose, a way of living. When I think of describing Woodstock, I think first of stories and of my friends. I think of Charlie's visits to the mental home and the lady who always comes charging up to him in chapel shouting, "Give back my cat, *then* I'll believe in God." And the beautiful young Negress there who kept smiling beatifically at Ed until he asked her why she was so happy and she replied she was so happy because at last she owned something really valuable, whereupon she showed him an envelope containing "the apple core from the Garden of Eden." And Justin's emergence, even while officially a student here, as one of Woodstock's best teachers. And Jim and Bruce and Leo's encouragement and delight in my publishing successes. And my own delight yesterday, realizing I have completed another book of poems, *One Eye and a Measuring Rod*. And David the Mad, who takes keen pleasure in the truth well put, telling me as I lay dying of the flu, "You're sick, you poor devil, and I think it's beginning to affect your body." Later, "You're feeling better today, I can tell. The circle of your malice is expanding to include other people." Which is very clever for a giraffe. And one last thing: my application to University of Chicago graduate school. I wrote them a lengthy, canny, crazy letter explaining that I am thirty-two years old and in the twenty-eighth grade and damned tired of filling out forms.

I included a pile of reviews and articles and my two books. They called me on the phone to tell me I was accepted. So let's drink to the University of Chicago. (Let's do. Even though, as it has turned out, I shall go to Harvard because of the enormous scholarship they've given me.)

Something should be said, too, about the incredible changes in theology, in the way it's studied and taught and lived, about the changes in our house. Woodstock took on the spirit and direction of Vatican II quite awhile before Vatican II was adjourned. Moral theology, at least here, has been completely rethought. It now proceeds from experience and from principles to which four years ago we merely tipped our caps. Canon law has been relegated to the fairly unimportant place it ought to have in a religion founded as a revelation of our Father's love for us and as a return of our love to the Father. Speculative theology remains the same, with the small difference that now everything is open for question, for investigation, not because we want to doubt or deny, but because we care a great deal about revelation and because truth is not worth much if it isn't your own. So we approach the problems of original sin, grace, redemption, Christ, in an open unfixed way that preserves the fascination the problems ought to have. Mystery thus remains mystery and conjecture remains conjecture; at the same time our understanding of religion is enriched by this scrutiny of the intersection of the divine and human. And so on. I can't praise the changes in theology here as I ought; I would sound excessive, as if I were suffering that gentle hysteria that precedes a priest's departure from the seminary.

Though human nature has suffered no radical revision and though we're still a good distance from paradise, the whole atmosphere at Woodstock is new and alive. Had I left Woodstock after my first-year theology and returned for my fourth, I would never have believed this was the same place, and I would have had serious doubts that these were the same people. In 1964 Woodstock was an unhappy house; Superiors were not generally liked; rules of daily life took precedence over living. Today the opposite is true. The talk of moving to Yale or Fordham is prompted by the notion that such a move would be good for Woodstock and Yale/Fordham and American theology, not by any notion that life here is crippling. Actually, and this is quite unusual for a house of studies, the men here are content; that is to say we spend more time getting upset over things wrong with us or with the world than we do blaming Woodstock for our problems. And we are blessed with magnificent Superiors. Felix (nobody refers to him as Father Cardegna) is the most extraordinary man. He came into the Rector's job with no evident qualifications except that he'd been a dull teacher and a very good confessor. And he astounded everybody by starting splendidly and growing daily bigger and deeper and more and more open until today he encompasses the entire community with his love for us and the harshest word I've heard spoken about him is that he ought to know enough to get away for a rest when he's about to collapse from overwork. He trusts us, treats us like grown and responsible men, favors—in a monarchical society—democracy. He's urged more and more apostolic activity in the city: we teach and preach and give retreats, we work in reformatories and hospitals and mental homes, we even go out to dinner when the walls begin to close in on us. All classes are optional, most classes are seminars. We can now get a glass of beer nights if we feel like it, with no possibility of anybody telling us it's bedtime and we must confess our delinquency to the community at dinner. And Felix is responsible for it all. He approaches his job looking always for what he can do, what he can give to make this a better theologate, make the men happier and more responsible religious. As a result the men here pray more, work harder, study longer, and live more joyously than in any house I've lived in. Because we are free. Liberty has supplanted legalism; we have freedom without chaos. It's hard to believe but it works.

I feel the difference in myself. I have never before been so free to write, to speak, to give myself. I don't have to pretend I'm something I'm not, don't have to worry that the kind of thing I write will be rejected by censors. Mental freedom completely emancipates me; because I know that I am free to print whatever I write, the whole sweaty effort of writing becomes less burdensome. I cannot imagine how I will

fare outside Woodstock. I can't help wondering if the stuffiness
and conformity of most religious houses I've lived in (not to
mention the actual unchristian repression—dare we say persecution—of one of them) will once again catch up with
me and I shall suffocate or choke to death on my rage or
perhaps disappear forever into my own pettiness. I don't think
so. I think it's too late. Thanks to Woodstock.

What else? My life as a priest, I guess, but I don't really
know how to talk about that. I am exactly the same as I have
always been, and then again I'm not. I'm rich now. I can give
things: the Eucharist, the Word in a special way, new life.
And I'm aware, too, that I'm not just me. People never come
to me as me; they come to me as a priest, as one who should
serve them. That puts a demand upon me and *makes* me what
I am supposed to be; people re-ordain me each time they bring
me their weakness and say help me. And I like it. I like preaching and the hours in the confessional when people are absolutely themselves (or try to be) and when I can love them
back to life. I like giving retreats and Bible vigils and that
stuff. A lot of priestly things have happened since my ordination: I have baptized a spanking new baby and I have crawled
into a car wreck and held in my arms an unrecognizably
mangled young man of twenty until the ambulance showed
up; and I anointed him. I have buried in Arlington cemetery
with full military honors a beautiful blond actress named Liza
Chapman Heath, dead at thirty-seven, who happened to be the
youngest commissioned Army officer since Custer. I have
buried my poor good uncle, singing for him a solemn Mass in
such ghastly voice that I half expected him to sit up and ask
me to stop. I have counseled nuns and a priest or two and
some great teen-agers. I have composed and used for small
private groups an English liturgy along the lines of what we
shall someday have in this country. And I am already bored
to death with the Breviary. So, considering I live in the forest
beyond the moat, I've had a good bit of priestly experience.

There are few teachers so effective as reality. And so my
thoughts today on several major issues—birth control, liturgy,
divorce, Catholic education, the religious life—are far different
from what they have been during the past years. For my change

in attitude I can thank confessions and counseling and just being available to people who want to talk. We are, I discover, in the early ages of Christianity.

I like being a priest. What I suffer from now is what I suffered from before ordination: a searing awareness of my hopeless inadequacy, my inability to give myself to the extent I must. Because I'm still the same clod, complaining of the cold, worrying that I am so lazy, defending myself against the ill opinion of people who don't even know I'm alive, wanting to squeeze all the life out of every minute just because . . . because. "Function in disaster," so Sister Elnora told me yesterday, "finish in style." I always seem to be working in the middle of a disaster area. No genuine sense of accomplishment ever. No peace in the way most people think of peace. No religious composure. A mess. Still there is the incontrovertible fact of Christ. And there are my family and my great good friends. And there is the chance to give. The whole point of being me, I suppose, is to live, and I'd be foolish to stop living just because I seem to exist at the slightly myopic eye of the tornado. Sister is right. The important thing is to continue to function. And who can tell? It's not impossible that I may yet (to the sound of God's laughter) finish in creditable style.